NO NEED TO KNEAD

Sage and Bread

NO NEED TO KNEAD

Handmade Italian

Breads in 90 Minutes

WRITTEN & ILLUSTRATED BY

Suzanne Dunaway

HYPERION

NEW YORK

For Don, this and other

LIBRARY OF CONGRESS CATALOGING-IN-PUBLICATION DATA

Dunaway, Suzanne, 1940–
No need to knead: handmade Italian breads in 90 minutes /
written and illustrated by Suzanne Dunaway.—1st ed.
p.   cm.
ISBN 0-7868-6427-3
1. Bread.   2. Cookery, Italian.   I. Title.
TX769.D795   1999
641.8' 15' 0945—dc21   99-24912
CIP

FIRST EDITION

Book design by Richard Oriolo

10 9 8 7 6 5 4 3 2 1

Contents

Introduction   1

     Why Bake Bread?   1

     Breaking the Rules (Myth and Mystique versus Reality)?   7

     Tools of the Trade   13

     Hands, Hunches, and How to Use Them   16

     Flour, Water, Yeast, and Salt—Down to Basics   20

     Just for Starters   32

Daily Breads   37

     Focaccia—Basic Dough for Flatbreads or Loaves   40

     Fougasse de Collioure   44

     Rosemary Filoncino   46

     Rosemary Oil   48

     Ciabatta (Slipper Bread)   49

     Kalamata Olive Filoncino   52

     Hazelnut-Sage Filoncino   55

     Filoncino Integrale   58

     Sourdough Caraway Rye   61

     Shimek Dill Pickles   64

     Pane Casereccio (Housewife's Bread)   65

     Whole Wheat Bread   68

Pane Rustico   70

French Baguette   73

Traditional Breads   77

Anadama Bread   80

My Mother's Cream Bread (Pain de Mie)   82

Buttermilk Bread   84

My Mother's Sourdough Biscuits   86

Fresh Fruit Purée   88

My Grandmother's Beaten Biscuits   89

Skillet Corn Bread   91

Cornmeal Spoon Bread   93

Sourdough Flapjacks   94

Buckwheat Blini   96

Boston Brown Bread   97

Suzanne's Version of Boston Baked Beans   99

English Muffins   100

Pizza   103

Basic Pizza Crust   105

Pizza Bianca alla Romana   108

Pizza Margherita   110

Pizza Napoletana   112

Pizza con Patate e Rosmarino   113

Pizza con Carciofi   115

Pizza Quattro Stagione   116

Pizza alla Griglia   118

Very Thin Pizza with Arugula Paste   120

Simply Perfect Tomato Sauce   121

Sweet Loaves and Others   123

Classic Brioches   127

Bigmama's Kolaches   130

Poppy Seed Filling   132

Prune Filling   133

Apricot Filling   134

Cottage Cheese Filling   134

Apricot Focaccia   135

Prune and Walnut Bread   137

Schiacciatta with Roasted Grapes   139

Suzanne's Roasted Grapes   141

Sourdough Lemon Cake   142

Golden Cornmeal Torta della Nonna   144

Gabriella's Ricotta Cake   145

Fresh Ricotta   147

Brownie Scout Chocolate Cake   148

Foolproof Chocolate Icing   150

Another Foolproof Chocolate Icing   150

Gingerbread Cake   151

Lemon Curd   153

Chocolate Tozzetti (Roman Dipping Cookies)   154

Wild Turkey Chocolate Ice Cream   156

Special Breads and Bread Sticks   159

Apricot-Plum Pudding   162

Hard Sauce   165

Panettone   165

Candied Orange and Lemon Zest   169

Russian Kulich   170

Pink Confectioners' Sugar Icing   172

Pashka   172

Quick Chappati for Curry   174

Ye-Wolo Ambasha (African Spiced Bread)   176

Nit'r K'ibe   178

Berberé   179

Truffle Rolls   180

Rosemary-Pepper Bread Sticks   183

Leftovers   187

Bread Salads   190
Panzanella (Bread Salad)   190
Tuna Panzanella   191
Fresh Scallop Panzanella   192

Bruschette   194
Bruschetta with Tomato and Basil   195
Bruschetta with Arugula and Prosciutto   196
Bruschetta with Sweet Peppers and Tuna   196
Bruschetta with Caponata   198
Bruschetta with Olive Paste   199
Bruschetta with Wild Mushrooms   200
Bruschetta with Roasted Garlic and Parmesan   202
Bruschetta with Rock Shrimp or Shellfish   204

Bruschettine   205

Bread Soufflés   206
Bread and Cheese Soufflé   206
Bread Soufflé with Salmon and Capers   207

Bread in Pasta and Rice   209
Penne with Broccoli and Anchovies   210
Rotelle alla Romana   212
Orecchiette with Rape and Hot Peppers   213
Pasta con le Sarde   215
Supplí   217

Bread Soups   219
Tuscan Bread Soup   219
Carrot, Celery Root, Onion, and Parmesan Soup   220
Pappa al Pomodoro   222
White Bean and Balsamic Vinegar Soup   223
Suzanne's Rich Chicken Stock   225

Bread for Dessert   226
Classic Bread and Butter Pudding   226
Chocolate Bread Pudding   228
Sautéed Apples and Cream on Toast   229
Pears in Caramel with Cheese on Toast   230

Exotic Croutons and Bread Crumbs   232
Croutons and Bread Crumbs   233

Bread for Children   237
Pie Crust Pinwheels   238
Your Very Own Bread   240
Egyptian Eggs   242
Log Cabin Scrambles   243
Alphabet Bread Sticks—Basic Recipe   244
Pain Perdu (Lost Bread)   246
Campfire Roly-Polys   247
Adam and Eve on a Raft   248

Acknowledgments   249
Index   253

No Need to Knead

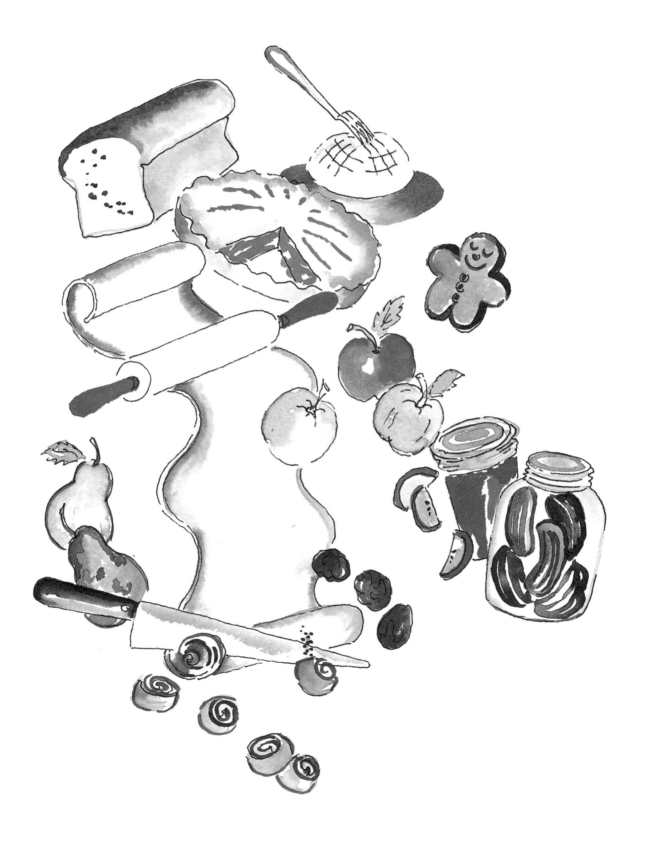

Introduction

Why Bake Bread?

I spent my childhood in the company of women who made bread daily, not just for special occasions. My mother, an avid collector of *Gourmet* magazines, began training me when I was five years old, giving me a little oak worktable and a miniature red-handled rolling pin to make cinnamon pinwheels from scraps of her extraordinary pie dough. One of my grandmothers, Bessie, taught me how to make beaten biscuits and spoon bread, while the other, my Czech grandmother called Bigmama, showed me how to wrap *kolache* dough around the buttery poppy seed filling that she kept on hand as other people keep salt on the table. Cooking with these women, I learned how pleasurable it was to create bread in one's own kitchen.

In my family, bread did not come in packages, just as butter did not come in boxes. Our farm butter came from the thick layer of cream skimmed off the milk from another Bessie, the cow. My grandfather brought the morning's milking to the back porch, and with a giant silver spoon, pulled the heavy top cream aside (into a blue bowl I still own and use for making bread), churned it into butter, and sculpted it into a half-moon mound, using a cold fork to decorate the butter with cross-hatching. All this just for my grandmother's daily biscuits and country loaves. He certainly knew where *his* bread was buttered.

Our world was filled with beautiful food on large family tables. Eating was an art and eating alone, unimaginable. The summer's apples, peaches, apricots, and berries were made into jams and gleaming, translucent jellies, ready for English muffins, airy biscuits, and country breads. I do not remember any bread that was not made in our kitchen: rye breads, white breads, sourdough biscuits (see page 86), Boston brown bread and cream bread (see page 82), made in a round baking pan and which, to my delight, yielded perfect little round sandwiches for my doll's tea parties. My mother's French toast, Pain Perdu, the recipe derived from an old New Orleans favorite (see page 246) was made with thick slices of her country white bread dipped in fresh farm eggs beaten to an amber liquid with cream and cinnamon.

The baking at Thanksgiving and Christmas for the gathering of our extensive clan began at least two weeks before any event. Swedish cookie presses, corn bread and plum pudding molds, and fancy bread pans were taken out of storage along with vintage tree decorations, all collected over many years. My mother often gave Christmas gifts from her kitchen and the most famous was her chili-pepper-corn-bread dressing for the turkey. Not only our turkey, but many friends' holiday turkeys as well! Along with large quantities of dressing, she would make fruitcakes, sugar cookies, butter cookies, rich little tidbits called sand toks, and of course, fresh biscuits, rolls, and bread. With memories like these, it's no wonder that I ended up with a bakery.

My new career began one summer afternoon when my friend Myra, having returned from a long trip and finding nothing to eat but a frozen focaccia, called to say in so many words that if I did not get my breads on the market, I was crazy—and then she hung up. Sell my bread? She had to be joking. Would anyone buy it? There was so much competition. I knew very little about running a bread business and even less about making bread for the masses, but when our local market started buying my focaccia and several other markets fell in step, I soon was making a thousand loaves a week in my kitchen, and everyone in the household including the cat was covered in flour from early morning to the next early morning.

Fortunately, my husband joined in, just to help out on a morning when I literally could not rise from the bed, and soon I found myself with an able partner. He left a successful screenwriting career of twenty-five years and never looked back. He says that he had to prove himself for six months before I would succumb to having a partner, but it was really fear on my part that a few focacce would not generate the possible riches and perks that Hollywood offers. With this in mind, we began to organize the finances (what there were of them), and we both started having daily "story meetings" about the future of our endeavor. It was only after my thumbs and my husband's middle finger gave out from stirring so often that it dawned on us to buy a small commercial mixer and to hire our first baker, Leonel Ramos, who is still, after five years, our very able chief of bakers. The thousand loaves, exhaustion, and an intractable cat forced us to move out of the house into 2,300 square feet in an industrial area. We bought the same mixer (only bigger), the same ovens (only bigger), and started Buona Forchetta Hand Made Breads, which are made the same way they were made at home—by eye and by hand.

The recipes are my own originals and interpretations, developed over years of trial and error, and I think people respond to them precisely because they are *not* like other breads. The crusts are lighter, chewier, user-friendly; the crumb is moist and stays fresh longer than most breads; ingredients are simple and to the point—no froufrou, as I call it. I leave it to the customer to add whatever he or she likes to the bread and steer clear of heavily flavored additions to the dough, such as mixed herbs, onions, garlic, cheeses, or sun-dried vegetables. These additions often flavor the plainer breads, which bake in the same ovens, and can be the cause of rancidity when breads are not stored well. Cheese, in particular, will go bad in packaged breads or crackers made without preservatives, and I will never use preservatives.

I often think that the way we make our bread at Buona Forchetta must look crazy to other bakers (we use no proofers, temperature-controlled equipment, deck ovens, or peels), and we regularly break every rule in the book about baking, yet our clients are loyal year after year, and the process of making handmade breads in new ways delights us.

No Need to Knead tells you how to make—without tears, anxiety, or special equipment—the same country loaves, filoncini, focacce, and other basic breads I sell at Buona Forchetta Hand Made Breads and other retail outlets and restaurants in the Los Angeles area. I have taught many students how to make these breads in my cooking classes and am so tickled when I hear that they make their own daily breads at home. These basic breads are not the complicated, multi-ingredient loaves found in so many bread books. They are not bread-machine doughs. They often take less time to make and taste better. They require no lengthy kneading to develop the dough—on the contrary, kneading often destroys the texture and the beautiful big holes I want to achieve. They require no special thermometers or equipment. They do not demand days and days of waiting for starters to ferment in order to get a loaf on the table. I grant that long-process breads are delicious, too (see "Daily Breads"), but they never have been my primary focus, especially knowing what I know now.

The majority of the recipes here evolved from going against the grain, so to speak, in order to achieve the moist, wonderfully textured breads I have eaten for years in Italy and France. Once you know the basic dough for a simple bread, you can let your imagination take over. There is very little you cannot put in bread, and I mention these ingredients in individual recipes, but remember that it is best to keep things as simple as possible and let the natural flavors of the bread emerge. By using your intuition, your own allotment of taste buds, and your skill, you will discover just what works and what does not.

For *No Need to Knead*, I selected the recipes I like to have on hand to make bread a special part of any meal. Many of the recipes are for various basic breads and the rest illustrate how I make use of the basics. I hope that some of my more unusual recipes will inspire you to think creatively about combining flavors, such as a spoon of hot chili powder added to Skillet Corn Bread (see page 91) to add body, or oven-roasted Red Flame grapes in the Sicilian Schiacciatta with Roasted Grapes (see page 139), to give this marvelous focaccia tartness. The easy Roman pizza dough (see page 105) is the basis for many savory and exotic flatbreads. The Truffle Rolls (see page 180) scented with white truffle oil (easily obtainable at specialty shops) will make anyone long to travel to the wondrous truffle grounds of Italy's Umbria and Piemonte. The Sourdough Caraway Rye, Pane Casereccio or Housewife's Bread, and Focaccia (see "Daily Breads") are easy enough to become part of every meal, each bread very different from the next. Even classics such as Russian Kulich and Italian Panettone (see "Special Breads") are my own very different versions of these festive breads. Beautiful, tasty, and memorable breads need not be difficult or daunting, but in order to have them taste different from all others, you must consider what you do that is unlike anyone else and then simply trust your instincts and your palate.

No fat, sugar, or dairy products are used in the basic doughs at Buona Forchetta. I believe something is wrong when you need a magnifying glass to read a food label or when you cannot pronounce most of the ingredients on it. A good baker can produce exquisite flavor without additives. A mediocre one cannot.

Many of my breads are made with what I call the cold dough method because it makes better bread with rich flavor. It is also a great time-saver for people with little to spare. You simply put the dough, covered tightly, in the refrigerator overnight to ripen and enhance its flavors. Almost any bread dough may be stored this way, mixed the day or a few hours before use, allowed to build its character in cold storage, then taken out and baked in short order. This is the quickest way to have bread on hand every day, whenever you want it, in very little time. Some doughs actually bake better when cold, because the steam created within the dough leaves the crumb of the loaf moist and chewy (my fougasse is a perfect example of this, see page 44). You, the baker, entertainer, mother, father, laundry schlepper, gardener, carpooler have nothing to do but stir up the dough, get on with the rest of your life, wait, and then bake the bread when you choose. Your simple home-baked loaf will be far superior to any store-bought, commercial bread and will take less time than a trip to the market.

I bake bread because my soul needs it, my senses need the smell, feel, and sight of bread every day, and it is the one food that, without adornment, endures on its own. I like to wake up knowing I am about to bake beautiful breads that can be shared. The timeless taste and feel of bread, as if bread has always been part of the universe, encourages me to create my own. Certainly my past has been filled with bread. With the recipes in this book, you can make a little history yourself.

I bake bread because bread plays its part in how we communicate with others: we sit at tables with total strangers in faraway lands and break bread; we offer bread to please friends, console children, and feed birds on a winter windowsill. Bread also brings new people into my life. In my travels, I sometimes come to a barren crossroad in the middle of nowhere that takes on new color the moment I find the local bakery. There, as always, is the center of the village and its life, and many long friendships have begun at such crossroads. Bread is my passport to unknown places and memorable characters. In my daily routine, I trade my bread for shoe repairs, quick consultations on everything from computer programs to organic gardening, fruit from my neighbor's trees, art supplies, or even emergency change for the parking meter. Bread and barter go together as perfectly as mozzarella and tomatoes.

I bake bread because it feels so very good to my body. Every one of my senses responds to a bowl of gently bubbling flour and yeast, looking like some primordial lava pool, to the cool silkiness of flour, to the sound of dough slapping hard against granite and wood, to the sweet nutty smells of flour, water, and yeast becoming bread—a magical metamorphosis that still holds mystery for me after all these years. I have never really completely understood my lust for bread baking and I now am wondering if I ever will—or if it even matters. I know that I feel content baking bread and when I share it with a friend, we both feel a little more joy in our lives.

I bake bread not only because I love good bread from my own hands (no one else's bread ever tastes like your own) but because I love surprises —and believe me, there are many when you bake bread. I like to be kept on my toes, I love thinking up new recipes, or seeing what evolves from an old one.

Bread is alive. Changeable. It moves. It grows. It often takes its own course and you simply have to follow, but it is also very forgiving, springing right back when you make mistakes. Fortunately, during my years of trial and error, I have made most of the mistakes for you. I had great fun doing it, and you won't have to work as hard. You'll have more time to invent your own bag of tricks to make baking a pleasure instead of a chore. In the end, what you will put on your table, to share with lovers, family, friends, is a little piece of yourself, right out of the oven.

Breaking the Rules
(Myth and Mystique versus Reality)

Because of the intuitive way I cook, I rarely analyze what is happening at the time, joyful for me but sometimes maddening for others. This could be a detriment to pinning things down precisely, but in writing this book, I was able to identify three tenets that I follow religiously. These are quite simple, especially when you think of the time it took to formulate them:

1. Maximize surface area in relation to volume.

2. For the best bread, use a dough that is far wetter than conventional bread dough.

3. Severely limit the kneading or mixing of any bread dough (except for the doughs for brioche or cracker dough, both of which benefit from sound beatings).

MAXIMIZE SURFACE AREA IN RELATION TO VOLUME

My scientifically inclined partner put this into an understandable formula for me, and this formula has become the very backbone of my philosophy of cooking. I am adamant about teaching this in my classes for the simple reason that *almost all food tastes better when this tenet is applied.*

Basically, by maximizing the surface area of any given volume, you achieve better taste. It works like this: a sphere has the least possible surface

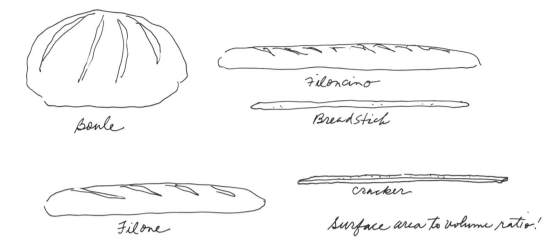

Boule

Filoncino

Breadstick

Filone

Cracker

Surface area to volume ratio!

area for its given volume. If you begin flattening the sphere into an elongated oval shape (*baguette*), the surface area will increase. If the sphere were made into an extremely elongated and flattened oval (focaccia), the surface area would still be greater. As you flatten the sphere more and more, it spreads out thinner and thinner, becoming a thin flat shape, like a cracker, thin focaccia, or pizza, with the maximum surface area possible relative to the given amount of dough. Elongated or flat breads have more crust than round balls of bread (which you may recognize as the word *boule* in French). I like crust and I know it provides flavor.

In keeping with this principle, I make elongated loaves called *filoncini* instead of *boule* or large round loaves. Some of my other loaves are actually cut down the middle and then pulled into a ladder shape (*fougasse*) in order to create even more surface area (in relation to volume) than a filoncino. Everyone loves crispy rolls because of their maximum surface area (crust) in relation to the volume contained (crumb). A *boule* divided in six equal pieces will have over 50% more surface area!

Now here is the paradox: A large round loaf of bread will keep fresh longer than a small, maximized-surface-area loaf because it has more moisture to draw upon from the larger area of crumb. To compensate for my desire to have more surface area and maximized crust, I make breads with a much wetter dough than most bakers, which gives me the best of both worlds. Of course, a small, elongated loaf with maximized surface area has the added advantage of being eaten much more quickly than a larger loaf so the problem of storage is moot!

Sometimes our customers buy two of the same bread at the market, assuring us that one will be gone by the time they arrive home. I have often had people come up to me in stores, cheerfully accusing me of being the cause of the half-eaten loaf in their shopping cart. It is a fact that Americans, in general, do not shop daily for bread as people do in other countries, and although breads keep well in a plastic bag overnight, it is my strong feeling that, if at all possible, bread should be eaten on the day it is baked.

Once you understand the principle of surface area, you will see that both bread making and cooking are more successful and appealing. Try a recipe one way and then try the surface-area approach, and see which one *you* think tastes better. I can only say that this has worked for me for years, at home and the bakery, where the success of our recipes and breads attests to it.

For example, imagine a whole roasted or sautéed eggplant, browned nicely on the outside but alas, soggy, collapsed, and wet on the inside. Compare this to flat thin slices or thin fingers of eggplant, sautéed exactly the same way, but which are crisp, separate elements, each one with its own integrity and flavor. The truth is that when a volume of food is reduced, the taste of the salted, peppered, or seasoned exterior sides (or planes) of the pieces that hit the olive oil, butter, grill, or what-have-you will always be the taste that stands out from the interior flavor, just as crust often takes precedence over crumb. (The exception to this theory might be a steak tartare or a white truffle, shaved raw over hot fettucine.) In Italy, one is known as someone who likes the *mollica* or one who eats the *crosta*. You are either a crumb or a crust person. What this says about your character is a matter of opinion, but it's a little like wanting white or dark meat, simply a matter of preference. I happen to like dark meat and crust, but I go for the *mollica* of the Pane Osso at my bakery because of its seductive flavor. Which part of a meat loaf do you love to bite? The soft, steamed inside or the crispy, crunchy crust?

I cut all my vegetables and meats to maximize their surface areas. I rarely cook anything whole, except potatoes, which I love baked in their skins and which, in my opinion, are one of the great discoveries of the

New World. But when I roast or sauté potatoes, I cut them all down to size for crispness. If you are assembling, for example, a bread soup (see "Leftovers") or any soup calling for onion, garlic, celery, carrot, and so on, you will have better flavor if first you dice the larger pieces of food and sauté them than if you simply throw big chunks of raw vegetable in the pot. Preference is preference, of course, and there will always be those who love large pieces of potato or onion or thick pieces of meat in their dishes and those who prefer smaller pieces—preferably grilled quickly, *tak tak* as the Italians say, for a little piece of savory crust with each bite. For me there is no contest.

WETTER DOUGH MAKES BETTER BREAD THAN CONVENTIONAL BREAD DOUGH

As I have explained, breads with maximized surface area do not stay as fresh as bread formed in a *boule;* the *boule* has a larger volume of crumb from which to draw moisture, especially if the crust is too thick. (Ironically, large balls of bread require longer baking time and inevitably emerge with thick crust: this will go stale more quickly than a thinner one, but deep inside, the bread will still be fairly fresh.)

My breads stay fresh even though they have more surface area for their given volume, without the additional crumb, because I make them from very wet dough, much wetter than most conventional bread recipes. This compensates for the additional surface area and subsequent moisture loss and gives me a nice balance between two extremes.

The recipe for the first real loaf of bread I ever baked (to impress my boyfriend when I was fifteen) did not look or feel right to me. Even the tiny ones I had baked for my dolls were superior. The recipe called for six or seven cups of flour, which seemed way too much for the water content, and to make it worse, I felt the instructions for mixing the dough would produce a heavy, dry, dull bread. I tossed in more water without considering the consequences, began mixing at my own risk, and learned a valuable lesson. When your intuitions tug at your apron strings, let them in, learn from them, and follow them, no matter what the results may be (and there can be some doozies!). In this case, fortunately, the decision to make a wetter dough resulted in tender, moist, and nicely textured loaves, which stayed fresh for several days—even though I had shaped the dough into two smaller loaves to satisfy my crust passion rather than a large round one. Over the years, I have experimented with many breads, using similar wet dough to achieve the seductive textures of the Italian breads I love so much—pizza bianca, pane casereccio, ciabatta, and focaccia.

Mind you, this was all happening long before focaccia and ciabatta recipes took over every bakery from New York to Los Angeles. For me, this was all new territory without many worn paths to follow. My research is usually done by tasting, and for years I sampled every pizza bianca and focaccia I could find, but the final product eluded me. When I visited my favorite *panifici* (bakeries) in Italy, the breads looked easy to make: stir up some dough, put some holes in it, wait, and bake it. When I tried it at home, mine never had the perfect texture and quality I wanted. I stumbled on the secret by accident.

SEVERELY LIMIT THE KNEADING OF BREAD DOUGH

When focacce and ciabatte finally hit the foodie list, most recipes did not have enough water to result in the chewy, open crumb texture of the loaves baked in Italy. No recipe I used looked, smelled, or tasted right. Each one told me to mix a fairly firm dough and then "knead well until smooth and shiny." This was simply not going to work for my purposes, plus there was no way on earth my own, much wetter dough could be mixed or kneaded in the conventional way. First it would slide all over as I handled it, and if I proofed it (let it rise) on a flat pan, it would creep into the corners of the pan when my back was turned.

One day long ago, I made my daily bowl of focaccia dough and then ran outside to check the tomato plants, which had just been planted and needed water. If you have a garden, you know how pleasurable it is to be distracted, and what with a little planting, a little weeding, and the beauty of the ruby-throated hummingbirds, the focaccia was forgotten. I rushed back to the kitchen to find that the dough was behaving like dough: taking off on its own. The yeasts were munching happily away on the sugar and protein in the flour and the dough had begun fermenting with or without me, kneaded or not, rising to a beautiful, light, shiny substance and doubling just as my firmer doughs did, emitting the wonderful nutty aroma of lively yeasts.

I was now at the conventional knock-down-the-dough-and-let-rise-again stage of bread making, but there was no way on earth that this dough was going to survive knock down, much less want to get up again. It dawned on me that if I did not knock it around too much, if I gently *poured* it out onto a baking sheet, the wonderful lightness of its texture might be preserved and it would need no second rise. I reasoned that a very hot oven, hotter than needed for most breads, would give a boost to the already risen dough and open up even more texture in the focaccia, just what I was trying to do. Into a very hot, 500°F oven it went (after first being carefully stretched with fingertips to make the traditional indentations of focaccia and to ensure an even bake), sprinkled first with extra-virgin olive oil (is there any other?), rosemary, and sea salt. What emerged finally was my first real focaccia (see page 40), mixed minimally, not kneaded, and with a flavor that eventually put our bakery on the map!

This is not to say that I eschew classic ways of baking or cooking—the classics are the basis for how I cook now—but after having cooked for more than thirty years, and having lived off and on in Italy for many of those, I have found that complicated, tedious recipes (on which I cut my teeth, mind you) do not necessarily produce the best-tasting results, whereas cooking and baking with simplicity and very fresh ingredients almost always does. There is a memorable saying in Roman dialect that can be used for food or for friends—*Parla come mangi*—"speak as you eat" or, as we say in Texas, don't be so highfalutin, give it to me straight, just as straight as your fork goes to your mouth. And it is a universal truth that Italian food is about as direct and full of truth as food can get.

None of my recipes requires days of preparation, special, complicated starters, or esoteric ingredients, and in this way, I cook as the Italians do. The flavors in my cooking and baking are allowed to shine through on their own without the necessity of a complicated formula or myriad herbs and spices, which can mask the beauty of good raw materials. This is not to say that other cuisines are always complicated, or that they are lacking, or that there are not hundreds of other ways to do things, but for me it is the Italians who have perfected the elusive, difficult art of simplicity. I say "difficult" because so many chefs lean toward menus with enforced complexity rather than allowing ingredients to speak directly. Italian breads from wood ovens, for example, are one of the wonders of the world, not to mention the various pizze and myriad focacce that are served in all regions of Italy. And yet they are the simplest foods imaginable, as simple as a perfect tomato or a freshly dug white truffle.

Tools of the Trade

This will be a quick read! I use a large bowl, a spoon with a hole in it, a measuring cup, a heavy skillet, a baking sheet, a rounded dough scraper, and a strong arm. My two favorite indulgences are a granite slab and a couple of those marvelous baguette baking pans with little holes in the bottom. Over the years, however, I have pared down my bread baking kitchen equipment to a few chosen items, most of which you probably already have in your kitchen, too. You will be surprised to learn how many cooking implements can be used for baking: ordinary glass dishes for pudding molds, cookie sheets for pizza, and various skillets for all sorts of great crusty breads, not to mention the indispensable coffee can for such recipes as Panettone and Boston Brown Bread.

There are, however, several specific items that you will find invaluable as you bake, not the least of which is a notebook and pencil to jot down your flashes of genius. A private cooking diary may be one of the best contributions to the continuity of your family's traditions, a very personal gift to pass on to children and friends. During her life, my mother wrote down her favorites on little cards and passed them on to me in a wooden recipe box, which I treasure more than my white truffle oil or saffron threads. I learned the hard way that I should have written everything down, beginning at the age of five, which would not have been an easy task, but I miss having a diary of the early years. (My first typed cookbook, written from ages eighteen to twenty-one, was entitled *Cooking for Myself—Fearless Cooking* and even had an appendix laboriously done by a friend, John Cooke, as a thank you for all the menus he had so willingly tasted over the years.)

It is also useful to have at least one willing taster with a good palate to give you additional feedback. Although I confidently rely on my own taste buds, I welcome input from those outside my kitchen whose suggestions might spur me on to even greater inventions, the most influential of these golden palates being my husband's, a master taster in his own right. At any rate, once surrounded by your army of pans, spoons, and bowls, you will discover as you go which ones work best for your breads.

This is not to discourage you from poking around kitchen shops; on the contrary, I am inspired by visits to my local purveyors of fine equipment, not to mention restaurant supply stores and garage sales—the best sources for those old seasoned cast-iron forms shaped like ears of corn called johnnycake pans and the beautiful pudding molds made in yesteryears. At garage sales, too, one can find lovely old pottery mixing bowls for stirring up biscuits or housing a *biga* or starter. Pottery is user-friendly to dough, at least I imagine, because its porosity retains warmth and cold equally well. I use a large old pottery bowl for my breads and starters primarily because it was my grandmother's and because it is a beautiful blue that makes me happy. I imagine my grandmother beating her biscuit dough or mixing her breads in her own kitchen over fifty years ago, and I feel a connection to the past that makes me smile. Did she dream and plan as I do when I mix the dough? Did her troubles and anxieties flee with each healing stir of the spoon? I cannot imagine that life was very different then for cooks, and the heirlooms of that time, the wondrous old tools of the kitchen, with the patina of generations, must be kept and treasured as one would treasure an irreplaceable piece of antique jewelry. My cracked plastic spoon, which started my business, means more to me than rubies.

Here, then, in order of appearance, are various tools you might need at one time or another:

THE NECESSITIES

- A large glass, ceramic, plastic, or stainless steel mixing bowl
- A large glass or plastic measuring cup
- A long, sturdy spoon, preferably with a hole in the middle (not easily found but they do exist, usually found at kitchen shops or department stores)
- A heavy 9- to 10-inch skillet—for baking bread
- A 13-by-18-inch baking sheet, for focaccia, pizza, flatbread
- A brush for applying olive oil to dough
- A dough scraper—preferably half-moon-shaped or rounded for lifting and turning the dough easily, also for nudging it out of its rising bowl with as little deflating as possible

Dough Scraper

- A small sharp paring knife to make slashes in tops of bread (works just as well as the French *lame*, which cuts at a 45-degree angle—just eyeball the angle and cut)
- Plastic wrap
- Freezer bags with zipper closures

OTHER USEFUL ITEMS

- Mixer—a good one like a KitchenAid with a dough hook attachment and a strong paddle for mixing lighter breads, such as brioche and panettone
- Food processor—I have a Robot Coupe, but all are good for pizza dough and other kinds
- A granite or marble slab
- Baguette pans—found at kitchen shops, usually with perforated bottoms for even baking

- Coffee cans—small and large, for baking tall breads
- Standard loaf pans—for sandwich bread or Pain de Mie
- Pudding molds—glass ones are now available at kitchen shops
- Small glass heatproof dishes—for steaming little breads or puddings
- Large shallow soup pot with lid—for steaming breads or puddings
- Spray bottles—to spritz bread for a crunchy crust, to spray infusions on breads or salads, or olive oil on pans. Pump sprayers for oil are available in kitchen shops.
- Scissors—to snip dough, cut up herbs, cut bread at the table
- Plastic or rubber spatulas
- Wire whisk—heavy-duty for aerating dough in the liquid stage
- Corn bread molds—seasoned cast-iron ones (they bake better), usually found in thrift shops
- Bread knife—serrated; a good one will last twenty years (I like my Japanese bread knife, which never needs sharpening)
- Grapefruit spoons—for hollowing out tomatoes, little rolls, fruits
- Small garden of fresh rosemary, basil, thyme, and parsley
- Bread baskets—in which to serve breads

You will have more to add to this list from your own experience and perhaps as many items to delete. The important thing to remember is that there are no rigid rules about what you use for baking. Experiment with what you already have, and then reward yourself with great gadgets after you have baked your first loaf.

Hands, Hunches, and How to Use Them

Anyone who likes to cook without getting her or his hands in the food will meet a real challenge when baking bread, but anyone who has played with modeling clay or made a lovely mud pie can turn out a golden loaf. There is no question in my mind that hands are superior to machines (even though at a trade show I watched in awe as a marvelous contraption invented by the Italians turned out several hundred fairly good ciabatte, but the baker was also there, pushing here and arranging there to make sure the bread was staying on the conveyor belt properly). It is always a shock to my cooking students to be handed a slippery duck carcass or Cornish game hen and then asked to disembowel the little creature, but for me, the texture of food is one of the first joys of the kitchen, just as hands are the first tools one uses. Plunging your hands into the buttery dough for Classic Brioches (see page 127) or feeling the smooth silkiness of fresh pizza dough as it stretches across the pan are only two of the many tactile pleasures of bread baking. And I still remember vividly a baker in Genzano simply dipping his hands into thick tomato sauce and smearing it over a six-foot-long pizza about to go into the wood oven.

Perhaps I love the feel of smooth, golden dough and the sensation of crashing it against granite because I was introduced to it at such an early age, when touching anything was a revelation. For this very reason, your kids will love helping you make bread (see "Bread for Children"), particularly the delightfully fun breads such as bread sticks and focaccia.

It goes without saying that it's best to plunge into any dough with clean hands. Everyone at Buona Forchetta is required to wash first thing in the morning before touching anything and then frequently thereafter during the day. It is wise, too, to wash your hands after handling eggs, just to be on the safe side, to prevent salmonella bacteria from spreading.

Hands are far more than serviceable appendages for holding implements; they are thermometers, sculpting knives and paintbrushes, power tools, messengers of good news, and ultimately, the bearers of gifts.

When it comes to gauging the temperatures of the starters you will make, and the dough and bread you create from them, your hands are far more reliable than gadgets—hence *thermometers*. When dough is very cold to the touch, it usually means it must be brought to room temperature before shaping and baking. On the other hand, some dough, such as the dough for Fougasse, is more easily shaped right out of the fridge. Only your hands can tell you what the next step should be. Your hands will feel the coolness or warmth of a baked loaf so that you know when to cut and serve it. Bread should not be cut warm when it is still very fragile. In his invaluable book *On Food and Cooking* (Charles Scribner's Sons, 1984), Harold McGee explains that the temperature of the "outer layer is very dry and close to 400°F (204°C), the interior moist and around 200°F (93°C). During cooling, these differences slowly even themselves out." To paraphrase McGee, it appears that if you cut into bread too early, it will collapse from the inequality of the internal gas pressure and the outer air pressure. When these pressures equalize, the bread is sufficiently cooled and may be cut without mishap and without exuding a mildly unpleasant smell of hot gas (this disappears as the bread cools; your nose, another invaluable tool, will tell you this).

You also use your hands to thump the bottoms of loaves to determine if they are cooked through. You use them to fold the bread dough over on itself three or four times to kick off the yeast action again; you stick your fingers in water, milk, and batter to test their temperatures. Best of all, you use your hands to break off fragrant bites of your own breads. Fresh bread pulled apart by hand always tastes best.

Your hands are your tools as an artist, like sculpting knives and paint-brushes (making bread is an art!), because it is with your hands that you will form dough into appealing, unusual shapes, which say as much about you as the earrings you wear or the way you speak. The shape of anything you cook sends a message to those who eat your food. For example, I am very partial to heart shapes for my biscuits (and polenta and cookies and anything else that can be shaped!) because anything having to do with love makes my own heart happy. My Grandmother's Beaten Biscuits (see page 89) will give you an empty canvas of dough on which to "draw" with your fork, making any kind of fanciful patterns. I love large, flat, square pizze because the shape gives me more area for tomato sauce and mozzarella than a round one—and my propensity for long, rustic, free-form baguettes may be interpreted as you see fit....

Your hands are *powerful tools*, because certain doughs need some pretty rough treatment, such as the aforementioned beaten biscuits. If you are going through a particularly trying time in your life, you can sometimes alleviate the symptoms with a good dough thrashing or brioche crashing. Whenever I teach a class there are always at least two or three students who mention how much they love to bang their bread dough around to change their moods. You may have deduced that with my no-knead policy, you would have to take up kick-boxing or primal scream classes to let off steam, but even without beating up everyday bread dough, you will discover plenty of areas in which your hands will be instrumental in helping you let off steam or simply allowing you to create, which always makes a body feel good. Rolling out Rosemary-Pepper Bread Sticks (see page 183) is certain to make you smile, as will shaping pizza or slapping Quick Chappati for Curry (page 174) into a frying pan and watching them bubble. And you will be amazed at how strong your hands become after several weeks of baking. Stirring and shaping dough builds muscle, strength, and dexterity in your hands, just as using heavy pans or copper cookware will develop great triceps, biceps, and a firm, pattable derrière.

Your hands are *messengers* because they are the conduit for your emotions, a very crucial element in anything you cook or bake. *Like Water for Chocolate*, a passionate book and film about food and love, is a perfect example of how emotions can either lift your cooking onto a higher plane or relegate it to the ninth circle of hell.

On the days that I head toward my kitchen, more weary from work than I might like to be, or agonizing over some imagined disaster, I try to remember that my mood will travel directly from my body to my delicate Truffle Rolls (see page 180), or possibly cause my Bread and Cheese Soufflé (see page 206) to fall. The sooner I can come up with a smile, the faster my dough will rise and the sweeter my sauces will be.

Hands as *gift givers* is self-explanatory. It is with your hands that your breads and pizze and savory dishes will be placed upon the table for family and friends, or even just for yourself. Although I am fortunate to have a partner with whom to break bread each day, I have on occasion sat down alone at the

table, and it has never occurred to me to give myself anything less than I would give my husband or dinner guests. I prepare Pomodori al Riso, one of my favorite Roman dishes, or Pasta con le Sarde (see page 215), make a salad of my garden lettuces and some of the rogue nasturtiums that grow among them, cut myself a piece of fresh Rosemary Filoncino, pour a glass of Pinot Grigio, and feast. All alone with good friends, the gifts from my own hands.

Flour, Water, Yeast, and Salt—Down to Basics

The columnist Herb Caen once wrote that describing pasta as nothing more than flour and water is like saying a sunset is only air, light, and dust. This same observation can be applied to bread, since it is nothing short of a miracle that such an amazing assortment of breads can be made from such simple ingredients as flour, water, yeast, and salt. Most of the delicious basic breads in "Daily Breads," such as focaccia, ciabatta, and pane casereccio are easily made from the four basic ingredients, and from these, one can spin off limitless variations. I think it is good to start with very simple breads and get more adventuresome as you gain confidence. You can rest assured that your bread will never taste like any other, no matter how humbly you begin. If every person in the universe were given the same flour, water, yeast, and salt and asked to make a loaf of bread, every single loaf would taste different from the next.

When attracting customers at demonstrations or expos, I often mention that there are no fats, sugar, or dairy products in my basic bread doughs (the *tozzetti,* our dipping cookies, do contain butter, free-range chicken eggs, and dehydrated cane juice but are considered a low-fat cookie because of the small amount, 3 grams, of fat). The curious crowd always has a few skeptics who seem relieved when assured that the fats in the olives and hazelnuts are the good monounsaturated kind. Finally they taste a tiny sample and suddenly there is no resistance at all! But it is so odd to me that there is always a section of the population that is wary of such a basic food as bread, and so overly concerned with fat.

If there is one message I try to get across when I talk to classes, clients, or curious crowds at a demonstration, it is that a well-rounded, moderate diet of fats, carbohydrates, and proteins, and especially a nice glass of red wine every now and then thrown in for good measure is just about the best way I know to keep healthy. Bread is an integral part of this diet. Certainly there are people who have diet restrictions and allergies, but generally speaking, bread is never the enemy. The only enemy is the abuse of food and perhaps little understanding of the wondrous role bread plays in our lives. There is the old cliché that "a piece of good bread does not make you fat—it is what you put on the bread that makes you fat." It is true.

Flour, water, yeast, and salt simply are not dangerous to your health, at least not when combined in a golden loaf. Many healthful breads are made with only flour and water, such as matzos served during Passover, some variations of the flour and corn tortillas throughout Mexico, and almost all plain crackers.

FLOUR

The kind of flour you use will make a difference in your bread, although even this is contested by some. The rather poor, soft flours of Italy, which are labeled 0 and 00 are used in some of my favorite bakeries in Genzano and are the basis for large, open textured loaves with the flavor of the *biga* made the day before (see "Just for Starters").
There are better flours milled in Italy from the region of Altamura, and there is durum flour used for making pasta, but in general, the Italians use minimal flour to get maximum results. This means that even if you have access only to an all-purpose supermarket flour, you will be able to make a better-

Hard and soft wheats

tasting bread using it in your home kitchen than the bread that comes in a package. I recommend, however, that you buy an unbleached hard wheat bread flour to make your breads superior; the flours milled for bread use have a protein content around 10 to 12 percent, which gives the dough strength and elasticity. All health food stores carry unbleached white and brown bread flours, both organic and nonorganic. As a rule organic flour comes from fields on which no spray or pesticide has been used and which has had no chemical fertilizers added to the soil for three years. You know you are getting as pure a product as you can get, short of growing it and milling it yourself, as, believe it or not, some *really* serious bread bakers do!

Flour is a substance containing protein, sugar, and enzymes. Basically, there are three wheats grown in America: hard wheat for bread, durum wheat for pasta, and soft wheat for pastry. The all-purpose flour you buy in supermarkets is a blending of hard and soft wheats, which meets many requirements in the kitchen, from biscuits and bread to pie crusts and cakes. It is not as high in protein as the bread flour you find in health food stores, but it has its own merits: pizza dough made with this flour will be far superior to pizza made with high-protein flour, because it will not have as much resistance and will be easier to stretch on the baking sheet. The softer wheat flour will also give pizza a delicate little crunch when you bite through the crust, much like that of a good pie crust, except more textured. There is no question in my mind that so-called inferior flour makes superior pizza.

For more detailed information on flour, I recommend *On Food and Cooking* by Harold McGee, already mentioned a few pages back.

WATER

In the No. 45 Winter Edition of *The Art of Eating*, one of the best culinary newsletters available, edited by a very erudite Edward Behr, I was thrilled to find confirmation that water is water is water, so far as baking goes. Short of having to use rusty water from an abandoned well or desert mirage water, tap water will work just fine in breads unless it has been labeled "contaminated."

I must admit that I love the sound of "spring water" or the names of several of the waters of Rome such as the Acqua Marcia ("festering water," actually my favorite, as it has a delicious taste!), Acqua Vergine (self-explanatory), or Acqua Acetosa ("acid water"). But after lugging a liter of Roman water back with me on the plane for seventeen hours, along with a kilo of Altamura flour, and then making bread with both Italian and American ingredients, I found there were no dramatic differences. In Italy, a memorable image of the baker in his undershirt, his muscles gleaming with sweat, paired with the fragrance of loaves baking in a 600-year-old oven and the centuries of crumbs under the stones of the *fornos* undoubtedly influences my taste buds. However, I have had great success baking a similar bread made with tap water in a gas oven, and the baker was fully dressed! Spring water makes no difference.

YEAST

Yeast or fermented dough added to flour and water makes *bread* dough. The little yeast babies (actually microorganisms) munch on the sugars naturally occurring in the flour and as they digest, throw off what are actually little farts of CO_2 and waste water, which break down the resistance in the dough, make it easier to handle and ferment it, and give it its final flavor. Yeasts are strange organisms. Even the guru Harold McGee says, "The behavior of yeast is not entirely understood." This will be evident to you as you bake. What yeast will do for your bread depends on which bread you are making. Some breads, such as pizza, require no more than a pinch of yeast, because you do not want a pizza to rise very high, while other breads need a little more help levitating, perhaps because of heavier ingredients or because you're in a hurry to pick up your kids at school or take your mother to the doctor and want the bread to rise faster.

Some yeasts are commercially grown on very specific sugar sources, such as sugarcane or beets; other yeasts may be found in the wild, such as yeast from grape must and various kinds of fruit. I have found by experimenting that either fresh, compressed yeast or dry yeast gets the job done equally well in a home kitchen. There is no need to get involved in the lengthy process of growing your own for starters—unless you want to. Wild yeast lives everywhere; as you read this, it is flying around your kitchen. It is not indigenous only to vineyards and cane fields, so even a little bowl of flour and water on a countertop can serve as attraction for the yeasts that live with you. The more you bake in your kitchen, the more your yeast community will thrive.

Both wet yeast (commercial yeast) and dry yeast may be frozen to preserve their powers, but I normally keep dry yeast in a tightly closed jar in the refrigerator, and keep a few cubes of compressed yeast in the freezer. Usually I buy bakers' yeast at the nearest health food store. If you are pressed for time, buy a rapid-rise yeast, which will enable you to make a decent focaccia in about 1½ hours, start to finish. All supermarkets carry bread yeast and all health food stores carry several kinds of bakers' yeasts, all equally good.

Yeasts love a tepid, not hot, water (105°F); it gets them into a frenzy. A pinch of sugar added to the water of compressed yeast will also give a jump start to its activity, a kind of antipasto for the little devils. When dough rises the first time, the yeast are busy multiplying and throwing off gases and liquids at a phenomenal rate; they do this best when you have used slightly cooler water in the mix (85 to 95°F).

SALT

Salt is added to almost all breads for flavor and also to help strengthen the dough. In the mix, salt can inhibit yeast action, however, and must be used sparingly. There are exceptions, of course, like the famous unsalted breads of Tuscany, which are made exactly as they were in the distant past when salt was an expensive commodity. I have always thought of the Fiorentini as stoics who made salt-free bread because in the Middle Ages only the very rich could afford salt, and so eating salt-free bread puts everyone on the same level. But I have seen even Fiorentini sneak a sprinkle of salt on their bread every now and then.

There is salt from mines and salt from the sea. I use commercial salt in my dough but coarse sea salt on top of my breads only because I like thinking about its origins. It seems less salty than iodized, commercial salt, but it is not imperative to use it in these recipes.

FATS, SUGAR, AND DAIRY

One of the great attractions to our bread at Buona Forchetta is that we use no fat, sugar, or dairy products in the basic bread dough. I use additional ingredients only for special breads (see "Traditional Breads," "Pizza," and "Sweet Loaves and Others") because I hold the strong belief that the best breads for everyday eating are made with only flour, water, yeast, and salt. In addition to these four basics, many bakers sometimes use fats, sugar, and dairy (which includes eggs) in their basic breads for preserving flavor, texture, and richness. These breads are often very fluffy and light with fine textures, but not the kinds needed for a good bruschetta.

Basically, sugar activates the yeasts more readily by giving them extra nourishment. Breads made with sugar retain more moisture and last longer, which is why it is used so often in commercial breads, which have to have an acceptable shelf life for the consumer. These breads also often taste sweet and leave a residue on the tongue. Sugar enhances the flavor of breakfast breads, rolls, and muffins, plus we like the little jolt it gives us in the morning. Because I was born with a salty tooth rather than a sweet one, I developed recipes such as cinnamon focaccia and Apricot Focaccia specifically for my own breakfast. There is no sugar in the dough itself—only the apricots, themselves both tart and sweet, and just enough sugar and cinnamon sprinkled on top to be satisfying.

I use cottage cheese in various recipes, including Bigmama's Kolaches (where it is used as a filling) and Gabriella's Ricotta Cake. I discovered that all cottage cheese benefits from a breath of air, so that after sitting out at room temperature for a specific amount of time, it acquires a lovely, slightly sour taste, similar to my grandfather's homemade cottage cheese, which had this flavor from the word go.

The commercial, often tasteless brands on the market today will change before your eyes when left out for a few hours. I remove the carton lid and leave it resting on top, and let the cheese sit at room temperature for sixteen to twenty-four hours, no more. If the top of the cheese turns pink, I scrape off about a half inch and use the rest—but it is unlikely that the cheese will color in twenty-four hours. When "aged" cottage cheese is used in cheesecakes, pancakes, fillings, or pasta sauces, the flavor of the recipe is 100 percent better. Trust me.

NUTS, GRAINS, AND SEEDS

As you start making more and more exotic breads, you may want to experiment with nuts, grains, and seeds, and throughout the book I have included recipes explaining how to do so. Walnuts, pecans, almonds, pistacchi, pine nuts, and even cashews are wonderful in bread. Cracked wheat, bulgur wheat, rye, millet, and grain mixtures may all be used in breads. Soak the grains for 15 minutes in a little tepid water to soften them, as you would for *tabbouleh,* and then add them to the dough. Poppy seeds, sesame seeds, and flaxseeds are all tasty in the dough itself but are normally sprinkled untoasted on top of breads. Use your own imagination and intuition to create the flavors you like.

You will have a better-tasting bread (and this applies to all recipes) if you toast all nuts and seeds before using them in the dough. I also toast all dry spices to release their flavors and, at the same time, seal them in. Primarily I do this to avoid the terrible raw taste of these ingredients, which almost certainly ruins a dish. Raw curry powder or cumin are good examples of how uncooked spices can overpower a dish and cause you to burp all day!

DRIED AND FRESH FRUIT

Dried raisins, apricots (my favorite), dates, currants, figs, peaches, and other fruits may be used in breads. I make my own raisins for Schiacciatta with Roasted Grapes (see page 139), and whenever possible, I try to dry other fruits on my own. Fresh fruits, such as the apricots in the Apricot Focaccia, are actually fresh-frozen Blenheim fruit from my local open market. Peaches, bananas, apples, pears, and plums may be used in their natural state, pitted and seeded of course, and sometimes peeled depending on the kind of fruit. I leave the skins on apricots and plums, for example, but peel peaches and pears, as in the recipe for Pears in Caramel with Cheese on Toast (see page 230).

VEGETABLES

If the olives are considered a vegetable, then I use a vegetable in my bread. Originally, when I was very naïve in my purist mode (and not wise enough to keep an open mind at all times!), I scoffed at olive bread or any kind of bread flavored with what I call "stuff." When my first fragrant kalamata focaccia came out of the oven and the toasted olives crunched under my teeth, I was a convert. Many different types of olives, including the green ones, go very well with bread dough. Many California and some French bakers often use tiny olives that are cured in oil and often flavored with herbs, but I prefer kalamata, cured in brine. In Rome, huge green olives are added, chopped or whole, to a large round loaf, which is unsalted to accommodate the flavor of the olives. Most Italian bakers in small towns leave the pits in the olives, so you have to be careful as you chew! At Buona Forchetta, we use only pitted olives, and to avoid unpleasant surprises, I recommend that you do, too.

Because too many flavors compete with the natural taste of bread, I use no onion, garlic, dried spices (the exception is the sage in our Hazelnut-Sage Filoncino), or any kind of cheese in my breads. I reason that breads made with these ingredients make the ovens smell funny and then flavor all the other breads. I prefer plain, simple breads and let the buyer put whatever he or she wants on them at home. If you must use onion, garlic, eggplant, or peppers in or on your bread, slice them thin and sauté or roast them first in a little olive oil. Dried vegetables such as tomatoes, eggplant, or peppers should be reconstituted in a little water before being added to bread dough. Once again, experiment with your own favorites and surprise yourself with new combinations.

MIXING

You will mix different breads in different ways, depending on the dough, but in general, for most of the breads in this book, mixing is kept to a minimum—just enough to dissolve the flour, salt, and yeast in the water and then a bit more to form a rough and ragged dough without lumps. The dough will always be more wet than dry. Sometimes, lumps are necessary to make the final product even better, such as when you are making light biscuits or pancakes. When you mix flour and water, you tangle up the gluten proteins in the flour (kneading attempts to straighten out this mangled mess). An overworked dough is tough and resistant (or too straightened out), making it difficult to form easily into biscuits, pancakes, or whatever.

Even in a commercial bakery, mixing is a strange blending of intuition and simply observing the dough to see what it tells you. When the gluten in flour is mixed with water, it begins to form strings; the strings attach themselves to the side of the bowl, like threads of taffy, and are not easily broken because of their strength and flexibility. When these strings come away easily from the sides of the bowl, the gluten in the flour is reaching its optimum state. At this point, I stop mixing, or continue for only a few seconds if I see white specks of raw flour, salt, or pale brown yeast not yet mixed into the dough. On the other hand, most commercial bakeries mix their doughs for longer than we do at Buona Forchetta, and these very elastic doughs tend to produce fine-grained loaves. Unless I am making a sandwich bread such as Pain de Mie (see page 82) or a steamed, tightly textured bread, I try to avoid fine-textured breads by undermixing and minimal kneading. Especially when making ciabatta or focaccia, the dough should be mixed and handled very gingerly in order to get the open texture that mops up and holds that last bit of pasta sauce or olive oil. In Italy, mopping up one's plate is called *fare la scarpetta*, "making the little shoe."

STIRRING

I stopped kneading and started stirring my breads when I developed my soft dough recipes. Conventional kneading simply did not work with these wet doughs. The kneading process changes the molecular structure of dough and creates a balance between plasticity and elasticity, plasticity being the strength of the dough, which is a result of mixing a liquid into flour, and elasticity being the ease with which dough can be handled and formed without excess resistance. I found that this balance can be achieved with simple stirring just as well as and often better than with kneading.

Stirring dough differs from lengthy kneading in that the dough's structure is not broken down as much, and the crumb of the baked bread will have a chewy, open texture, rather than a tight, closed one; a good brisk stir is often all the exertion you will have to use to start your dough toward being a loaf. I think of stirring as gently coaxing the dough to form its malleable structure, a kind of caress with a spoon or paddle instead of an assault with a dough hook or firm hands, thereby damaging the yeast by overheating it, or damaging the dough by overworking it. Every baker has his own opinion of how to stir, and I am only telling you mine because it has worked so well for me. There are exceptions to any rule. Brioche is a perfect example of dough that requires more manhandling than any of my daily breads. Brioche dough is extremely resilient and strong because of its high fat content (eggs and butter), and gets even more so when lifted off a flat surface and crashed down again. It can be kneaded quickly, although I would more aptly call it "slammed," since it responds well to lifting off and crashing against a surface such as Corian, marble, or granite.

Intuition tells you that to get more crust, you must minimize the crumb—i.e., make thin, flat focaccia or long, skinny Rosemary Filoncini instead of fat loaves. You might have a hunch that your yeast is not as active as it should be when you note that there is no bubbling and the surface of the mixture is flat and dull. You may test it by feeding it a little sugar or flour to see if it gets livelier. That's a small hunch, but the small ones will sharpen your intuition for the bigger, more significant ones, and big hunches often make the difference between average cooks and great cooks. Think, as you bake, of what other recipes tell you to do and ask yourself: Do the instructions seem logical or even feasible? Can you imagine the results? The tastes? Do they feel to you to be way off base? Compare these instructions to what *you* would do instead.

When you feel doubtful about your bread making, ask yourself a few simple questions and use your senses to gauge the process: How does my dough look? Normally, it should be rough and ragged when you begin and then turn supple and smooth as you stir. Does it have life or does it simply lie in the bowl, limp and flaccid, stringy and without elasticity? How does it smell? Rich and yeasty or unpleasant and gaseous? How does the raw dough taste? Slightly salty with the nice nutty taste of flour—perhaps a little sour but pleasant—or gassy and acrid from too much fermentation, yeast, or salt?

Trusting your intuition as you bake and cook can be a formidable task, especially for the less confident. It sometimes helps to seek the opinions of family and friends, or someone whose taste buds you trust, but in the end, it is only *you* who will really know how you want your breads and dishes to taste. Coraggio! Have some fun! This is only cooking, not manning the space shuttle.

Fortunately, mixing and baking are forgiving activities. If the dough is fighting you, walk away and let it relax for a few minutes while you do the same. If you smell something too soon after putting it in the oven, the oven is probably too hot. If you don't smell anything at all after half an hour, most likely the oven isn't even on! These things do happen, although infrequently, but nothing has to be a disaster if your intuition is working well. When you mix up a batch of dough that is so difficult to manage that you want to throw in your spoon, use the recipe for My Grandmother's Beaten Biscuits (see page 89) to turn it into an exotic homemade cracker, or add a little water and flour to see if it responds to feeding. If the pizza dough becomes too soupy after a few days in the fridge and has a gray pallor to its complexion, throw in some more flour and watch how the texture and color suddenly come alive and the dough regains its elasticity.

It is when you are most in doubt that you must call upon your intuition. Never compare your breads to others, just keep on your own path, and listen to yourself and the answers will bubble up like yeast from your subconscious. Failures provide marvelous opportunities to improvise and hone your intuition. Mistakes often do not need correcting but can instead be the inspiration for a new and exciting bread or dish. Chili powder in the Skillet Corn Bread; hazelnuts and sage in the filoncini; apricots in the focaccia or roasted grapes in the Schiacciatta, all are the fruits (not to make a pun) of intuition. I am sure that the first humble breads thousands of years ago were the result of an accidental spill from a sack of grain into a forgotten basin of water. A few nights later as the cook labored over dinner, he or she mused over the bubbling dough. "Hmm, let me just put this funny stuff on the fire and see what happens…."

CLARIFICATION OF TERMS

Throughout this book, the terms listed here are identified as follows:

Diced means cutting ingredients into small (½ inch), medium (¾ inch), or coarse (1 inch) squares.

Minced means chopping very small, smaller than dice.

Mashed means puréed unless otherwise stated.

Dried spices are *always* toasted or roasted before using.

Flour is unbleached white bread flour or all-purpose flour unless otherwise stated.

Butter is unsalted unless otherwise stated.

Eggs are large and at room temperature before using.

Vegetable shortening is the semisolid kind that usually comes in a can, such as Crisco.

Olive oil is always extra-virgin or cold-pressed extra-virgin.

Mozzarella is always the fresh kind, packed in water (not, as the Italians charmingly call it, *sottovuoto*, "under empty," meaning vacuum packed in plastic). Hard American mozzarella has nothing to do with fresh mozzarella and will give you a different taste and texture.

Salt and pepper are not mentioned except as ingredients but it is understood that you will use them to your taste. Salt as an ingredient means table salt.

A *dash* of something is, to be a bit more technical, a little slosh or approximately 1 to 2 tablespoons of anything, as in "a dash of vinegar." When salt is used, it is a pinch instead of a dash.

Heaping means a rounded measurement, as in "a heaping teaspoon of salt." A heaping teaspoon of salt is a little curved, not flat.

Rough and ragged, pertaining to dough, means that the dough is just barely mixed with a few turns, still a little tattered looking, not yet smooth and shiny.

Cream is heavy cream, not half-and-half or dairy substitutes.

Milk need not be scalded before using. Scalding milk in the old days was to kill anything dangerous in it, and now there is nothing dangerous in it! Room temperature is fine, although warming milk before using in a recipe can sometimes help the yeast action or help to melt butter added to it, but is not necessary.

Coffee should be strong, real coffee, preferably Italian or French roast, not instant coffee. Use instant if it is the only thing available.

Parmesan is always cheese and is always Reggiano Rocca (if you can find it).

Balsamic vinegar should be the best you can afford.

Mascarpone is always cheese, found in the dairy section of large supermarkets or Italian specialty stores, but crème fraîche may be used as a substitute.

TIPS ON BAKING AND COOKING:

When dough has risen the first time, do not deflate it but only fold it over on itself a few times for the second or third rise.

A gear-operated, handheld eggbeater is the best tool for whipping whites. If the whites are beaten in a copper bowl, they easily beat to a high volume.

A few dried porcini mushrooms in your cornmeal makes a wonderfully flavored polenta, Anadama Bread, Skillet Corn Bread, or Cornmeal Spoon Bread (see page 93).

A sprig of rosemary or thyme in the water in which beans are soaking imparts a lovely, subtle taste to the finished product.

Just for Starters

Let me start with this: Everyone seems to have his or her own view of what a starter is. The subject can make your head swim. My view is that any kind of flour, water, and yeast (commercial or otherwise) mixture that is left to ferment before using it in the final recipe is a starter—a jump start for your dough, just as cables give a jolt of electricity to an engine. (Gold rush hopefuls, eventually nicknamed "sourdoughs," in the old West used to spit in their starters to give them a boost! I do *not* suggest this!)

The French have a term for a starter, *levain*, and the Austrians, *poolish*, and in the *levain*'s first stage, a *chef* and several other names to boot. I plan to concentrate on simple terms and straightforward techniques for making starters. Simply, a starter is an active mixture of flour, water (or milk, yogurt, grape juice and grape skins, or any one of hundreds of variations, depending on the baker), and the specific yeasts attracted or added to it, which cannot easily digest maltose (a sugar) and which thrive best in an acid environment.

The sour or tart taste of most starters is from lactic acid produced by very distinct bacteria. For example, the lactic acid–producing bacteria in the San Francisco Bay Area of California produces that region's world-famous sourdough breads. They are literally called *Lactobacillus sanfrancisco*, a name I have always loved, and these bacteria are *not found anywhere else*, which is why the bread in San Francisco tastes different from its many impersonators. The yeast in this particular starter is called, according to author Harold McGee (*On Food and Cooking*), *Saccharomyces exiguus* and is *not Saccharomyces cerevisiae*, or brewer's yeast (used in making beer), which is also used for bread. Beer yeasts are all over the place, as you will discover when you bake.

For the starters in this book, we are going to use various methods. First is a *straight dough method*, which does not require any starter. Next is an *old dough method*, which uses a previously made dough (such as dough from the day before) as starter. Third is a *sponge*, which is simply a thicker mixture than a liquid starter. Last is a *biga*, which is the Italian name for a certain kind of starter resembling a sponge. That's about all.

If you want in-depth, professional definitions for these and other terms, I suggest you read *The Village Baker* by Joe Ortiz (Ten Speed Press, Berkeley), learn the terms he has so carefully laid out for aspiring bakers, and if you are an aficionado who has all the time in the world, experiment with every starter that catches your fancy. Have fun with them. However, if you have limited time and still want superior results, learn my simple methods and then elaborate on them as you wish, time willing.

It does not really matter what you call something if you simply want to make bread. When you run across a name of something that is made with flour, water, and sometimes yeast, and has to sit for several hours, overnight, or several days before being used in bread dough, you know that you have a fermentation or a starter. A sourdough starter (as in the sourdough of San Francisco) is very specific, and, in fact, will change with the particular yeasts of the region. Some starters are more liquid than others and are called "starters," others are more spongy and are called "sponges." It's that simple.

STRAIGHT DOUGH METHOD

The process of making bread with flour, water, yeast, and salt mixed together, left to rise, and then baked is called the *straight dough method*. Breads made with previously fermented flour and water (a starter, a sponge, or some dough from a previous mix) cannot be called breads made from the straight dough method. The straight dough method most often produces a soft, airy loaf, much like the bread from a bread machine, but even with a straight dough method, one can get a chewier texture and more interesting crust if the dough is wetter and *not* kneaded, as in focaccia.

OLD DOUGH METHOD

Breads made with a mixture that incorporates a piece of the dough from a previous batch of bread are made by the *old dough method*. The focaccia at the bakery is made this way. We mix up focaccia dough each day and reserve a certain amount of it to use in the next day's focaccia as the jump starter and to add flavor. In the beginning, when you start to make bread, simply mix up about a quarter of the recipe for the bread and let it sit overnight in a covered bowl. The next day, use that piece of dough to make the same recipe, using the precise measurements in the recipe. You will have a quarter more dough than the recipe normally produces, right? Simply save that amount for the next time you bake, and so on.

The old dough method may be continued for years, if you bake on a regular schedule. The old dough may lose its life if left too long in cold storage, but more often than not, adding equal parts of flour and water to the seemingly dead dough will give it life. To confuse you, some Italian bakers call their old dough *biga*; the French appropriately call it *vieille pâte* (old dough). In our bakery we call it *levadura*, but that's because almost everyone speaks Spanish! Whatever you call it, it is an already fermented dough from one day to be used in the next day's bread.

SPONGE

A sponge is a thick mixture of flour, water, and yeast (not as thick as dough but not as liquid as *biga* or sourdough starter) that is allowed to ferment before using it in a bread recipe, usually for 4 to 5 hours or overnight. Its finished appearance is very like that of a sea sponge, with a texture full of holes and an active surface. Panettone uses a sponge, as does a brioche dough.

BIGA

The Italian name for starter is *biga;* the French call it *levain* and often stir a little yeast into the mix to encourage development. Some bakers feel that *biga* does not give bread the same complex flavor that a lengthy sourdough process does, but I disagree with this. It is my *biga* that makes our Pane Casereccio and our Pane Trattoria different from others. Our breads made with *biga* are some of the tastiest around, and they stay fresh much longer than breads made by the straight dough method because of their moisture content.

Just why do we want to use a starter of any kind to make our breads? Basically, starters, sponges, or old dough are used for achieving more complex flavor and, as mentioned, to jump-start the recipe. Not that straight yeast doesn't work just as well, but it is the consensus of bakers the world over that if these little yeast babies are allowed to feast for longer periods of time, they impart special flavor to the bread that is simply not achieved with a straight dough method. However, a perfectly wonderful focaccia and basic bread can be made relatively quickly without prefermentation (starters), and then, if you choose to wait overnight to make your bread, the bread will automatically have an even better flavor because of the time you have given the little yeasts to munch away in the wee, small hours.

My bread recipes give you more choices and flexibility than most, in that they use this yeast action to produce several different-tasting breads from one basic recipe (see "Daily Breads").

THINGS TO REMEMBER ABOUT STARTERS

- Flour, water, and a pinch of yeast mixed together and left for 6 hours to overnight will give many breads a better flavor, but not necessary for great bread.

- If you are making a sourdough starter from someone else's recipe, it really should be bubbling when used, not limp and flat looking, and certainly not pink. A pinkish tinge means it has gone too long and the acid has polished off the yeast.

- Starters do not have to be kept for generations. New ones are better than old ones as they have more life, and besides, the yeasts from a starter made years ago have already been replaced by new yeasts. Is it the same starter as fifty years ago? It's like the hammer: the top breaks so you buy a new top, then the handle breaks so you replace the handle. Is it the same hammer?

A mystique has been built around starters and fermentations, but basically anyone can jump-start a loaf of bread with any easily made starter; there is no mystery to it. Just get into the kitchen and start experimenting (or read Harold McGee for technical support!).

Hazelnut / Sage

Kalamata Olive Filoncino

Filoncino integrale

Panini

Rosemary focaccia

Fougasse

Rustico

Cinnamon focaccia

Daily Breads

WHEN I LIVED IN ROME, my mornings began with a stop
at the local *panificio*, the bakery, where I could gather the latest gossip,
gaze upon the Caravaggio countenances of my neighbor's children,
and flirt wantonly with the handsome bakers, their faces dusted with
flour like the masks of medieval actors on a fragrant stage. The six-foot-
long *pizza bianca* (see page 108) would first be placed on a wooden
paddle, carefully pleated, like a piece of fabric, liberally brushed
with olive oil, and then quickly pulled to its full length over the stone
floor of the oven. The owner would hack off great chunks of *pane
casereccio* for the housewives' lunches, and children would inevitably
be munching on fresh little anise-flavored *biscotti* or pieces of just-
baked *pizza bianca*, a morning favorite of every Italian, young and old.

How different from shopping at our supermarkets, where the shelves are lined with packaged breads, soft, cottony, and most inedible (except for the whole-grain specialty breads that every now and then make a good piece of toast). We have been known for years as the country of Wonder bread, Twinkies, and doughnuts, and it is no wonder that there are national rampages against the presence of some of our junk-food restaurants in countries such as France and Italy. Our culture has never been one to embrace artisan bread. Not, at least, until now, and boy, are things changing!

In existence for only a mere 250 or so years, we Americans have the daunting but exciting task of creating our own food history, and we are fast catching up in the realm of daily breads. We have marvelous bakers who can hold their own among the world's masters, while ironically the French, after hundreds of years, lament the loss of their crusty, dense, and flavorful baguettes, the backbone of any French meal. The French baguette is probably the most influential bread in modern American bread making. Everyone wants to make a baguette like the lovely artisan ones found nowadays only in small village bakeries in France or select city bakeries. But if the country breads of Italy were more prevalent here, I am sure that they would be the breads we would emulate more often; it is these breads that I want to eat every day. It is a formidable challenge, however, to encourage education about bread to a country of people who grew up with sliced, white, tasteless loaves. Now, when you watch someone bite into your own homemade Rosemary or Olive Filoncino, you will, I believe, find a willing convert and student.

Education begins, of course, with children. For heaven's sake, give children a great-tasting bread in their lunch boxes instead of calorie-rich, sugar-filled snacks or sliced commercial breads. I often do demonstrations in supermarkets or at events to acquaint the public with breads from Buona Forchetta, and I am struck by one thing that happens over and over again: mothers with children are very open to having their babies taste new flavors, but it is the children themselves who surprise me. They taste a piece of rosemary focaccia or olive bread and almost always ask for more, proving themselves to be much more adventuresome than many adults. Some will come back to my table time after time (in fact, sometimes I'm not sure their mothers know they are there!), grab a handful of samples when I'm not looking, and run.

Daily breads, for me, are those that you can eat with all foods or that become the meal itself. A simple, well-baked loaf is far more satisfying to me than all the honey-wheat-berry-walnut-raisin-and-garlic breads in the world, although I have my favorites with flavors, such as the Hazelnut-Sage Filoncino in this chapter or the spiced African bread in "Special Breads." But what I want to eat daily is a very chewy, flavorful, and simple loaf such as the Pane Trattoria (for restaurants), or the Pane Osso we make at the bakery: no fat, no sugar, no nonsense, just bread with a great taste and substantial texture, or a simple focaccia with olive oil, fresh rosemary, and salt.

A perfect example of how I created one of my own daily breads is the evolution of Fougasse de Collioure, a wondrous, chewy, ladder-shaped bread that I first tasted in the south of France near the Spanish border. When I returned home, my heart had unfortunately stayed behind, and I began work on a recipe for my beloved fougasse so as not to die from nostalgia. Just as the air, water, and flour of Italy are different from ours in Los Angeles, so are they in France, but one of our clients is a chef from Perpignan, near Collioure, and he has put his stamp of approval on our fougasse. It is much chewier than the French one, with a rich, nutty, almost buttery flavor from the fermented dough. Other fougasses contain herbs or olives, which you can always add to the basic recipe, but the thing itself, without enhancement, is one of our best sellers at the bakery.

Upon returning to Collioure after several summers away, we found that the fougasse was not the same, or that our tastes had changed; the crusty, rich fougasse we were making had spoiled us for others, probably because our flour is substantially different from theirs or perhaps because we begin with a different sponge and develop a little more flavor. It turned out that the only baker who could make the original fougasse had sold out and left the area; his bakery was for sale and the whole town was in turmoil over the loss of its best bread. My husband had to tie me down to keep me from becoming an expatriate, fougasse-baking, American interloper in Collioure (the beaches aren't bad, either). Fortunately, I can now bake my own ladder bread at home, and so can you, along with many other unusual breads that have taken shape in my kitchen after years of travel and tasting.

Having daily bread on the table does not mean meticulous, precise measurements, days and days of ripening starters, temperature-controlled environments, and closets of equipment, all of which have their place. A more than memorable loaf may be yours in 1½ hours, start to finish, without effort. Of course you may choose to have a longer rising time or simply put your dough on hold overnight until you are ready to bake, and yes, you will get a more complex and richer flavor, but let me say to all cooks who feel intimidated by lengthy processes, complicated instructions, and the seemingly arcane language of the baking world: plunge in! Have no fear! Making bread is a piece of cake. With the recipes that follow, making your own simple, daily bread will be as much a part of your day as making the morning coffee.

Focaccia: Basic Dough for Flatbreads or Loaves

1 LARGE OR 2 SMALL LOAVES; 1 LARGE OR 2 SMALL FOCACCE

This user-friendly dough is about as basic as you can get. It was the dough that inspired me to start my bakery in Los Angeles and was the dough that everyone seems to like. One morning at the Farmer's Market in Santa Monica, when I was setting up my bread concession, I dropped a focaccetta (sandwich size) in the street and watched with horror, as did several others, as a pickup truck, Mercedes, and large van rolled over the just-baked bun. We could actually see its shape spring back, resilient and just as fresh as ever, much like the Samsonite luggage that when dropped from thirty stories bounces back without a scratch! This is very hardy dough.

With it you can make loaves of bread, flatbreads, crisp breads, little sandwich buns (focaccette), the French ladder bread fougasse, exotic hamburger buns, bread sticks, and more. You can also forget it in the refrigerator or leave it to rise a little too long and it will bounce back very easily, even after the Mack truck is gone. It is very forgiving, and I have witnesses to prove it.

2 cups lukewarm water (85 to 95°F)
2 teaspoons active dry yeast
4 cups unbleached bread flour
2 to 3 teaspoons salt
2 to 3 teaspoons olive oil
2 tablespoons chopped fresh rosemary
1 teaspoon kosher or sea salt

Measure the water into a large bowl. Sprinkle the yeast over the water and stir until dissolved. Stir in 2 cups of the flour and the salt and stir briskly until smooth, about 2 minutes. With a strong wooden spoon or one of those rare mixing spoons with a big hole in the middle, stir in the remaining 2 cups of flour for about 2 minutes longer, just until the dough pulls away from the sides of the bowl and the flour is incorporated. The dough will be fairly wet and tacky (sticky), but when it pulls away from the sides of the bowl and forms a loose ball, you'll know the dough has been stirred sufficiently. If it seems too sticky, stir in an additional ¼ to ½ cup of flour.

Same day method: Cover the bowl with plastic wrap and let the dough rise in a warm place until doubled in volume, 30 to 40 minutes. Proceed with the shaping instructions.

Overnight method: Cover the bowl and refrigerate overnight. The dough will rise in the refrigerator and acquire flavor from the slower yeast action. Remove the dough 2 hours before shaping and let stand, covered, in a warm place. The dough will rise for the second time. Proceed with the shaping instructions.

To shape into loaves: Preheat the oven to 500°F. Oil a seasoned nonstick, oven-proof 9-inch skillet or two 5-inch skillets.

Pour the dough into the large pan or divide it equally between the two small-

Focaccia dough can be used for every shape

continued

er pans by loosening the dough with a spatula and then carefully scraping it from the sides of the bowl, keeping the dough as inflated as possible. If you are using two pans, cut the dough off at the edge of the bowl with the spatula as it falls into each pan. The shape that the dough takes on as it falls into the pan is fine. Brush the tops of loaves with olive oil, sprinkle with rosemary and sea salt, and set aside to rise until doubled, about 15 to 20 minutes.

To bake loaves: Place the bread in the preheated oven and reduce the oven temperature to 400°F. Bake for 30 to 35 minutes or until nicely browned and the loaf sounds hollow when tapped with your finger. Remove loaf from pan and cool on a rack.

Cut dough off at edge of bowl.

To shape into focaccia: Preheat the oven to 500°F. Oil one or two nonstick 13-by-18-inch baking sheets.

Pour the dough onto the sheet(s), carefully scraping it from the sides of the bowl with a rubber spatula. Brush the dough with 2 teaspoons of olive oil. To make the traditional focaccia with indentations, dip your fingers into cold water or olive oil and insert them straight down into the dough. Make holes in the dough by pulling it to the sides about 1 inch at a time. Pull the holes at random to form little craters all over with the pan showing through where you have put your fingers. As you work, stretch the dough into a 1-inch-thick oval. (If you are using just one baking sheet, the focaccia will cover almost the entire sheet.) Brush the loaf with another teaspoon of olive oil and sprinkle with the rosemary and sea salt. Focaccia does not need to rise, but if you forget it for a few minutes, don't worry. It will bake beautifully despite a little neglect.

To shape into dinner rolls: This is the easiest way to make rolls with any dough. Follow the instructions for the Overnight Method. Preheat the oven to 500°F. Spray a French bread pan with nonstick spray or rub with olive oil. A 3-section pan will yield 9 or 12 rolls, depending on the size you choose to cut off.

Take a good handful of the chilled dough and gently stretch it out into a rectangle approximately 2 inches wide and 8 inches long. Snip off 2-inch pieces of dough and drop them into the grooves in the pan, using three to a groove. You may shape them after cutting if you like, but I prefer the free-form look of the unshaped rolls. Brush with olive oil and sprinkle with fresh rosemary. Let rise until doubled in volume. (If you wish to make rolls from room-temperature dough, pour the dough into the grooves of the pan, cutting off the dough with a scraper after a 3-inch piece of dough has "fallen" into the groove. Proceed again down the groove, letting the dough fall into its roll shape [see illustration]. Rolls made like this need to rise only for about 15 minutes before baking. They will have a good spring and be very tender with a crisp crust.)

Pour dough and cut off rolls into pan

To bake the focaccia and rolls: Place the pan(s) in the oven and reduce the oven temperature to 450°F. Bake for 15 to 20 minutes, until the focaccia has a nice, golden-brown color mixed with a little darker brown around the indented area. Bake the rolls for 12 to 15 minutes, or until golden brown on top. Cool on a wire rack. Cut focaccia into wedges or rectangles and serve warm.

NOTE: For a breakfast focaccia, mix 1 teaspoon cinnamon with 1 cup coarse brown sugar and sprinkle over focaccia in place of rosemary and salt.

Fougasse de Collioure

3 SMALL LOAVES

This is a moist, chewy ladder bread that I discovered and enjoyed for the several summers I spent in the little French medieval town of Collioure, near the Spanish border. There, in an apartment looking out over not one but three beaches, I grilled local sardines and made thick ratatouille with the luscious red peppers, sweet onions, and rich black eggplant of the Roussillon region and then piled all onto fresh-split *fougasse* from the local baker (when he was still there!).

The Fauves (in French, *fauve* means wild animal), so named because of their wild and sensual colors and shapes, painted the magical evening light in Collioure as it illuminated the red, blue, and yellow Latine-rigged boats rocking in the harbor. I imagine that the artists might have munched on fougasse during breaks from the canvas, the bread accompanied by many bottles of good Roussillon wine. The exquisite food of the region incorporated Fauve-colored vegetables and fish, and the daily bread always included fougasse, as well as the usual baguettes. For eight years, I did not go back, and then in July 1997, I returned with children and grandchildren and found that every one of our friends was still there on the beach, in practically the same places where I had bid them *au revoir*, with *their* children and grandchildren, and still enjoying the warm fougasses and *bunyettes* (little round, flat sugar breads) from the local boulangerie. My fougasse has a little more body and texture than the French one, because our flour is made from a harder wheat with more elasticity than the flour milled in France. Since this is a bread that is mostly crust, it does not keep as long as larger loaves do, but the flavor is buttery and rich without any fat used in the dough. My husband calls its unusual shape a "figure 12," a figure 8 with a circle added. For an unusual appetizer, stud it with anchovies before baking.

1 recipe prepared Focaccia Dough (page 40), minus the rosemary
2 teaspoons olive oil
Kosher or sea salt

Follow the recipe for Focaccia through the first rise. Fold the dough over 3 or 4 times and cover tightly with plastic wrap. Refrigerate the dough overnight so it can rise again.

To shape the fougasse: Preheat the oven to 500°F. Remove the dough from the refrigerator and, using a scraper, carefully scoop the dough out onto a clean surface. Cut it into 3 pieces. Let them rest for 10 minutes. Rub another baking sheet with olive oil.

Grasp one of the pieces in each hand and stretch it to form a fairly flat 12-by-6-inch oblong or rectangle. Pull it gently so as not to break it. Lay this on the oiled baking sheet. With kitchen shears, cut the dough into 3 equal lengths, approximately 2 inches wide and 12 inches long. Make 3 vertical slashes with scissors along each piece of dough (see illustration). With your fingers, stretch the slashes open to form a kind of ladder shape (a "figure 12"). Let the dough rest for 15 minutes.

Cutting slits in fougasse

To bake the fougasse: Brush the loaf with the olive oil and sprinkle with salt. Place in the oven and reduce the oven temperature to 450°F. Bake for 15 to 20 minutes until golden brown. Cool on a wire rack.

NOTE: Watch that the fougasse does not brown too quickly. Fougasse needs high heat because there is so much crust and so little crumb. If it does not brown in 20 minutes, increase the oven temperature to 500°F and check that it browns quickly without burning.

Opening cuts in fougasse

Rosemary Filoncino

There is nothing like the fragrance of rosemary (except perhaps white truffles). Rosemary is one of the few herbs used in cooking to which I am addicted! It calms and soothes me—and just a whiff can take you on a little private vacation to Italy, where the smell of *rosmarino*, as it is called, permeates the air near almost any trattoria. You can imagine the cook turning quail or little flattened chickens on the grill or tossing new potatoes in rosemary and olive oil, ready for the roasting pan along with a *branzino* (sea bass).

I use it in many foods: breads, chicken, lamb, veal, and even in sorbet. I make a fragrant rinse for my hair (great for brunettes) from crushed rosemary leaves. When breads are brushed with olive oil and sprinkled with fresh, chopped rosemary, the rich flavor is often mistaken for that of sweet butter.

This baguette is made from the same dough as the focaccia, but because the flavor of a bread changes when its shape changes, you will find that this long, cylindrical loaf has a bit more crumb, a slightly more buttery taste, and is useful for slicing into small rounds for canapés or little toasts. This bread also makes a great long sandwich, bruschetta, or breakfast *tartine* split lengthwise, toasted, and served with jam.

2¼ cups lukewarm water (85 to 95°F)
2 teaspoons active dry yeast
4½ cups unbleached bread flour
2 to 3 teaspoons salt
3 tablespoons rosemary oil

2 teaspoons olive oil

4 tablespoons chopped fresh rosemary

1 teaspoon kosher or sea salt

Measure the water into a large bowl. Sprinkle the yeast over the water and stir until dissolved. Stir in 2 cups of the flour and the salt and stir briskly until smooth, about 2 minutes. Stir in the rosemary oil.

With a wooden or plastic spoon, stir in the remaining 2½ cups of flour for about 2 minutes longer, just until the dough pulls away from the sides of the bowl and the flour is incorporated.

The dough will be fairly wet and tacky (sticky), but when it pulls away from the sides of the bowl and forms a loose ball, the dough has been stirred sufficiently. If the dough seems too sticky, stir in an additional ¼ to ½ cup of flour.

Same day method: Cover the bowl with plastic wrap and let the dough rise in a warm place until doubled in volume, 30 to 40 minutes. Proceed with the shaping instructions.

Overnight method: Cover the bowl and refrigerate overnight. The dough will rise in the refrigerator and acquire flavor from the slower yeast action. Remove the dough 2 hours before shaping and let stand, covered, in a warm place. The dough will rise for the second time. Proceed with the shaping instructions.

To shape into filoncino: Preheat the oven to 500°F. Spray a three-loaf baguette pan with nonstick spray or rub with olive oil.

With your left hand (or right hand if you are left-handed), hold the bowl and tip it over the opening of a groove and pour the dough along and into the groove by loosening the dough with a spatula. Carefully move along the groove as the dough pours, keeping it as inflated as possible. With the spatula, cut the dough off at the rim of the bowl as it falls into the groove (see illustration). The dough should form a nice, rounded

CUT OFF DOUGH HERE

FRENCH BAGUETTE PAN

continued

cylinder that fills the groove and stands about ½ inch above the rim of the pan. Fill the other two grooves. Brush the tops of loaves with the olive oil, sprinkle with rosemary and salt, and let rise about 15 to 20 minutes or until cylinders of dough are nicely rounded and puffed.

To bake loaves: Place the bread in the preheated oven and reduce the oven temperature to 400°F. Bake for 30 to 35 minutes, or until the filoncini are nicely browned. Tap the baguette pan on a flat surface to loosen the loaves and cool them on a rack.

Rosemary Oil

MAKES 1 CUP

Strip 6 long branches of fresh rosemary when the leaves are very green. Chop the leaves fine. Very gently, heat 1 cup of extra-virgin olive oil, just until warm. Off the heat, stir the rosemary leaves into the oil and let sit for 2 to 3 hours. Strain the oil and use. Store in a lidded glass jar or bottle.

Rosemary

Ciabatta

Slipper Bread

1 LARGE LOAF, OR A PAIR OF "SMALLER OLD SLIPPERS"

This loaf is called ciabatta because its shape resembles a comfortable old slipper. Perhaps you should make a pair, but wait until they cool to try them on. This name probably is not an accident. I imagine that some flustered baker in a hurry one morning threw his dough out flat on the table, made a few swift folds at the ends to give it shape and into the oven it went. While the bread was baking, he hoisted his slippered feet up on the table and then 20 minutes later, after contemplating his old houseshoes, he pulled the bread from the oven and gave it its charming name.

Ciabatta originated in the north around Lago di Como, but has become popular in other parts of Italy. It seems to be just short of a mad craze here in America because it is a lovely chewy bread, made from a very soft dough that gives it its wonderful texture, full of holes like the pane casereccio. It takes more time to make than most bread, but most of that time is spent waiting, not working. Ciabatta has a nutty, yeasty, seductive flavor that will make you want to eat it every day. Brush a slice with olive oil, grill it, and experience nirvana.

A good ciabatta dough should be very soft and resilient with a silky, elastic feel. In order to get the best flavor in a ciabatta, let the dough rise once, fold it over on itself two or three times, let it rise again, and then refrigerate it overnight to rise a third time, following the directions for overnight method. It is an extremely wet dough so when working with it, coat it with a little flour for easy handling. Three rises enhance the flavor

continued

of the bread, but one will do if you have no time; the result will be slightly less tasty. The dough is mixed with a *biga,* which must be made the night before to be ready for the ciabatta the next day.

BIGA

½ teaspoon active dry yeast

1 cup lukewarm water (85 to 95°F)

2 cups unbleached bread flour plus 2 tablespoons rye flour

CIABATTA

1½ cups lukewarm water (85 to 95°F)

2 teaspoons active dry yeast

4 cups unbleached bread flour

2 teaspoons salt dissolved in 1 tablespoon water

½ cup flour, for the baking sheet and top of ciabatta

To make the biga: Mix the yeast with the water and stir well. In a glass bowl, mix the two flours with the yeast mixture, stirring well to aerate the mixture and form a wet dough. Cover tightly with plastic wrap and let ferment overnight at room temperature. In the morning, it will be bubbly and fragrant.

To make the ciabatta: Measure the water into a large mixing bowl. Sprinkle the yeast over the water and stir until dissolved. Stir in the *biga.* Add the flour and dissolved salt, and stir until the flour is thoroughly incorporated and the dough is smooth with the consistency of very thick biscuit batter. It will be a rather sticky, soft dough. Cover the dough and let it stand in a warm place until doubled in volume, about 1 hour.

With a scraper or spatula, fold the dough by gently lifting it up from underneath and turning or folding it over on itself two or three times. Folding the dough gives the gluten a rest and stimulates the little yeast babies so that they moisten the dough as they convert sugar (from the flour) into gas and water. Cover and let rise a second time for 40 to 45 minutes until doubled in volume (the second rise takes less time as the yeasts are very active at this point) or cover and refrigerate until time to bake. At least 2 hours before forming, remove the dough from the refrigerator. During this time it will rise again. It is then ready to shape and bake. The dough should be very soft and silky.

To shape the ciabatta: Flour a baking sheet with a nice thin layer. Carefully turn the dough out onto the baking sheet in one long glop, being very careful to keep it as inflated as possible. The dough should be about 3 inches thick at the highest point. Flour your hands, throw a little flour over the dough to give it a light coat, and lift each end of the dough, gently stretching it into an oblong about 4 inches wide and 13 to 15 inches long. Or cut the dough in half and form 2 ciabatte. Flour two 13-by-18-inch baking sheets and place one ciabatta on each. The dough should be about 1½ inches thick in the middle. (Some of the classic ciabatte are stretched to make the outer ends of the rectangle thinner than the middle and then folded toward the middle, making the dough into toe and heel of an old slipper [see illustration], but I leave mine alone. The resulting baked shape is rough and casual looking, like an old beat-up shoe.) Let the slippers rise until doubled in volume, about ½ hour.

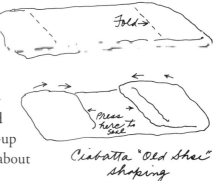

Ciabatta "Old Shoe" shaping

Preheat the oven to 500°F. Just before putting it in the oven, slip your hands under each end of the ciabatta and push it a little toward the center, flipping it over softly onto its other side. This will enable it to rise evenly in the oven. Dust thoroughly with flour and bake.

To bake the ciabatta: Place in the oven for 15 minutes. Reduce the oven temperature to 450°F. Bake for 15 minutes longer or until nicely browned. Remove to a wire rack and cool completely before cutting. The texture of the crumb and crust should be moist and chewy, with the crumb shiny and inviting, just waiting to become a bruschetta. Grill a slice, remove from grill and rub it with garlic, and top with fresh tomatoes and basil.

Kalamata Olive Filoncino

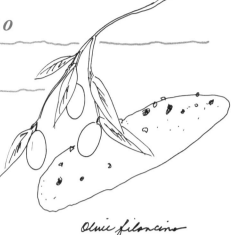

Olive filoncino

I had originally made Kalamata Olive Filoncino as a focaccia, but each time I looked at it, its circular shape seemed a little homely, much too flat and full of dark indeterminate spots. Because of the surface area and internal volume, flat bread, such as focaccia, bakes differently from a round loaf with more crumb, and a change in shape can make a great difference to its taste and appearance.

When the olive dough was formed into a baguette, the olives in the dough popped out slightly as it rose, so that when it baked, the olives became crisp, almost crunchy, like an olive chip. The outside was lovely and shiny (the baguettes baked all together threw off large quantities of moisture), glittering with sea salt. Our olive bread had finally found its true personality. Because the olives were so good when toasted, we subsequently made the olive baguettes into yet another product, little thin-sliced melba toasts called *bruschettine*. We did the same with our Hazelnut-Sage Bread.

There are olives and there are Kalamata olives. Our Kalamata Olive Bread is one of the most popular at Buona Forchetta, and I feel it is because of the quality and taste of the olives we use. Not every olive reacts well with flour and yeast, not to mention being baked! There is a sweetness to a good brine-cured olive, in contrast to the acrid, often bitter taste of the olives marinated in oil used by many bakers. The bread is stained with the rich dark juice of the briny olives released during baking. Use other kinds of olives if kalamatas are not available and the result will be different. But don't worry, you will most likely come up with a delicious, new bread! Even martini olives work in a pinch. Use the olives, drink the martini.

1¼ cups lukewarm water (85 to 95°F)

2 teaspoons active dry yeast

4½ cups unbleached bread flour

1 teaspoon salt

¾ cup chopped Kalamata olives (or leave some whole, if you like)

2 tablespoons olive paste (see Notes)

¾ cup Kalamata olive brine (see Notes)

2 teaspoons olive oil

1 teaspoon kosher or sea salt

Measure the water into a large bowl. Sprinkle the yeast over the water and stir to dissolve. Stir in 2¼ cups of the flour, salt, olives, and paste, and stir until smooth, about 2 minutes. Add the remaining 2¼ cups flour and the brine and stir. The dough will be fairly wet and sticky, the consistency of a very thick batter. If the dough seems too wet, add an additional ¼ to ½ cup of flour.

Same day method: Cover the bowl with plastic wrap and let the dough rise in a warm place until doubled in volume, 30 to 45 minutes.

With a scraper or spatula, fold the dough by gently lifting it up from underneath and turning or folding it over on itself three or four times. Let the dough rise a second time in a warm place until doubled in volume, 30 to 45 minutes. Proceed with the shaping instructions.

Overnight method: Cover the dough and refrigerate overnight. The dough will rise in the refrigerator and acquire flavor from the slower yeast action. Remove the dough from the refrigerator 2 hours before shaping and let stand, covered, in a warm place. The dough will rise for the second time. Proceed with the shaping instructions.

continued

To shape into loaves: Preheat the oven to 500°F. Spray a three-loaf baguette pan with nonstick spray or rub with olive oil.

With your left hand (or right hand if you are left-handed), hold the bowl and tip it over the opening of a groove and pour the dough along and into the groove by loosening the dough with a spatula. Carefully move along the groove as the dough pours, keeping it as inflated as possible. With the spatula, cut the dough off at the rim of the bowl as it falls into the groove. The dough should form a nice, rounded cylinder that fills the groove and stands about ½ inch above the rim of the pan. Fill the other two grooves. Brush the tops of loaves with the olive oil and sprinkle with kosher salt.

To bake loaves: Place the pan in the oven and reduce the oven temperature to 400°F. Bake for 25 to 30 minutes, until the top is browned and the loaves sound hollow when tapped. Remove baguettes from the pan and cool on wire racks.

NOTES: If you prefer loaves with crisper undersides, remove the loaves from the pan and return them to the oven, placing them directly on the oven rack, for about 5 minutes. Cool on wire racks.

Make olive paste by putting 2 cups pitted olives in a blender and puréeing it until smooth but still a little textured. Excess may be used for tapenade or on pizza or sandwiches.

A strong olive brine is used to pack the olives. If the brine with the olives you buy does not measure ¾ cup, add water to measure the full ¾ cup and add ¼ teaspoon salt.

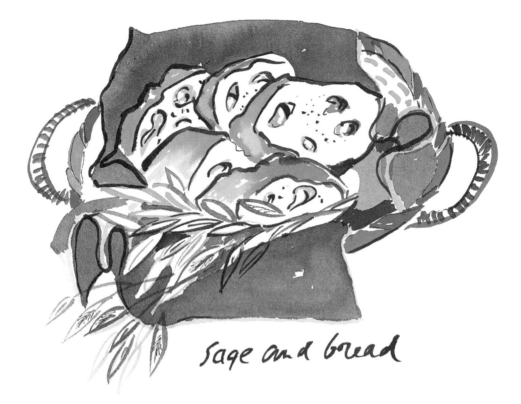

sage and bread

Hazelnut-Sage Filoncino

3 BAGUETTES

My Hazelnut-Sage Filoncino was born out of pure, unadulterated laziness. The prospect of stuffing a 12-pound goose at Thanksgiving and no time at all to plan for several guests had me in a frenzy. I found myself longing for that other leisurely life, before I ran a business, when I made holiday wreaths from the garden, hand-painted the Christmas stockings, and attempted to prepare for holidays in the manner of Martha Stewart. (Well, sort of like Martha Stewart.) How simple it would be, I mused, to simply stick the hazelnuts and sage in the bread dough, bake it, and then use that

continued

for stuffing. And any leftover bread would certainly liven up my bread basket.

I am fortunate to have a backyard full of wild sage and so I plucked a good cupful, toasted it in a little olive oil, and threw it in the dough to create a new recipe. The resulting bread is one of our most popular, especially at Thanksgiving and in winter when it can be used to stuff all manner of birds, pork chops, or what have you. It also makes exotic croutons for salads, bread crumbs for scaloppine or chicken breasts, or for adding a crunch to sautéed vegetables.

Try it for French toast or simply toasted, plain, with a little marmalade. The hazelnuts brown along with the bread and lend such a rich taste to the bread that no butter is needed. Any bread made with sage, rosemary, or thyme will bring out the taste of a tart fruit jam or jelly. I particularly love the marriage of bitter orange marmalade and the round sweet taste of sage and nuts. A bruschetta of Hazelnut-Sage and goat cheese is another delicious way to serve this bread.

1½ cups roasted hazelnuts

1 tablespoon crushed, dried sage leaves (I dry fresh sage leaves in a slow oven)

2 cups lukewarm water (85 to 95°F)

2 teaspoons active dry yeast

4½ cups unbleached bread flour

2 to 3 teaspoons salt

2 tablespoons hazelnut oil (found in supermarkets or specialty stores) (optional)

2 teaspoons olive oil

1 teaspoon kosher or sea salt

1 tablespoon crushed hazelnuts (optional)

In the food processor, chop the nuts with the dried sage for 5 to 6 seconds, until the nuts are the size of small peas. Remove half the mixture to a dish, and then pulverize the remaining nuts and sage until fairly smooth.

Measure the water into a large bowl. Sprinkle the yeast over the water and stir until dissolved. Stir in 2¼ cups of the flour, salt, the nut mixtures, and the hazelnut oil, if using, and mix until smooth. Add the remaining 2¼ cups flour and mix just until the flour is incorporated. If dough is too sticky, stir in an additional ¼ to ½ cup of flour.

Same day method: Cover the bowl with plastic wrap and let the dough rise in a warm place until doubled in volume, 30 to 40 minutes. Proceed with the shaping instructions.

Overnight method: Cover the dough and refrigerate overnight. The dough will rise in the refrigerator and acquire flavor from the slower yeast action. Remove the dough from the refrigerator 2 hours before shaping and let stand, covered, in a warm place. The dough will rise for the second time. Proceed with the shaping instructions.

To shape into loaves: Preheat the oven to 500°F. Spray a three-loaf baguette pan with nonstick spray or rub with olive oil.

With your left hand (or right hand if you are left-handed), hold the bowl and tip it over the opening of a groove and pour the dough along by loosening it with a spatula. Carefully move along the groove as the dough pours, keeping it as inflated as possible. With the spatula, cut the dough off at the rim of the bowl as it falls into the groove. The dough should form a nice, rounded cylinder that fills the groove and stands about ½ inch above the rim of the pan. Fill the other two grooves. Brush the tops of loaves with the olive oil and sprinkle with salt and crushed hazelnuts, if using.

To bake loaves: Place the pan in the oven and reduce the oven temperature to 400°F. Bake for 25 to 30 minutes, until the top is browned and the loaves sound hollow when tapped. Remove baguettes from the pan and cool on wire racks.

Filoncino Integrale

Integrale rolls

Sourdough was the rage in the 1960s when I lived in Berkeley and San Francisco. There was nothing more exotic and sexy than a picnic on the beach with cracked Dungeness crab, just out of the steamer pot on Fisherman's Wharf, and a round of the famous sourdough that put San Francisco bread on the map. A little cold split of Chablis didn't hurt either. The *Bacillus sanfrancisco*, as I mentioned before, is famous the world over because of the particular flavor it imparts to San Francisco's breads. Perhaps it's the ocean moisture or the placement of the city on its particular coastal soil, but no one seems to be able to duplicate it, even though there are many impostors.

Many beautiful-looking sourdough breads, slashed just so and often shining with a steam patina, will not necessarily have good flavor, just as a breathtakingly beautiful body may house a vapid soul. For example, many, many commercial producers of sourdough bread try to emulate the original large crusty San Francisco sourdough loaves, and, in fact, they often come up with a pretty good facsimile. On the outside. The inside is a whole other ball game. (My husband actually makes little compact soccer balls out of most sourdough breads at restaurants and shoots them around the table, making goals between wineglasses. Naturally, you may gather from this that we are very sophisticated diners....)

Perhaps I am the only bread maker in the world less than enthusiastic about sourdough breads, but there are so many replicas of the original that I find other original breads more interesting. The sourdough flavor can often be overwhelming; there is no other taste in the bread except sour or tart. The fermentation upstages the many levels on which a bread can be savored.

My recipe for sourdough whole wheat uses a mild starter that produces a chewy, moist loaf with a very subtle flavor. It's pleasingly lemony and nutty at the same time. I am partial to this bread, even though it is made with a semisourdough starter, because I know that the final product will taste completely different from what you know as sourdough bread and will not overpower the flavors of the whole wheat flour and your own kitchen yeast.

BIGA
½ cup whole wheat flour
½ cup rye flour
½ teaspoon active dry yeast
1 cup lukewarm water (85 to 95°F)

FILONCINO
1¼ cups lukewarm water (85 to 95°F)
2 teaspoons active dry yeast
1 cup *biga*
4 cups unbleached bread flour
Whole grains or nuts (see Notes) (optional)
2 teaspoons salt
¾ cup whole wheat flour
2 teaspoons olive oil
1 teaspoon kosher or coarse sea salt

continued

To make the biga: Mix the flours, yeast, and water, stirring until very smooth. Cover tightly with plastic wrap and let sit overnight at room temperature. In the morning, it will be bubbly and fragrant.

To make the bread: Measure the water into a large mixing bowl. Sprinkle the yeast over the water and stir until dissolved. Stir in the *biga*. Add 2½ cups of the bread flour and the salt and stir until smooth, about 2 minutes. At this point, add any whole grains or other additives (see Notes). Add the remaining 1½ cups of bread flour and the whole wheat flour and stir until smooth and dough pulls away from the sides of the bowl. Cover the bowl and let the dough rise until doubled in volume, 30 to 45 minutes.

With a scraper or spatula, fold the dough by gently lifting it up from underneath and turning or folding it over on itself two or three times. Folding the dough gives the gluten a rest and stimulates the little yeast babies so that they moisten the dough as they convert sugar (from the flour) into gas and water. Cover and let rise a second time, for 40 to 45 minutes, until doubled in volume.

To shape into loaves: Preheat the oven to 500°F. Spray a three-loaf baguette pan with nonstick spray or rub with olive oil.

With your left hand (or right hand if you are left-handed), hold the bowl and tip it over the opening of a groove and pour the dough along the groove by loosening the dough with a spatula. Carefully move along the groove as the dough pours, keeping it as inflated as possible. With the spatula, cut the dough off at the rim of the bowl as it falls into the groove. The dough should form a nice, rounded cylinder that fills the groove and stands about ½ inch above the rim of the pan. Fill the other two grooves. Brush the tops with the olive oil and sprinkle with salt and let rise for 15 to 20 minutes or until the cylinders of dough are nicely rounded and puffed.

To bake loaves: Place the pan in the oven and reduce the oven temperature to 425°F. Bake for 20 minutes, until the top is browned. Remove from oven and cool on wire racks.

NOTES: Add any of the following to enhance the loaves:

- ½ cup cracked wheat, rye, or bulgur, soaked in water for 2 hours and drained, or wheat bran

- ¾ cup walnuts, pecans, or hazelnuts, roasted and chopped medium fine
- ¼ cup nut meal

For a breakfast bread: ⅔ cup roasted grapes (see p. 141)

If you add weight to this bread by adding ingredients, you will need to add 1 more teaspoon of yeast to the basic dough in order to give the dough help during the last rise.

Sourdough Caraway Rye

1 ROUND LOAF OR 2 SMALL BAGUETTES

My mother, who could not eat wheat because of migraines, had various rye breads, rye crisps, and crackers in the house so as not to aggravate her allergies (and to further compensate for her sacrifice, she kept a bottle of rye whisky for the cocktail hour). Of course, my mother ate wheat anyway, but this introduction to rye products at any early age inspired me to make this light bread, intensified and made better with molasses and a little bitter chocolate. This rye bread is very different from my Czech grandmother's heavy German-style rye breads, scented with caraway, and from the famous New York Jewish ryes, which I discovered in college. My rye bread crust is chewy, not hard, and the crumb not too fine but still welcoming enough to a warm slice of corned beef, some mustard, and a good dill pickle. When making rye bread, you can control the strength of the caraway, add raisins, or even cut the rye for a more pleasing texture. In any event, you should feel satisfied that you have conquered one of the most difficult breads to make. Rye flour does not contain much gluten, and so you must use some white or wheat flour with it to get a rise out of it or be

continued

satisfied with a really dense bread. One of my tester's grandchildren appropriately christened this bread "The Chocolate Bread."

BIGA

1 teaspoon active dry yeast

1½ cups lukewarm water (85 to 95°F)

1½ cups unbleached bread flour

½ cup rye flour

BREAD

½ cup lukewarm water (85 to 95°F)

1½ tablespoons active dry yeast

2 cups unbleached bread flour

1 scant cup whole wheat flour

½ cup rye flour

2 tablespoons dark molasses

2 teaspoons unsweetened Dutch-processed cocoa powder, such as Droste

⅓ cup caraway seeds, toasted, plus 1 tablespoon for crusts

1 teaspoon kosher or sea salt

1 tablespoon olive oil

To make the biga: In a glass bowl, mix the yeast with the water and stir well. Add the bread flour and rye flour to the yeast mixture, stirring well to aerate the mixture and form a wet dough. Cover the bowl tightly with plastic wrap and let the dough ferment overnight at room temperature. In the morning, it will be bubbly and fragrant.

To make the bread: Measure the water into a large bowl. Sprinkle the yeast over the water and stir until dissolved. Add the *biga,* flours, molasses, cocoa powder, ⅓ cup caraway seeds, and salt, stirring until all the flour is incorporated and the dough pulls away from the sides of the bowl. Rub a little olive oil on your hands, and press the dough once or twice with the heel of your hand to incorporate the flour. Fold the dough over on itself once or twice to form a smooth ball.

Same day method: Cover the bowl with plastic wrap and let the dough rise in a warm place until doubled in volume, 40 to 60 minutes. Proceed with the shaping instructions.

Overnight method: Cover the bowl and refrigerate overnight. The dough will rise in the refrigerator and acquire a mild, sour-rye flavor from the slower yeast action. Remove the dough 2 hours before shaping and let stand, covered, in a warm place. The dough will rise for the second time. Proceed with the shaping instructions.

To shape into loaves: Brush a skillet, baking sheet, or baguette pan with olive oil. Using a spatula to loosen the dough from the sides of the bowl, pour the dough into the skillet or grooves of the pan, using the bowl and gravity to allow the dough to fall into the grooves as you move the bowl along it. Divide the dough equally among the three grooves. You may lift the dough and stretch it if needed. The dough is very easy to handle and shape. Keep the dough as inflated as possible.

Brush the dough with the olive oil, sprinkle with salt and the remaining 1 tablespoon caraway seeds. Let rise for 40 minutes.

To bake loaves: Preheat the oven to 500°F. Place the pan in the oven and reduce the temperature to 400°F. Bake for 25 to 30 minutes, until the top is browned. Remove from oven and cool on wire racks.

Shimek Dill Pickles

2 QUARTS

Rye bread with dill pickles a perfect marriage

My Czech grandmother, Bigmama, made the best dill pickles in the world using only crisp, summer cucumbers, salt, garlic, hot peppers, dill, vinegar, and water. This caused my Prussian grandmother, Mommie, great envy. Having appropriated Bigmama's recipe and claimed it as her own, Mommie would serve her own great country bread and the plagiarized Czech pickles, declaring, in her very southern-belle accent, that "Theah is nuthin' in the world bettah than bread and buttah and *mah* pickles on a nahss slahsse of frai-esh rye brai-ed." I feel I have to toss in the pickle recipe to give you the full impact of this wonderful marriage.

4 pounds pickling cucumbers (see Note)
2 cloves garlic, halved
2 small hot red peppers
1 large or 2 small bunches fresh dill
½ cup salt (you may use a scant ½ cup for less salty pickles)
1 cup cider vinegar
7 cups water

Scrub cucumbers well, wipe them dry, and refrigerate overnight.

Divide the cucumbers between two sterilized quart jars, standing the cucumbers upright in one layer and then upright in a second layer on top of the first. Pack tightly without breaking the cucumbers. Drop 2 garlic halves and 1 pepper into each jar. Put a handful of dill in each jar over the top of the vegetables. Put the jars in the sink.

In a large saucepan, mix the salt, vinegar, and water and bring to a rolling boil over medium-high heat. Simmer for 5 minutes, then pour the boiling water mixture over the cucumbers until it reaches the top and spills over. Screw the lids on the jars and allow them to cool. Refrigerate for 2 weeks before serving. The pickles will be crisp and flavorful, never soft and mushy.

NOTE: Use tiny cucumbers for cornichons or medium-size kirby cucumbers. Large cucumbers do not work as well.

Pane Casereccio

Housewife's Bread

2 LOAVES

In almost every trattoria in Italy, the first thing brought to the table is bread. This usually is fairly good bread, but if you ask, there is probably another kind of bread lurking in the kitchen, the *pane casereccio*, "bread of the home"—enormous round loaves of artisan bread that are most likely baked nearby in wood ovens. If you can find a wizened old winemaker who can bring you bundles of cuttings from his vineyard in Frascati, and if by chance you have a 600-year-old stone oven in your backyard and sweet water coming from the

continued

Pane casereccio

nearby mountains, running down through Roman aqueducts, then no doubt you'll be more successful than I was at duplicating the wondrous breads of Genzano, which inspired me to create this recipe. Barring the perfect setting, and ingredients, this will do very nicely.

When this bread is rounded and oblong, it is called a *pagnotta*, but in my bakery, the loaves come out looking like bones so we call them Pane Osso (as in osso buco).

BIGA

1 teaspoon active dry yeast
1 cup lukewarm water (85 to 95°F)
½ cup whole wheat flour
1 cup unbleached bread flour
3 tablespoons rye flour

BREAD

2 cups lukewarm water (85 to 95°F)
5 cups unbleached white flour
2 teaspoons salt
½ cup wheat bran, for baking sheet and tops of loaves

To make the biga: In a glass bowl, mix the yeast with the water and stir well. Add the whole wheat flour, bread flour, and rye flour to the yeast mixture, stirring well to aerate the mixture and form a wet dough. Cover bowl tightly with plastic wrap and let mixture ferment overnight at room temperature. In the morning, it will be bubbly and fragrant.

To make the bread: Measure the water into a large bowl. Add the *biga*, flour, and salt, stirring until all the flour is incorporated and the dough pulls away from the sides of the bowl. Rub a little olive oil on your hands and fold the dough over on itself two or three times to form a smooth ball.

Same day method: Cover the bowl with plastic wrap and let rise in a warm place until double, about 30 to 40 minutes. Fold the dough over on itself again a few times to trap air in the loaf and let the dough rise again until doubled in volume, 30 to 40 minutes. The dough should be shiny and contain nice big bubbles. Let rise a third time for 30 to 40 minutes. Proceed with shaping instructions.

Overnight method: Cover the bowl and refrigerate overnight. The dough will rise in refrigerator and acquire flavor from the slower yeast action. Remove the dough 2 hours before shaping and let stand, covered, in a warm place. The dough will rise for the second time. Continue with shaping instructions.

To shape into a pagnotta: Preheat oven to 500°F. Dust a baking sheet well with about half of the wheat bran or two tablespoons flour.

Pour the dough onto the pan by loosening it with a spatula and then carefully letting it fall onto the surface of the pan, keeping the dough as inflated as possible. You will have a rounded shape on the pan that should be fairly risen from the last rise. Cut the dough in half with a pair of scissors and shape each piece of dough into a long oblong by lifting and pulling it gently. Let the two loaves rise for about 30 minutes or until double in bulk. Very carefully, loosen the loaves with a thin spatula. Slide your fingers under the ends of each loaf and quickly, very gently turn it over in place. Some air will escape, but do not worry, the bread will rise beautifully in the oven. Spritz with water and dust the tops of the loaves well with the remaining wheat bran.

To bake loaves: Place bread in the oven, and then lower oven temperature to 400°F. Bake for 30 to 40 minutes or until the pagnotta is nicely browned. Turn off the oven, open the oven door, and let the bread sit in the oven for 10 minutes longer if you wish a thicker crust. Cool on a wire rack.

Whole Wheat Bread

1 LARGE OR 2 SMALL LOAVES

This is a bread I developed years ago when I was just beginning to make breads. It is a straight dough method, which produces a softer crumb than breads made with starters—the kind of bread ideal for tuna fish sandwiches or BLTs. But this will not taste like just any whole wheat bread because of the coffee, which imparts a lovely, rich toasty flavor to it. One rise will produce a soft sandwich bread. You may also use the covered bread pan method (see My Mother's Cream Bread [Pain de Mie]) to keep the shape perfectly square for party bread. I happen to like the little rounded top on sandwich bread, however, because it shows that a human being, not a machine, actually formed the loaf. One of our customers once told my husband that something called "whole wheat bread" just wasn't sexy, so we changed the name of our sourdough whole wheat to "Filoncino Integrale." Now it's sexy, but no one can pronounce it!

When I first made whole wheat bread, I put all sorts of wild things into the dough, such as nuts, seeds, herbs, raisins, and other dried fruit. You are free to do so, but I found that it is best made plain and simple, great for a grilled cheese sandwich or any cold filling. Additions already mentioned or any whole grains will turn this into a lovely breakfast loaf. From ½ to 1 cup of raisins or nuts—toasted nuts, of course—or ½ cup of grains can be worked into this dough after the first rise. It's up to you to experiment.

1 cup lukewarm water (85 to 95°F)
2 tablespoons active dry yeast
1½ cups warm milk
2 tablespoons olive oil or melted butter
2 tablespoons honey or molasses

1 tablespoon very strong espresso (syrupy is best)

3½ to 4 cups unbleached bread flour

1 tablespoon salt

1 cup whole wheat flour

½ cup rye flour

2 teaspoons olive oil

1 teaspoon kosher or sea salt

Measure the water into a large bowl. Sprinkle the yeast over the water and stir until dissolved. In another bowl, combine the milk, olive oil, honey or molasses, and espresso. Add the yeast mixture and about 2 cups of bread flour and the salt, and stir briskly until smooth. Add the remaining bread flour, whole wheat flour, and the rye flour and stir for about 2 minutes longer, just until the dough pulls away from the side of the bowl and the flour is incorporated.

Same day method: Cover the bowl with plastic wrap and let the dough rise in a warm place until doubled in volume, 30 to 40 minutes. Proceed with the shaping instructions.

Overnight method: Cover the bowl and refrigerate overnight. The dough will rise in the refrigerator and acquire flavor from the slower yeast action. Remove the dough 2 hours before shaping and let stand, covered, in a warm place. The dough will rise for the second time. Proceed with the shaping instructions.

To shape into loaves: Preheat the oven to 500°F. Oil one seasoned nonstick, oven-proof loaf pan, one 9-inch seasoned skillet, or two 5-inch skillets. Pour the dough into the loaf pan or seasoned skillet, or divide it between the smaller pans by loosening the dough with a spatula and then carefully scraping it from the bowl, keeping the dough as inflated as possible. With the spatula, cut the dough off at the edge of the bowl as it falls into the skillets. The shape that the dough takes on as it falls into the pan is fine. Brush the top of the loaf or loaves with the olive oil, sprinkle with salt, and let rise until doubled, 25 to 30 minutes.

To bake loaves: Place bread in the preheated oven and reduce the oven temperature to 400°F. Bake for 30 to 35 minutes until nicely browned and bread sounds hollow when tapped with your finger. Remove from pan and cool on a wire rack.

Pane Rustico

2 LOAVES

In the early days of the bakery, this bread was a very large-holed rustic, oblong loaf. Unfortunately, I lost the original loaf over some months as new bakers came to us from other bakeries and, accustomed to other techniques, beat the hell out of the dough. We went round and round for several weeks about our lost rustico, and finally what emerged was, for me, a compromise—a great sandwich loaf (which we wanted anyway) with a fine texture and a beautiful brown crust showing in the slashes. All in all, I am pleased with this bastard child because it makes wonderful nutty-tasting French toast, bruschette, and extraordinary grilled sandwiches, and I am thrilled that the original rich taste of the crumb itself was not lost in translation.

Pane Rustico

1 teaspoon active dry yeast

1 cup lukewarm water (85 to 95°F)

¾ cup unbleached bread flour

4 tablespoons rye flour

BREAD

2 cups lukewarm water (85 to 95°F)

5½ cups unbleached bread flour

2 teaspoons salt

¼ cup flour, for baking sheet and tops of loaves

To make the biga: In a glass bowl, mix the yeast with the water and stir well. Add the bread flour and rye flour to the yeast mixture, stirring well to aerate the mixture and form a wet dough. Cover tightly with plastic wrap and let ferment overnight at room temperature. In the morning, it will be bubbly and fragrant.

To make the bread: Measure the water into a large bowl. Add the *biga*, flour, and salt, stirring until all the flour is incorporated and the dough pulls away from the sides of the bowl. Rub a little olive oil on your hands and fold the dough once or twice with the heel of your hand to incorporate the flour. Fold the dough over on itself once or twice to form a smooth ball.

Same day method: Cover the bowl with plastic wrap and let the dough rise in a warm place until doubled in volume, 30 to 40 minutes. Fold the dough over on itself again a few times to trap air in the loaf and let the dough rise again until doubled in volume, 30 to 40 minutes. The dough should be shiny and contain nice big bubbles. Let it rise a third time for 30 to 40 minutes. Proceed with the shaping instructions.

Overnight method: Cover the bowl and refrigerate overnight. The dough will rise in the refrigerator and acquire flavor from the slower yeast action. Remove the dough 2 hours before shaping and let stand, covered, in a warm place. The dough will rise for the second time. Proceed with the shaping instructions.

continued

To shape into a pagnotta: Preheat the oven to 500°F. Dust a baking sheet with 2 tablespoons of the flour.

Turn the dough onto a floured work surface, keeping the dough as inflated as possible. Cut the dough in half with a pair of scissors and shape each piece into a rectangle. Fold the top third of the rectangle over the middle third and the bottom third over that, like a book, pressing out the air bubbles. Seal the dough using the palm of your hand. Place the loaves on the floured baking sheet and dust the loaves with the remaining flour. Let the two loaves rise for about 40 minutes, or until doubled. With a very sharp paring knife, make three diagonal slashes across the tops of each loaf, cutting at a 45° angle about ¼ inch deep.

To bake loaves: Place the bread in the oven, and then lower the oven temperature to 400°F. Bake for 30 to 40 minutes, until the tops are nicely browned. Cool on a wire rack.

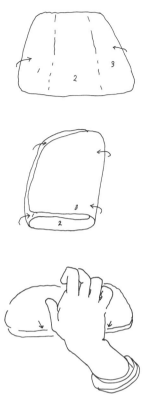

Seal fold with heel of hand.

When bread has risen, cut quick, shallow slashes down the length of the loaf. These allow bread to expand evenly when baking.

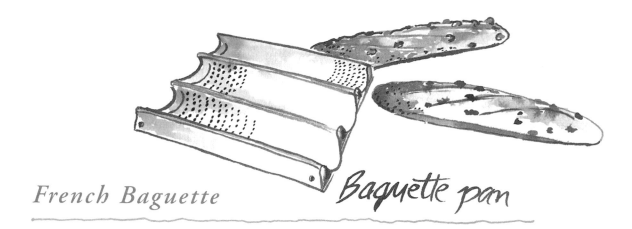

French Baguette

Baguette pan

2 LOAVES, OR 3 FICELLES (SMALLER BAGUETTES)

The baguettes you may have eaten in Paris some years ago have become more and more difficult to find all over France! Fortunately, many bakers are reviving the recipes of the past in an effort to restore order to French life. Good baguettes may be found at Poujauran bakery in Paris and in small, country bakeries such as Boulangerie Artisanale des Maures in Cannet-des-Maures.

My father introduced me to Europe when I was eighteen, and I can still remember the café where I was served a glass of 1959 Burgundy with a perfect omelette and an even more perfect salad, with a hint of mustard in the dressing. I also remember biting through a sandy crunch into what seemed to me to be glorified white bread, made extraordinary by its creamy flavor and, of course, the exciting street life of Paris swirling around me. When I want real French bread, I want only *that* French bread. This recipe comes very close except that, alas, our Los Angeles bakery does not front the Boulevard Saint Germain. The secret is to use everyday flour you can find in any supermarket and let the dough have three rises to develop flavor.

continued

2 cups lukewarm water (85 to 95°F)

2 tablespoons active dry yeast

5 cups all-purpose or unbleached bread flour

2 to 3 teaspoons salt

Measure the water into a large bowl. Sprinkle the yeast over the water and stir until dissolved. Add 2 cups of the flour and stir briskly until smooth, about 2 minutes. With a wooden or plastic spoon, add the remaining 3 cups of flour and the salt, stirring for about 5 minutes longer, until the dough pulls away from the sides of the bowl in strands and the flour is completely incorporated. If the dough feels too wet, stir in an additional ¼ to ½ cup of flour. The dough should be smooth and shiny.

Same day method: Cover the bowl with plastic wrap and let the dough rise in a warm place until doubled in volume, 30 to 40 minutes. Fold the dough over on itself two or three times and let the dough rise a second time until doubled in volume, about 30 to 40 minutes. Repeat this process one more time. Proceed with the shaping instructions.

Overnight method: Cover the bowl and refrigerate overnight. The dough will rise in the refrigerator and acquire flavor from the slower yeast action. Remove the dough 2 hours before shaping and let stand, covered, in a warm place. The dough will rise for the second time. Proceed with the shaping instructions.

To shape into baguettes: Preheat the oven to 450°F. Spray a two- or three-loaf baguette pan or a baking sheet with nonstick spray.

Turn the dough out onto a floured work surface. Divide the dough into two or three pieces to fit the baguette pan. Let the dough rest for 15 minutes. With the palms of your hands, begin rolling each piece into a long cylinder the length of the baguette pan, as you would roll soft clay. Place each cylinder in the baguette pan or on the baking sheet. Let the loaves rise until doubled in volume, about 30 minutes. With a sharp paring knife, cut 3 long slashes down the length of each loaf, beginning at one end and making sure that the next slash slightly overlaps the first and so on. Spritz with water.

To bake loaves: Place the bread in the preheated oven and reduce the oven temperature to 400°F. Bake for 30 to 35 minutes, or until the baguettes are nicely browned. Tap the baguette pan on a flat surface to loosen the loaves and cool them on a wire rack.

Traditional Breads

I HAVE SELECTED THESE BREADS among the many thousands I could have picked because they were *our* family's traditional breads, the ones my mother loved and also the ones I liked best after moving to California and starting to bake in my own kitchens. Some of my favorites are from other countries, and I have worked with these recipes to make each one the best of its kind for our kitchens, but I know you will contribute your own personal touch and tradition to many.

This chapter could have been a book in itself if I had included all of my relatives' and friends' favorites. What family does not have a dozen special recipes that have been passed down from cook to cook, through word of mouth or scribbled on a recipe card or scrap of paper and then tucked in a cookbook, only to be found years later by a delighted offspring?

It was one of these finds sometime in the 70s in one of my mother's regional cookbooks that inspired me to experiment with Boston Brown Bread. The only Boston bread I had ever eaten came in a dog-food-size can and was extracted the same way: take off both ends and push the contents onto a plate; serve with canned baked beans. When I baked and tasted the homemade version, I could not believe the difference—akin to the difference between eating canned corn and kernels fresh off the cob, sautéed in butter. The same experience applied to English muffins, inspired by the ones my mother made for us on special mornings. Store boughten (as they used to be called in the South) products were one thing, but fragrant muffins hot off my own grill spoiled me for anything else. Just watching them rise gave a lift to my own heart and made me realize how lucky I had been to have had a mother who derived such pleasure from making good food for her children and who created so many of her own original recipes as she went.

When my mother died, I had no idea how much it would affect my life; the depth of my sadness was unfathomable to me. Grief is not something we know before the fact, and it took me more than a year to accept that she was really gone and that I could not just pick up the phone to say hello, wish you were nearer, or to ask just how she got her jelly to set. We had had some stormy years, but the three years before her death I allowed all of my affection and admiration for her to surface and to embrace her amazingly strong spirit, difficult as it (and I!) sometimes could be. I could not imagine life without a mother, *my* mother, the mother who had been, at times, my enemy and adversary but who had, at the same time, given me a love of laughter, music, art, reading, gardening, and especially, cooking and baking.

My mother made enduring friends throughout her life, and with great pleasure fed them all. When she taught me that "a way to a man's heart is through his stomach," she was more than serious. It was a God-given fact, something every Southern woman knew, just like when it was acceptable to wear white shoes (after Memorial Day), when to wear velvet (*not* after February), or when to let a man win at cards (never!). Everyone knew her to be a wizard in the kitchen, and she traded recipes throughout her life with everyone from housekeepers and gardeners to chefs at local restaurants. She was always sending me articles and clippings on food and wine (I have previously mentioned the vast collection of *Gourmet* magazines, which is now mine), and in our chats every few days during the last years of her life, we gleefully argued the merits of buffalo as opposed to sirloin strips to make a true Texas chili, or whether quick-rise yeast could really be trusted, with an occasional interjection from her on the danger of Democrats in government (she was an obstinate Republican who loved Ronald Reagan), or on how all forms of department store courtesy had gone down the tubes since she was a girl. She took aerobics classes at age seventy-two and had a darling figure, despite a passion for chocolate, heavy cream in her coffee, and butter on everything.

I cherish my inherited gift of her well-worn wooden recipe box, filled with the best picks of everything from A to Z, fresh applesauce to zwieback pie crust. It was in this treasure chest that I also found some of her favorite breads (see My Mother's Cream Bread [Pain de Mie]) and biscuits (see My Grandmother's Beaten Biscuits). These recipes are not only the best of their kind, but are fun to make. I hope they also become part of the tradition you are creating for your future generations. When you balk at having to cook dinner for the umpteenth time or hesitate before making your own Skillet Corn Bread for the Thanksgiving turkey stuffing, remember the wondrous gifts you are giving your children by perfuming the house with the smells of the holidays, bread, or simmering sauces. Remember, too, that what we share with others through traditions in our kitchens is not easily lost or diluted with time; it is a groundwork for a strong future. Your children will have memories to give their children and boxes of their own recipes to pass on to the next generation of cooks.

When, as a child, I was sick or discouraged or even just needing my usual good-night kiss, I would close my eyes and feel the gentle touch on my forehead of my mother's miraculous and gifted hand. It always smelled of bread.

Anadama Bread

This bread is sentimental for me, as it was the first really impressive bread I ever made. I was fifteen and already impatient for out of the ordinary bread, not just white loaves in square pans. For some reason, Texans just love anything using cornmeal, from catfish to hush puppies, and this bread has a cornmeal base with a little flour added for body. You may vary the ingredients, using different kinds of cornmeal and flour, or by adding nuts or raisins, if you like.

2 cups water
1½ teaspoons salt
½ cup stoneground yellow cornmeal
3 tablespoons melted unsalted butter or olive oil
¼ cup honey or dark molasses
2 tablespoons active dry yeast
½ cup lukewarm water (85 to 95°F)
5 to 6 cups unbleached bread flour

In a large pot, bring the water and salt to a boil over medium-high heat. With a wire whisk, slowly stir the cornmeal into the water, making sure it does not lump. When it has thickened, remove it from the heat and stir in oil or butter and honey or molasses. Transfer to a large mixing bowl and let cool completely.

Dissolve the yeast in the lukewarm water. Stir into the cornmeal mixture. Stir in the flour, a cup or so at a time, mixing well as you go to incorporate it. This will form a firm dough that should not be too dry. When the dough pulls away from the sides of the bowl, stir well a few more times, rub oil on your hands, and transfer the dough to a clean oiled bowl.

Same day method: Cover the bowl with plastic wrap and let the dough rise in a warm place until doubled in volume, about 1 hour. Proceed with the shaping instructions.

Overnight method: Cover the bowl and refrigerate overnight. The dough will rise in the refrigerator and acquire flavor from the slower yeast action. Remove the dough 3 hours before shaping and let stand, covered, in a warm place. Proceed with shaping instructions.

To shape into loaves: Preheat the oven to 500°F. Oil one seasoned nonstick, oven-proof 9-inch skillet or two 5-inch skillets. Shape the dough into 1 large or 2 small round loaves. Place the loaf or loaves in the oiled pan or pans and let rise for about 40 minutes or until doubled. Brush the tops of the loaves with olive oil, if desired

To bake loaves: Place the bread in the oven and reduce the oven temperature to 400°F. Bake for about 40 minutes or until nicely browned and loaf sounds hollow when tapped with your finger. Remove the loaf from a pan and cool on a wire rack.

My Mother's Cream Bread

Pain de Mie

2 LOAVES

My mother had a cylindrical metal bread mold with indentations that indicated where to cut the slices from the baked bread. Although outwardly I often scoff at soft, spongy white breads, inwardly I adore the cucumber and salmon salad tea sandwiches made in England, and the heavenly triangular *tramezzini*, filled with tomato, mozzarella, artichokes, and tuna served at all bars in Italy. Both are made with the lowest form of soft white bread, crusts removed.

When I was a kid, my cousins and I loved cream bread to make little round grilled cheese sandwiches, cinnamon toast, or fried egg sandwiches, which squirted yolk when you bit into them. Cream bread does not really have cream in it, only milk and butter, which I suppose could be construed to be cream when mixed together. At any rate, this is easy white bread at its best, the kind to be toasted and spread with caviar. You can always munch a few carrots along with it to make up for your decadence.

2 tablespoons active dry yeast
¼ cup lukewarm water (85 to 95°F)
¼ cup sugar
5 to 6 cups all-purpose flour
2 cups warm milk
¼ cup melted unsalted butter
1 large egg, beaten (optional)
1 tablespoon salt

In a 1-cup measure, stir together the water, yeast, and 1 teaspoon of the sugar and let the mixture foam to the top of the container. Pour into a large mixing bowl, add 2½ to 3 cups of flour, the milk, remaining sugar, butter, egg, and salt. Beat well until thoroughly mixed. Add the remaining 2½ to 3 cups of flour and stir until the dough pulls away from the sides of the bowl and the dough is shiny and smooth. Cover the bowl and let the dough rise until doubled in volume, 30 to 40 minutes.

Turn the dough out on a lightly floured board and beat on the dough with your fists for a few minutes. Give it a good punching to achieve a fine texture. Return to the bowl, cover, and let the dough rise again, until doubled.

Butter two 8½-by-4-by-4-inch loaf pans. Divide the dough in half and form each into a loaf, pressing each flat on top. Place the bread in the pans. Butter the underside of a baking sheet, place it over the bread pans, and set aside for about 30 minutes until the dough touches the baking sheet.

Preheat the oven to 400°F. Place the pans in the oven, covered with the baking sheet weighted with a brick to keep the dough from pushing up the pan. Reduce the oven heat to 375°F and bake for 30 minutes. Remove the baking sheet and oil it lightly. Invert the pans on the baking sheet and bake for another 15 to 20 minutes until the loaves sound hollow and feel solid when tapped. Turn right side up and cool on a wire rack.

Buttermilk Bread

2 LARGE LOAVES

During my childhood, there was always buttermilk in the refrigerator. Everyone drank it on hot afternoons in Texas; my grandfather made his own from Bessie's milk. (Bessie was the cow named affectionately, I think—but I'm not quite sure—after my headstrong grandmother, Elizabeth, the one who stole the pickle recipe.) It was the milk of choice for biscuits, bread, chicken gravies, ham gravies...whatever called for milk. I thought the buttermilk was horribly rich because of the little flecks of golden butter that floated in it, and only learned later that it was not only low in calories but contained all those good things for your tummy that are also in yogurt and other milk products with acidophilus. But when I was a child, buttermilk made me gag; as an adult, I learned to love it along with most cultured milks and to rely on its magic to make my own crème fraîche, unbeatable biscuits, and this marvelous bread.

BIGA

2 tablespoons active dry yeast
½ cup lukewarm water (85 to 95°F)
2 cups warmed buttermilk
2 cups unbleached bread flour

BREAD

2 tablespoons melted butter
1 tablespoon honey
2 teaspoons salt
3 to 3½ cups unbleached white flour
2 teaspoons olive oil

To make the biga: In a glass bowl, mix the yeast with the water and stir well. Add the buttermilk and bread flour to the yeast mixture, stirring well to aerate the mixture and form a wet dough. Cover tightly with plastic wrap and let ferment overnight at room temperature. In the morning, it will be bubbly and fragrant.

To make the bread: Add the butter, honey, and salt to the *biga* and mix well. Stir in the flour until the dough is smooth and pulls away from the sides of the bowl. Add up to an additional ½ cup of flour, if dough is too moist.

Rub your hands with oil and lift the dough from the bowl to a lightly floured board. Push it with the heels of your hands and flip it over, folding it on itself two or three times. Put the dough in an oiled bowl, covered, and let rise until the dough is doubled in volume, about 1 hour.

Oil two 8½-by-4-by-4-inch loaf pans. Divide the dough in half and form each into a loaf. Place the bread in the pans. Brush the dough with olive oil, cover, and let rise until the dough reaches the rim of the pans, 30 to 40 minutes.

Preheat the oven to 450°F. Place the pans in the oven and bake for 30 to 40 minutes until the loaves sound hollow when tapped. Cool on a wire rack.

My Mother's Sourdough Biscuits

My mother, Evelyn, made her own rules. She kept her own version of sourdough starter in the refrigerator at all times, ready for breads, biscuits, and pancakes, but her starter was very different in texture and flavor from those on the market now. Perhaps it was the addition of a little sugar and salt that separated hers from the rest, but it had a wonderfully sour and nutty flavor all at once, and with care and feeding, remained active for many years. In the 1950s, she even took it down to our local baker and insisted he start making sourdough bread for Houston—which he did and, as far as I know, still does. I do not put salt or sugar in my starter, but it's nice to have my mother's recipe on hand for experiments, and just to have her near. Try them both and see which one you like best. In time, you will certainly come up with one of your own.

EVELYN'S SOURDOUGH STARTER

1 cup lukewarm water (85 to 95°F), plus 1 cup to refresh starter
½ tablespoon active dry yeast
1 cup unbleached bread flour, plus 1 cup to refresh starter
1 teaspoon sugar
Pinch of salt

MY BIGA

½ cup lukewarm water (85 to 95°F)
½ cup unbleached bread flour
2 teaspoons rye flour

BISCUIT DOUGH

2 cups unbleached bread flour

1 tablespoon baking powder

1 teaspoon salt

Pinch of baking soda

¼ cup (½ stick) chilled unsalted butter, cut into pieces

2 tablespoons chilled vegetable shortening (see page 30)

Additional flour, as needed

2 tablespoons unsalted butter, melted

To make Evelyn's starter: In a crock or glass jar with lid, mix 1 cup of the water and the yeast until foamy. Add 1 cup of flour, then sugar and salt, and stir well. Cover and let stand for 1 day at room temperature. Stir down the mixture, cover, and store in the refrigerator until ready to use.

To make my biga: Mix the water and flours and stir well to aerate the mixture and form a wet dough. Cover tightly with plastic wrap and let ferment overnight at room temperature. In the morning, it will be bubbly and fragrant.

To make the biscuit dough: Combine the flour, baking powder, salt, baking soda, chilled butter, and shortening in a food processor fitted with the metal blade and pulse 2 or 3 times until the mixture is the size of small peas. (Or, cut in the butter and shortening with a pastry blender or 2 knives using a crisscross motion.) Add ½ cup of Evelyn's sourdough starter or my *biga*, and process just until the dough is moistened, much like a pie crust. If you need more liquid, add a few teaspoons of milk or cream. Turn the dough onto a lightly floured board.

Preheat the oven to 400°F. Butter two 8-inch or 9-inch cake pans or 1 rectangular baking pan. Roll the dough, without pressing too hard, into a flat circle about ½ inch thick. Cut out biscuits with a biscuit cutter or a 2½-inch-diameter water glass. Place biscuits side by side in the pans and brush them with melted butter. Bake for 15 to 18 minutes, or until browned. The biscuits will be about 1 inch high. Serve hot with butter and slices of fresh fruit or homemade fresh fruit purée.

If you used my mother's starter, reconstitute it with 1 cup water and 1 cup flour and keep it refrigerated.

Fresh Fruit Purée

many choices
for fresh fruit purées

ABOUT 2 CUPS

I love the freshness of fruit purées. There are those with a sweet tooth and those with a sour one—and I am among the latter. For me, dessert is a fresh peach in one hand and a piece of warm buttered bread in the other, a kind of poor man's shortcake. It is low, low in calories and does not make you feel the way a lot of sugar does—a sudden high and then a crash about half an hour later. At any rate, this is a nice alternative to sweet jams or preserves, spread on biscuits or fresh bread. Serve with pound cake or over pancakes, too. These purées are also useful for making sorbet or ice cream or lining a tart shell before adding fresh fruit.

2 cups fresh raspberries, strawberries, blueberries, peeled and cubed apricots or peaches, or whatever fruit you like
½ to ¾ cup sugar, according to taste
A few drops of fresh lemon juice

In a heavy saucepan, heat the fruit and sugar over medium-high heat until boiling. Reduce the heat and simmer for 2 to 3 minutes. Cool.

Transfer the fruit to a food processor and process for a few seconds or until jamlike. Add lemon juice to taste. Add more sugar to make a thicker consistency, but I prefer the taste and texture of a thinner purée.

NOTE: A teaspoon of vanilla gives this a little flair.

My Grandmother's Beaten Biscuits

Kitchen Sink Therapy might well be my next book title. Nowhere else, except perhaps the garden, do I find such auspicious outlets for aggressions, occasional sadness, or simply the peacefulness to think creatively about grand things (grandiose, most likely). This theory applies well to recipes that require bashing around, such as brioche or veal scaloppine, but when making beaten biscuits, you can really wail. Any covert emotions you might have buried will be aired and purged as you bash the bloody hell out of this dough. Have ready one of those nice wooden French rolling pins—a long cylinder without handles—or at least a good heavy mallet. The bottom of a frying pan works well, too, but be careful not to crack marble or granite counters.

A picture of my formidably plump grandmother punching this dough around the kitchen still lingers in my memory, especially when I remember that this same ferocity could be unleashed just as easily when the grandchildren got too rowdy. She even made us cut our own switches—but of course we cut tiny little things that only stung our pride. A few minutes later, we would all be nestled in her large, comforting bosom, eating biscuits and jam.

continued

BIGA

½ cup water

Tiny pinch of yeast

½ cup flour

BISCUITS

1½ cups unbleached bread flour

2 teaspoons sugar

½ teaspoon salt

½ cup (1 stick) chilled unsalted butter, diced into medium-size cubes

2 tablespoons chilled vegetable shortening

½ cup ice water

To make the biga: In a glass bowl, mix the water and yeast and stir well. Add the flour to the yeast mixture, stirring well to aerate the mixture and form a wet dough. Cover tightly with plastic wrap and let ferment overnight at room temperature. In the morning, it will be bubbly and fragrant.

To make the biscuits: Sift together the flour, sugar, and salt and place in the bowl of a food processor fitted with the metal blade. Add the butter and shortening, and pulse two or three times until the mixture is the size of small peas. Or, cut in the butter and shortening with a pastry blender or 2 knives, using a crisscross motion. Add the *biga* and ice water and process just to blend. Turn the dough out onto a lightly floured board or other hard surface (not tile).

Preheat the oven to 400°F.

Start hammering the dough with the rolling pin or mallet. If necessary, add just enough flour to keep the dough workable but not sticky. Beat the dough well for about 5 minutes until it is glossy and has little air bubbles in it. Roll the dough out very thin into a long rectangle about ¼ inch thick. Take the ends and fold them toward the center over on themselves, forming 3 layers. Roll out the dough again and repeat one more time. Prick the dough all over with a fork. This is the fun part—make any design you wish. Cut out biscuits with a biscuit cutter or 2½-inch-diameter water glass. Lay on an unbuttered baking sheet and bake for about 20 minutes, but do not let them get too much color or they will harden. These biscuits do not rise as others do, but stay rather flat. If you happen to be out in your garden gathering even more lofty thoughts than you did at the sink, and the biscuits bake longer than planned, they will have metamorphosed into exotic crackers, great with cheese or spreads.

Skillet Corn Bread

8 SERVINGS

At our house, the idea of making a big pot of black-eyed peas without corn bread is unthinkable. Where I grew up in Texas, corn bread was first cousin to ham, greens, Thanksgiving stuffing, or, as it is called there, dressing. Corn bread hush puppies with maple syrup were given to my brother and me for a special breakfast. The idea that anyone would throw such a delectable treat to the whining dogs and say "Hush, puppies!" was unimaginable to me, but that was the story my mother told of their origins. As for the corn bread, it had to be made in a skillet or a corn pone mold, called a johnnycake pan, a wonderful black cast-iron pan that has indentations that look like ears of corn. The seasoned ones are found at the Salvation Army or thrift shops, if you're lucky, but new ones are still made by Ware. To season a new pan, oil it well and put it in a hot, hot oven (450°F) for about an hour. Just be sure to make enough corn bread for the next day because, split and toasted for breakfast, it's almost as good as hush puppies.

continued

2 cups stoneground yellow cornmeal

2 teaspoons salt

2 teaspoons sugar

½ cup unsalted butter or vegetable shortening, melted, or olive oil

2 cups boiling water

2 large eggs, beaten

⅔ cup sour milk or buttermilk (plain milk will do but sour is better)
(see Note)

1 cup unbleached bread flour

1 tablespoon baking powder

½ teaspoon baking soda

½ cup cooked fresh corn kernels

2 tablespoons unsalted butter

Preheat the oven to 425°F.

In a large mixing bowl, combine the cornmeal, salt, sugar, and butter and pour the boiling water over them, stirring well. In another bowl, stir the eggs into the milk and beat well.

Mix the flour, baking powder, and baking soda together. With a wooden spoon stir the milk and flour mixtures alternately into the cornmeal mixture just until moistened. Do not overmix. Stir in the corn kernels.

Heat a 10- to 12-inch iron skillet on the stove until smoking. Add the butter. When melted and bubbling, pour the batter into the skillet. Cook on top of the stove for about 1 minute and then transfer to the oven and bake for 20 minutes, or until corn bread is golden brown.

NOTE: To sour milk, add 1 tablespoon of cider vinegar to 1 cup of milk.

If you are making corn bread for stuffing, add 2 tablespoons of chili powder to the skillet when the butter is melted and cook it for about 2 minutes. Stir this into the batter, pour batter back into the skillet, and bake as directed. This will give your stuffing zip without overpowering the onion, celery, and sage. My mother used chili powder in all kinds of places to improve the flavor of whatever it was, and no one could guess her secret.

Cornmeal Spoon Bread

Spoon bread is a Southern dish that seems to be dying out. I remember eating it at school in Virginia—I will not mention the school's name, because I was desperately trying to escape from its conventions and go to radical Berkeley—but the occasional treat of spoon bread made some days tolerable. Not even the ethereal lightness of a rich cornmeal soufflé could change my despair at being where I was rather than sitting in the Cock and Bull coffeehouse in New York's Greenwich Village in a black turtle neck sweater, smoking pink cigarettes, and looking sultry. Fortunately, I soon found myself in Berkeley, the antithesis of where I had been, and succumbed to making spoon bread as a nostalgic remnant from my anguished youth—or is that redundant?

3½ cups milk
1½ cups stoneground yellow cornmeal
¼ cup butter, melted
1 teaspoon salt
4 large eggs, separated
½ cup cooked corn, optional but definitely a plus
Pinch of ground red pepper

Preheat the oven to 350°F. Generously butter a 9-inch baking dish.

Bring 2 cups of the milk to a boil over medium-high heat. With a wire whisk, stir the cornmeal into the milk. Continue stirring over very low heat until the mixture is smooth. Add the butter, salt, and remaining 1½ cups of milk, stirring slowly to mix well. Stir in the egg yolks, mixing well. Transfer the mixture to a large bowl to cool completely.

continued

Beat the egg whites until stiff but not dry; they will be glossy and hold small peaks easily. Carefully fold them into the cornmeal mixture, cutting them into the cornmeal with a spatula and then lifting the mixture up and over itself to trap air. (This is the classic technique for soufflés.) Fold in the corn, if using, and hot pepper. Carefully scrape the mixture into the dish and bake for about 35 minutes, or until risen and well browned on top. Naturally, you must dish this out with a spoon.

Sourdough Flapjacks

4 SERVINGS

My grandfather, Poppie, called them flapjacks and flapjacks are what he made, never pancakes. He was a traveling oil man, and, having had adventures all over the world in his youth, retired at a young age to a farmhouse outside Houston with Bess, my grandmother, Bessie, the cow, Inky, the stallion, and a pig or two for bacon. Every now and then some old bow-legged cowboy would show up, ostensibly to break a horse or help out with the butchering—or maybe just to sit on the porch with Poppie and eat flapjacks.

STARTER
1 cup lukewarm water (85 to 95°F)
1 cup unbleached bread flour (see Variation)
2 tablespoons sugar

3 tablespoons butter, melted, plus more for the griddle

1 tablespoon honey or molasses

1 teaspoon baking soda

1 teaspoon salt

1 large egg, beaten

To make the starter: Measure the water into a bowl. Add the flour and sugar to the water and stir to aerate the mixture and form a wet dough. Cover tightly with plastic wrap and let ferment overnight at room temperature. In the morning, it will be bubbly and fragrant.

To make the flapjacks: Stir the butter, honey or molasses, baking soda, salt, and egg into the starter. Do not overmix.

Brush a hot griddle with melted butter and ladle the batter onto the griddle to form 3-inch circles (or Mickey Mouse ears or pigs). When little bubbles appear on the surface and the edges firm up, turn the flapjacks, as in "flap" them over, and cook the other side for about another minute. Serve with maple syrup or molasses.

VARIATION

For a richer flavor, make the flapjacks with ½ cup of bread flour and ½ cup of buckwheat flour.

Buckwheat Blini

Buckwheat Blini with caviar

One of my weaknesses is for caviar. Anytime, anyplace. I even have a special connection in Los Angeles who finds exquisite caviar at very good prices. I, in turn, keep him well supplied with bread. He is leaning on me to make blini for him that he can freeze and sell along with his black jewels. Try these blini the way they should be eaten: with caviar. If you are a purist, try the caviar on toasted Rustico or My Mother's Cream Bread. These blini freeze very well, wrapped in foil to keep out the air. Just bring them to room temperature before using and heat for 5 minutes in a medium oven (350°F).

1 cup buckwheat flour
1 cup all-purpose flour, sifted
1 teaspoon salt
1 tablespoon active dry yeast
¼ cup lukewarm water (85 to 95°F)
2 cups warm milk
3 large eggs, separated
2 tablespoons butter, melted
1 teaspoon sugar

In a medium bowl, mix the flours and salt together.

In a large bowl, stir the yeast into the water. Add 1 cup of the milk and half the flour mixture and mix well. Cover the bowl and let dough rise for 2 hours.

Beat the egg yolks with the remaining cup of milk. Add the butter and sugar and mix well. Stir into the batter with the remaining flour. The batter will not be very thick. Add a little more milk, if necessary. Stir well and let stand, covered, for 30 minutes.

Whip the egg whites until stiff but not dry; they will be glossy and hold small peaks easily. Fold them into the batter.

Brush a hot griddle with melted butter and ladle the batter onto the griddle to form 3-inch circles. When little bubbles appear on the surface and the edges firm up, turn the pancakes over and cook the other side for about another minute.

Boston Brown Bread

2 LARGE OR 4 SMALL LOAVES

I can't tell you why I love this bread. It probably is served in Boston, although when I lived there one summer, I headed straight for oyster bars and seafood restaurants, forgetting to research the classic Boston baked beans that must accompany it. You may want to serve it with your own version of beans; I find most baked beans too sweet and cloying and prefer the pintos my mother used to make, or even Italian cannellini. With beans or without, this is a great bread for teatime or anytime, spread with butter or without any adornment.

continued

¼ cup unsalted butter, softened, for buttering molds

1 cup unbleached bread flour

1 cup stoneground yellow cornmeal

½ cup rye flour

½ cup whole wheat or graham flour

2 teaspoons baking soda

1 teaspoon salt

½ teaspoon baking powder

1½ to 2 cups buttermilk

½ cup dark molasses

1 cup chopped raisins or dates

Prepare two 1-pound coffee cans or four 3-inch round heatproof glass bowls, each about 3 inches deep, by buttering them generously with the softened butter. Have ready a large pot with a tight-fitting lid and a steaming rack large enough to hold the molds for steaming (you may need two pots).

In a large mixing bowl, combine the bread flour, cornmeal, rye flour, and whole wheat flour, baking soda, salt, and baking powder, and stir well. Add the buttermilk and molasses and stir until well incorporated, but do not overmix. Stir in the raisins or dates.

Spoon the batter into the molds, filling each about two-thirds full. Cover tightly with foil and secure with kitchen twine. Pour enough water into the pot to come about 2 inches up the sides and bring to a boil over medium-high heat. Carefully place the molds on the rack, reduce the heat to a simmer, cover the pot, and steam the bread for about 2 hours, adding more hot water as needed to maintain the level.

Lift the molds from the pot, remove the foil, and set them on wire racks to cool completely in the molds. Remove from the molds by running a knife around the sides; the bread will slide or lift out easily. Serve sliced thin.

NOTE: Glass bread steamers are available at kitchen shops or from the Baker's Catalogue, 1-800-827-6836.

Suzanne's Version of Boston Baked Beans

8 SERVINGS

This recipe is similar to the one my mother made in Texas—about as far from Boston as you can get, in a culinary sense. Beans are infamous for their repercussions. My sister-in-law taught me first to bring them to a boil, then let them cool, then pour off the water and refill the pot with fresh cold water. Some of the culprit goes out with the water, supposedly. It seems to work.

1 pound dried pinto beans
1 small sweet onion, chopped fine
1 cup dark beer
2 tablespoons olive oil
1 tablespoon dark molasses
1 tablespoon honey
1 tablespoon dark brown sugar
2 teaspoons salt
1 level teaspoon dry mustard
¼ pound salt pork, bacon, or pancetta, cut into thin ½-inch slices

In a large pot, cover beans with water and bring to a boil over high heat. Remove from heat and let cool. Pour off water and cover the beans with fresh cold water. Add the onion and bring to a boil over high heat. Reduce the heat again and simmer for about 45 minutes until the beans are soft but firm enough to hold their shape.

Drain the beans and transfer to a casserole with a tight-fitting cover. Stir the beer, olive oil, molasses, honey, sugar, salt, and mustard into the beans. Add enough boiling water to cover. Lay the salt pork slices on top of the beans to cover. Cover the casserole and bake for 4 to 5 hours, keeping the liquid covering the beans during cooking (I use water, dry white wine, more beer, or whatever liquid I choose). Remove the cover during the final 30 minutes to get a nice crust on the beans.

English Muffins

2 DOZEN

My stepdaughter, Nicole, who lived in Rome, requested that I bring English muffins in my luggage every time I visited (as well as chocolate chips, fresh tortillas, and Cheddar cheese, which made for an interesting suitcase aroma). I have yet to whip these up right on the spot in my Roman kitchen since Babbington's Tea Room is just up the street in the Piazza di Spagna and their muffins are very good. Nevertheless, homemade English muffins, with bitter marmalade and unsalted butter, will undoubtedly spoil you forever for store-bought.

BIGA
½ cup milk
½ cup unbleached bread flour
Pinch of yeast

MUFFINS
¼ cup lukewarm water (85 to 95°F)
1 tablespoon active dry yeast
1 cup warmed milk
¼ cup unsalted butter, melted
1 tablespoon sugar
1 large egg, lightly beaten
1 teaspoon salt
4¼ cups sifted unbleached bread flour
½ cup stoneground yellow or white cornmeal

To make the biga: Combine the milk, flour, and yeast and stir well to aerate the mixture and form a wet dough. Cover tightly with plastic wrap and let ferment overnight at room temperature. In the morning, it will be bubbly and fragrant.

To make the muffins: Measure the water into a large bowl. Sprinkle the yeast over the water and stir until dissolved. Stir in the warm milk, melted butter, sugar, egg, and salt. Add the *biga* and mix well. Stir in the flour and stir briskly until the dough pulls away from the sides of the bowl. If necessary, stir in an additional ¼ to ½ cup of flour. Turn the dough out and press with the palms of your hands two or three times, turning it over on itself. It will be smooth and shiny. Return the dough to the bowl.

Same day method: Cover the bowl with plastic wrap and let the dough rise in a warm place until doubled in volume, 30 to 40 minutes. Proceed with the shaping instructions.

Overnight method: Cover the bowl and refrigerate overnight. The dough will rise in the refrigerator and acquire flavor from the slower yeast action. Remove the dough 2 hours before shaping and let it stand, covered, in a warm place. Proceed with shaping instructions.

To shape the muffins: Sprinkle the cornmeal on a board or flat surface. Put the dough on the cornmeal and roll it out to a thickness of ¼ inch. With a cookie cutter or 3-inch-diameter glass, cut the dough into rounds and sprinkle with cornmeal. Cover the rounds with a dry towel and let rise until doubled, about 30 minutes.

To cook the muffins: Heat a large, heavy griddle on the top of the stove. The griddle should be very hot. Carefully slide a spatula under each muffin and slide it onto the hot griddle and cook for 3 or 4 minutes. Lower heat and continue cooking until well browned on bottom. Turn and cook on the other side for 3 or 4 minutes longer until browned. Cool completely on wire racks. Split the muffins with your fingers or a fork only. Remember the old Thomas Brothers slogan, "Never knife an English muffin!"

NOTE: English muffin molds that you place on the griddle with the dough inside may be found in kitchen stores, but I prefer the free-form kind.

Pizza

Pizza

OH, WHAT A PERFECT FOOD is pizza! I never ate pizza until I began going to Italy once or twice a year, and now I place it up there with baked potatoes or a great omelet. I'm talking about real pizza, not the cheesy, gummy, oversauced, oregano-laden, tough pizza made in most pizza parlors. You get the picture. I have strong feelings about what pizza is and how it should be made. The pizza of Rome is my favorite, made with the fresh buffalo mozzarella found only between Rome and Naples, but the pizza you make at home will be a close second—if only because you can regulate the thickness of the crust and put only the freshest ingredients on top.

Everyone has a favorite pizza, but most people, including the restaurateurs who put pizza on their menus, have never actually tasted the real thing: simple dough, light sauce, fresh mozzarella, and a sprinkle of fresh basil. If they had, they would not dream of offering the public what passes for a pizza.

My food history guru, Charles Perry, wrote in *The Journal of Gastronomy* some years ago that pizza came from the Greek word *picea* (pitch, a flattened cake), which became *pitta*, then *pissa*, so I guess we have the Greeks to thank for one of the world's most popular foods. Of course, anyone with eyes and an appetite could see that a nice piece of dough, flattened and baked, cried out for something to top it, if only a splash of good olive oil and a little salt. What you put on your pizza is your business, but once again I encourage you to keep it simple: do not suffocate your pizza with too much sauce, heavy meats, or gloppy cheeses.

Pizza does not agree with everyone, often the result of overcooking the cheese and tossing too many ingredients on top to fight with one another. In most pizza parlors, hard, waxy, commercial mozzarella is used, and the casein in the cheese changes structure when cooked, making it more indigestible than it is when eaten uncooked. Fresh mozzarella will do the same thing, although not as radically, and so should be added just before the pizza is ready in order to keep the cheese smooth and creamy. Keep in mind that a light hand with what you put on top will yield a crispy, savory pizza that will not keep you up all night. Try using three or four ingredients instead of seven or eight—the same approach you might use in making any good, simple dish—and you will be able to taste each individual flavor instead of having a stew on top of a piece of dough. Pizza is not bouillabaisse. Pizza is only a simple bruschetta that you put in the oven.

Basic Pizza Crust

This pizza dough is not like any other. It takes exactly two minutes to make and is made from dough that is refrigerated overnight or for as long as a week to acquire flavor. This gives it a slight tang, and all-purpose flour plus olive oil gives it crisp texture. You may also use the dough to make quick breads.

If the dough remains in the refrigerator for more than three days or so, you will need to liven it up with a little flour, as the yeast will have dined on most of the nutrients in the flour—only by feeding them new carbohydrates will you get a response from them. Simply let the dough come to room temperature, take it out of the plastic bag, roll it in a couple of spoonfuls of all-purpose flour, and take a few seconds to work the flour into the dough with the palms of your hands. The dough will lose its pallor and become shiny, smooth, and resilient again. Let it rest for 30 minutes before using, so that it can be easily stretched.

Pizza dough must have oil for the short, crisp texture that complements the acidity of tomato sauce and the creaminess of fresh mozzarella. Many chefs flavor dough with various other ingredients, but I am a staunch purist who prefers her pizza dough plain and simple without the distractions of onion, herbs, or spices. Everyone, however, should do exactly as he or she likes with pizza. That's the fun of it. I only give you the building blocks, and what you make of them is your own creation. The following recipe is for the classic thin pizza of Rome, my favorite, and, along with the pizza of Naples, the best pizza in Italy. In the following recipe, I use 1 cup of flour for each main-course serving, but more often

continued

than not, I make some extra dough to freeze or to have on hand to make flat, thin antipasto focaccia.

1 teaspoon active dry yeast
1½ cups lukewarm water (85 to 95°F)
4 to 4½ cups unbleached all-purpose flour
6 tablespoons olive oil
1 teaspoon salt

In a container that pours easily, sprinkle the yeast over the water and stir until dissolved. Put the flour, olive oil, and salt into the bowl of a food processor fitted with the metal blade. Blend for a few seconds and then add the yeast and water, blending just until the dough pulls away from the sides of the bowl. The dough will be slightly sticky to the touch. Dip your fingers in a little olive oil and lift the dough from the bowl, shaping it into a ball. Put the dough in an oiled bowl.

Same day method: Cover the bowl with plastic wrap and let the dough rise in a warm place until doubled in volume, about 60 minutes.

Overnight method: After first rise, transfer the dough to a plastic freezer bag and seal tightly, leaving a little air in the bag. Alternatively, ignore first rise completely and place the dough directly in bag. Refrigerate overnight or up to 1 week. The dough will rise in the bag and take on a lovely, sour taste. Let the dough come to room temperature before using.

To shape and prepare pizza: Coat two 13-by-18-inch baking sheets with olive oil. Divide the dough in half and stretch each piece on a baking sheet into a 12-by-6-inch rectangle in the following manner: using your palms and starting from the center of the dough, gently press and stretch the dough outward from the center to form a thin ⅛-inch-thick crust slightly thicker at the edge. Push the

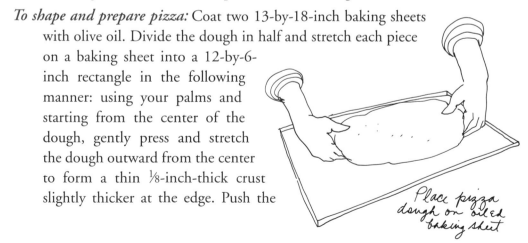

Place pizza dough on oiled baking sheet

dough up around the edges to make a ⅛- to ¼-inch lip to hold the sauce. Choose from the following recipes to complete your pizza.

To bake the pizza: Preheat the oven to 525°F.

Place the pizza with topping on the lowest rack of the oven and increase the oven temperature to 550°F. This will give an extra boost of heat to the bottom of the pizza and brown it nicely. Bake for 7 to 10 minutes, depending on the thickness of the crust. The crust edges should be well browned and the cheese bubbling and browned. If, when the pizza is done, the bottom seems a little soggy, place the baking sheet on a stove burner over medium heat, moving the pan continually back and forth over the heat and watching carefully until the pizza begins to send off steam. At this point, the bottom will be well browned and the crust crisped. A wood-burning oven would really do the trick, but alas, not many of us have that luxury! By cooking the bottom of the pizza on the stovetop, you duplicate as well as you can the stone floor of a wood-burning oven. This technique works for other dishes as well.

NOTE: If you prefer to use quick-rising yeast, the dough will only need about 30 minutes to rise. If the dough rises and you cannot top and bake it right away, flatten it, cover it with a light cotton towel, and let it rest at room temperature for at least 30 minutes or until needed.

To use a pizza stone, make 3 pizze from the dough, rolling each one only to the size of the stone. Heat the stone in the oven. Place the pizza on a wooden peel coated with cornmeal or flour and put on the toppings. When the oven is hot, slide the pizza off the peel onto the stone in one motion. Bake for the same amount of time in the recipe. (I do not use pizza stones only because I like to make bigger pizze.)

Pizza Bianca alla Romana

This is my favorite pizza: simple, beautiful, and satisfying—particularly about eleven in the morning when hunger pangs begin. Midmorning, the smell of pizza bianca permeates the air in Rome, since any baker worth his salt is making it. It is the "snack" of Italy. I have never liked the idea of snacking, much less the word itself, but if there is one thing I will eat between breakfast and the late lunches in Italy, it is pizza bianca. Italians do not eat breakfast, per se, which is why the pizza bianca has become practically an icon. Thin, delicious, chewy pizza with a brush of olive oil and a sprinkling of coarse salt can't be all bad. And it's a heck of a lot healthier than candy bars or potato chips washed down with a diet soda.

The dough for this pizza is a little more bready than the basic pizza dough. If you prefer, use the basic pizza dough to make pizza bianca.

BIGA
1 cup unbleached all-purpose flour
1 cup lukewarm water (85 to 95°F)
1 teaspoon active dry yeast

PIZZA
3 cups unbleached all-purpose flour
1 cup lukewarm water (85 to 95°F)
6 tablespoons olive oil
1 teaspoon active dry yeast
1 teaspoon salt
¼ cup extra-virgin olive oil
1 tablespoon coarse salt

To make the biga: Stir together the flour, water, and yeast until it forms a wet dough. Cover with plastic wrap and set aside until doubled in volume, about 1 hour.

To make the pizza: Stir together the flour, water, olive oil, yeast, and salt. Add the *biga* and mix well until smooth and shiny. This may be done in a food processor. Transfer to a glass bowl, cover, and let rise until doubled, about 1 hour.

Keeping the dough inflated as much as possible, turn it out on a baking sheet and stretch it to the edges, making little indentations all over with your fingers (see illustration). Let the dough rise until doubled in bulk, about 30 minutes. Brush with the extra-virgin olive oil and sprinkle with the coarse salt.

To bake the pizza: Follow the instructions on page 107.

Pizza Blanca

Push straight down into dough and stretch dough out to sides of pan.

VARIATIONS

Pizza con Rughetta (arugula) or Salvia (sage)

Stretch the pizza dough extra thin, brush with extra-virgin olive oil, and bake at 500°F for about 9 minutes, until well browned and crispy. Sprinkle with more olive oil and strew fresh arugula leaves or ½ cup fresh sage leaves, sautéed until crispy in a tablespoon of olive oil, over the hot surface. Serve immediately.

Pizza con Olio di Tartuffo

Bake as for Pizza con Rughetta. Dust with rock salt before baking. Drip truffle oil over the hot surface of the crisp pizza and serve immediately.

Pizza con Cipolle

Sauté 2 cups of onions, sliced thin, in ½ cup of olive oil until softened. Sprinkle with ½ teaspoon of sugar and cook for a few minutes longer until browned. Spread over the pizza dough and bake as directed on page 107.

continued

Pizza ai Funghi

Sauté 2 cups of brown mushrooms, sliced thin, or a mixture of your favorite mushrooms, such as chanterelles, morels, white cap, portobello, etc., in ½ cup of olive oil until well browned. Add 1 to 2 cloves of minced or sliced garlic and cook just until translucent. Add 2 tablespoons of fresh lemon juice, salt, and pepper. Spread over the pizza dough, sprinkle with 1 tablespoon fresh, chopped basil, and bake as directed on page 107.

Pizza Margherita

ONE 13-BY-18-INCH PIZZA

The number one choice in Italy for pizza (after Pizza Bianca) is Pizza Margherita. Once again, it is the absolutely fresh ingredients from the dairy and the garden that make this pizza so extraordinary. Here in California we actually have a fresh mozzarella packed in water, which resembles a cow's milk cheese in Italy called *fior di latte*, literally, "flower of milk," which believe me, it is! It is produced at a marvelous cheese company called Italcheese, started by Virgilio Ciccone. Italcheese is making *real bufala mozzarella* from *real* buffalo, the same cows that produce the exquisite fresh mozzarella made at dairies between Rome and Naples. There is also a company in Texas that produces *bufala*. Please, please search for mozzarella packed in water to use on pizza, not hard, packaged mozzarella. If you must use this kind, put the cheese on the pizza just before it is done, so that it will not overbake and turn rubbery.

⅔ cup Simply Perfect Tomato Sauce (page 121), or your favorite tomato sauce

Dough for 1 pizza crust, ½ recipe Basic Pizza Crust (page 105)

6 ounces fresh mozzarella packed in water, chopped fine

1 cup fresh basil leaves, chopped fine or snipped into ½-inch strips

2 tablespoons olive oil

Preheat the oven to 550°F. Stretch the dough on an oiled baking sheet, as explained in the recipe for Basic Pizza Crust.

Spread a thin, even layer of tomato sauce over the dough. Sprinkle the mozzarella and chopped basil evenly over the sauce and sprinkle with olive oil. Bake on the lowest oven rack for 7 to 10 minutes, or until crust is golden and the cheese is bubbling.

Pizza Napoletana

ONE 13-BY-18-INCH PIZZA

Following the Italian custom, Sunday night is pizza night in our house—one of the rare moments of stability in my otherwise unpredictable life. The rest of the week is hectic, surprising, sometimes trying (the oven goes out or the starter goes limp or the head bagger at the bakery goes on vacation!), often exhilarating, but with a pace that could discourage even a player on the Roma soccer team. On Sundays, at least I know what I am to do. I know that I must have fresh basil. I know that mozzarella must be in the refrigerator, and I know that I must have anchovies for the pizza, although one of my cookbooks, written in Italian by a baker, says that capers and fresh oregano are also used to top Pizza Napoletana. I go back and forth with this one, but I have the first three in my larder come hell or high water.

There is no limit as to how many anchovies anyone can put on a pizza. At our house, anchovies are used liberally, not only on our pizze but in many other dishes, too. When on occasion I run out of them, I have been known to use impostor squiggles of anchovy paste as stand-ins for my coveted Italian anchovies packed in olive oil. My real favorites are those packed in salt in large square tins, usually found in good Italian food shops, but the ones in little cans do just as well. For those pizza lovers who must also watch their salt intake, give the anchovies a quick 5-minute soak in cold water to wash off as much salt as possible but still retain the flavor.

Dough for 1 pizza crust, ½ recipe Basic Pizza Crust (page 105)
⅔ cup Simply Perfect Tomato Sauce (page 121), or your favorite tomato sauce

6 ounces fresh mozzarella packed in water, chopped fine

½ cup fresh basil leaves, chopped fine (see Note)

8 to 10 anchovy fillets

2 tablespoons olive oil

Preheat the oven to 550°F. Stretch the dough on an oiled baking sheet as explained in the recipe for Basic Pizza Crust.

Spread a thin, even layer of tomato sauce over the dough. Sprinkle the mozzarella and chopped basil evenly over the sauce. Lay the anchovy fillets every 4 inches or so to cover the entire pizza or lay them in a lattice design for a more elegant presentation. Sprinkle the pizza with olive oil. Bake on the lowest oven rack for 7 to 10 minutes, or until crust is golden and the cheese is bubbling.

NOTE: If you must, in a pinch substitute fresh oregano leaves or parsley, chopped fine, for the basil.

Pizza con Patate e Rosmarino

ONE 13-BY-18-INCH PIZZA

My first *pizza a taglio* (pizza by the piece) was eaten in a narrow little Roman street near the Parliament, a street offering every amenity you would need to live a happy life—a book shop, a shoe repair, a beauty supply, a tiny *alimentari* (grocery store), a hardware store, a blacksmith, a fragile little *nonna* who knitted exquisite sweaters, and to top it off, a wood-burning pizza oven known as a *forno al legno*. When I saw my favorite

continued

vegetable, sliced thin and strewn with rosemary over the top of a 3-foot-square pizza, I wanted to move next door on the spot. Potatoes and rosemary on pizza are as satisfying as a layer of fresh cream over raspberries or fresh butter melting on hot bread. This is a filling pizza and does not even need the mozzarella, but you can choose which you like best. You will also find amazing *pizza a taglio* in Florence.

¼ cup olive oil
8 small red new potatoes, sliced thin
½ sweet onion, minced
¼ cup fresh rosemary leaves, chopped fine
Dough for 1 pizza crust, ½ recipe Basic Pizza Crust (page 105)
⅔ cup Simply Perfect Tomato Sauce (page 121), or your favorite tomato sauce
6 ounces fresh mozzarella packed in water, chopped fine

In a large skillet, heat the oil over medium-high heat and sauté the potatoes until golden, about 10 minutes. Add the onion and rosemary and cook for 5 or 6 minutes longer until the potatoes are well browned and the onion is tender but still crisp. Remove from the heat to cool.

Stretch the dough on an oiled baking sheet, as explained in the recipe for Basic Pizza Crust.

Spread a thin, even layer of tomato sauce over the dough. Arrange the potato-rosemary mixture evenly over the sauce and sprinkle with mozzarella. Bake on the lowest oven rack for 7 to 10 minutes, or until the crust is golden.

NOTE: When onions are very sweet in late summer, add them sliced raw to pizza, cooking only as long as the pizza takes to bake. In this way they retain their freshness and crispness. In Italy, the sweet red onions of Sicily are used for this special pizza.

Pizza con Carciofi

ONE 13-BY-18-INCH PIZZA

Another passion of mine is the artichoke. The artichoke fields outside Rome are like vast silver-green seas that go on for miles. I once wrote an article about artichokes and found that they had been discovered by asses in a field of thistles. Just after this miraculous find, the Roman senators forbade the commoners to eat them (naturally, they wanted them all for themselves), and the remark went around that "asses had discovered them and asses were still eating them," no reflection, of course, on those of us who make whole meals of them whenever we can. We have round baby artichokes in California, which I prefer to the huge, globe type because they are very tender and sweet, but I am still trying to persuade growers at our farmer's market to plant the beautiful, elongated Italian ones that are deep green and streaked with violet. These can be eaten raw with a little olive oil and salt and are perfect for pizza.

10 fresh baby artichokes

3 tablespoons fresh lemon juice

6 tablespoons olive oil

2 cloves garlic, minced or sliced

2 tablespoons minced fresh mint

Salt and pepper

Dough for 1 pizza crust, ½ recipe Basic Pizza Crust (page 105)

⅔ cup Simply Perfect Tomato Sauce (page 121), or your favorite tomato sauce (optional)

6 ounces fresh mozzarella packed in water, shredded or chopped (about 1½ cups)

continued

To prepare the artichokes: With a sharp, serrated knife, trim the discolored parts of the stem and cut each globe in half, discarding the tips of the pointy leaves. Peel and discard the outer green leaves to expose the yellow, tender part of the globes. Slice each artichoke in thin slices from top to bottom. Put them in a bowl, sprinkle with 1 tablespoon of the lemon juice, and set aside until ready to use.

In a large skillet, heat the olive oil over medium-high heat, drain the artichokes well, and sauté them until golden brown or until quite crispy on the edges. Add the garlic and mint and cook for 2 to 3 minutes longer. Season with salt and pepper. Sprinkle with the remaining 2 tablespoons of lemon juice and set aside to cool.

To make the pizza: Preheat the oven to 550°F. Stretch the dough on an oiled baking sheet, as explained in the recipe for Basic Pizza Crust.

Spread a thin, even layer of tomato sauce over the dough, if using. Distribute the cooled artichoke slices over the pizza and sprinkle with the mozzarella. Bake on the lowest oven rack for 7 to 10 minutes, or until the crust is golden and the artichokes are nicely browned.

NOTE: For a more exotic pizza, add sliced, sautéed potatoes (what else?). *Mentuccia,* an Italian mint, may be found at nurseries.

Pizza Quattro Stagioni

ONE 13-BY-18-INCH PIZZA

This pizza is called Four Seasons pizza because each quadrant of the pie is graced with a different ingredient, such as a combination of prosciutto, cheese, artichokes, and mushrooms. I used to think it was named for *The Four Seasons* by Vivaldi, and that each ingredient represented a season of the year—a challenging task, if you think about it. You may use any four vegetables or even four cheeses if you like (change the name to Pizza Quattro Formaggi), but once again, try to stick to the simplest and most complementary combinations.

Dough for 1 pizza crust, ½ recipe Basic Pizza Crust (page 105)

⅔ cup Simply Perfect Tomato Sauce (page 121), or your favorite tomato sauce

6 ounces prosciutto, sliced very thin

1 cup baby artichokes, sliced, prepared, and cooled as for Pizza con Carciofi (page 115)

1 cup mushrooms, prepared as for Pizza ai Funghi (page 110)

½ cup chopped or shredded fontina, mozzarella, Parmesan, or Taleggio cheese

½ cup fresh basil, chopped fine

¼ cup olive oil

Preheat the oven to 550°F. Stretch the dough on an oiled baking sheet, as explained in the recipe for Basic Pizza Crust.

Spread a thin, even layer of tomato sauce over the dough. Arrange the prosciutto, artichokes, mushrooms, and cheese on the pizza on each quarter of the dough, to make Quattro Stagioni. Sprinkle basil over any or all of the quadrants, depending on your taste. Sprinkle with olive oil. Bake on the lowest oven rack for 7 to 10 minutes, or until the crust is golden and the cheese is bubbly.

Pizza alla Griglia

ONE 13-BY-18-INCH PIZZA

Brick on end
or place pizza up on bricks direct

This grilled pizza is a lovely change from oven-baked pizza, and a fair facsimile of the pizza crusts made in wood-burning ovens in Italy. You must have a barbecue with a lid for good results, even better if the barbecue also has a temperature gauge, which should read 400 to 450°F for a crusty pizza. If your grill rack is not adjustable, simply place two patio bricks flat on the barbecue grill to hold a second grill (for the pizza) farther from the coals (see illustration). I take advantage of the hot coals to roast peppers for the pizza, but you may just as easily grill thin slices of eggplant, zucchine, or any other vegetable you like, including green tomato slices, which make a spectacular pizza. If you do, omit the tomato sauce and substitute the fresh, grilled tomatoes, spreading them over the crust before adding the cheese and basil.

1 large or 2 medium-size red or yellow bell peppers
6 tablespoons olive oil
2 cloves garlic, chopped
3 tablespoons balsamic vinegar
2 tablespoons chopped flat-leaf parsley
Salt
Dough for 1 pizza crust, ½ recipe Basic Pizza Crust (page 105)
½ cup Simply Perfect Tomato Sauce (page 121), or your favorite tomato sauce
4 ounces fresh mozzarella packed in water, chopped
½ cup chopped fresh basil leaves

Prepare a charcoal or gas grill. Position the grill rack so that it is 6 or 7 inches above the coals.

To prepare the peppers: Roast the peppers on the grill, turning them often until they are blackened. Transfer them to a plate and cover them with a damp cloth for 5 minutes (I simply cover them with a clean cloth and spritz it). Rub the skins from the peppers; they will slip off easily. Scrape out the seeds and slice into ½-inch-thick slices.

In a skillet, heat 4 tablespoons of the olive oil over medium-high heat and sauté the peppers until nicely browned. Add the garlic and cook a few minutes longer. Add the balsamic vinegar and cook for about 2 minutes or until vinegar evaporates and the peppers caramelize. Remove from the heat, add the parsley, and season with salt. Let cool.

To make the pizza: With lightly floured hands, press the dough into two 12-inch rounds, forming a lip around the edges. Make sure the dough is not sticky by dusting it with a little flour, if necessary. Transfer the rounds to a floured baking sheet (or dust it with cornmeal, which acts as little ball-bearings to enable the pizza to slide off easily). Let it rest for 10 minutes.

Brush the pizza crust with 1 tablespoon of the remaining olive oil. Brush grill with oil and slide the pizza crust onto it. Close the lid of the grill and bake for about 5 minutes, watching to see that the fire is not too hot and burning the underside. If fire is too hot, let coals burn out a bit or spritz them with a little water before proceeding. Open lid and spread the pizza with sauce, arrange the peppers on top, sprinkle with mozzarella and basil, and sprinkle with the remaining 1 tablespoon of olive oil. Close the lid for 5 to 7 minutes longer, or until the edges are crisp and browned and cheese is melted. Remove with large metal spatula and serve in wedges.

Pizza on the Grill

Very Thin Pizza with Arugula Paste

My whole garden was cannibalized one season by some seemingly innocuous seeds from Capri which, for two years, would not even germinate. But when they did, they produced prodigious plants of wild arugula (*Arugula selvatica*), which have a delightful small jagged leaf and a very peppery spicy flavor to which one becomes instantly addicted. I cannot eat a salad without it, and in searching for ways to use it, invented this very healthy condiment. I am sure it is packed with vitamins just because of its intense green color. Domestic arugula does just as well.

My pizza dough must be stretched very thin to make this, so that it becomes very crisp, like a cracker, when baking.

½ recipe Basic Pizza Crust (page 105), stretched to fit 13-by-18-inch baking sheet
4 cups torn fresh arugula leaves
⅔ cup olive oil
Juice from 2 lemons
½ garlic clove
½ teaspoon salt
Olive oil, for brushing on pizza dough

Preheat the oven to 450°F. Let the pizza dough rise for 15 minutes while you make the arugula paste.

In the bowl of a food processor, combine the arugula, olive oil, lemon juice, garlic, and salt, and process to a smooth paste.

Brush the pizza dough generously with olive oil and bake for 9 or 10 minutes, until nicely browned and crisp in places. The surface will be uneven and will cook unevenly but will look pretty. Cool in the pan for a few minutes, break in pieces, and serve with the arugula paste (see Note).

NOTE: Try this recipe with olive paste or substitute cilantro for arugula to make your paste.

Simply Perfect Tomato Sauce

2 CUPS

For years, I have debated with friends and chefs about the controversial pinch of sugar added to tomato sauce. My stepdaughter, Nicole, who is Italian and a marvelous cook, says that a pinch of sugar is imperative, and so I am in the habit of using it and I cannot do without it. I use the sugar to complement and temper the acidity of the tomatoes, but even in the summer, when I often harvest pound after pound of very sweet Roma sauce tomatoes, I still use my pinch. Although this sauce is ideal for pasta or pizza, a spoonful of it is also useful in finishing other sauces or livening up soup stocks. You might just want to dip your focaccia in it as is.

2 tablespoons olive oil
½ cup minced sweet onion
One 16-ounce can crushed Italian tomatoes, or 2 pounds fresh Roma tomatoes, chopped or crushed
½ teaspoon salt
Pinch of sugar

In a 12-inch sauté pan or deep stainless steel skillet, heat the oil over medium-high heat. Sauté the onion until translucent. Add the tomatoes with their liquid, the salt, and sugar and simmer for 15 to 20 minutes, or until thickened.

Sweet Loaves and Others

ALTHOUGH MY TASTE RUNS TO salty (as does my humor, on occasion), there are several sweet breads that I find irresistible. Some recipes come from my family, and represent loaves we have eaten for generations, while others are from way out in left field and simply appeal to me as being sensational breads, cakes, or cookies—breads you would want to have in a solid, eclectic repertoire.

A word on sugar: white sugar is brown sugar is honey is molasses is sucrose is glucose (or dextrose) is fructose. There exist very few differences between them, except what we think about them. I meet many people who have a pathological fear of white sugar and only want raw or "natural" sugars in their diets.

I believe that everyone should have exactly what he or she wishes, but chemically, sugar is sugar is sugar, and if you really want to eat the one that is best for you (in the most minute way), eat molasses!

White sugar is composed mainly of sucrose, with a tiny bit of fructose, a few minerals, and some water. Brown sugar is mainly sucrose, too, except with a bit more fructose and a slightly higher percentage of minerals. Molasses is about a third sucrose, a third minerals and fructose, and a third water, carbohydrates, and nitrogen—so if a tiny jolt of nitrogen is prescribed in your diet, eat molasses.

Moderation is a useful word in a world of food fanaticism. The sugar we derive from fruits may appear to be more healthful than the sugar in a slice of chocolate mousse cake, but in reality your body does not differentiate among kinds of sugar, so having a moderate slice of dessert every once in a while is not cause for panic. If you eat more calories than you burn, you will gain weight, no matter what kind of food it is, but small servings of a sweet once or twice a week are not necessarily dangerous. At any rate, sugar is the "standard currency of chemically stored energy for all plants and animals on earth," says food scientist and author Harold McGee, and as such, should be treated with respect and consideration in our foods. Along with consideration, add moderation.

The argument I have with recipes for breads that contain sugar in any form is that most of them call for too much. This goes for many, many desserts, too. I have to mention here that my favorite cooks, the Italians, do not really have as many recipes for sweets or desserts as do some other countries in the Western world. They very often finish their meals with a bowl of beautiful fruit or a little cheese, and rarely dilute the beauty of a perfectly balanced menu with a sticky, heavy, creamy, buttery, and oversugared sweet. There are a few delectable exceptions, such as tiramisú, Sardinian *sabadas,* and the wildly sweet Sicilian cassata, but still, the basic ingredient in tiramisú is mascarpone, a cheese, and there is not much sugar added because of the savoiardi cookies or ladyfingers used as the base of the dessert. The cream that many cooks insist on adding is absolutely not a part of an authentic tiramisú. And a Sardinian favorite, *sabadas,* are filled with dolce Sardo, a cheese.

A good thing is a good thing, and too much of a good thing always tastes exactly as you would expect. By now, you know that I have strong opinions on cooking, and the use of sugar is no exception. Even the Italians, who are capable of making a very good gelato, sometimes (depending on the gelato shop) go overboard with sugar so that the beautiful flavors of the fruit, nuts, or chocolate are sometimes masked by a cloying sweetness. The same applies to breads: Our goal is to keep the taste of the main ingredients in the limelight without upstaging them with sugar.

A perfect example of how sugar is used delicately to counterbalance the lovely, buttery quality of the dough is My Czech Grandmother's Kolaches in this chapter. You could say that a *kolache* is a kind of turnover and, just as some turnovers or dumplings can be as heavy as lead, the dumplings sinking to the bottom of a soup rather than floating lazily on top, there are also many versions of *kolaches* that one could easily use as paperweights. Fortunately, my grandmother had a light hand with dough, which is very important to keep in mind with dessert dough. Any bread or pastry containing butter or sugar must be handled as if you were mixing fragile butterfly wings. Schiacciatta with Roasted Grapes is an exception, as it requires many little dents, made with the fingers, to rise evenly, much like pizza or focaccia.

Cakes, too, must be mixed with a deft hand so as not to beat all of the life out of the batter, especially Gabriella's Ricotta Cake and the Sourdough Lemon Cake, which require egg whites to be beaten and then folded into the batter.

When I began experimenting with starters in cakes, using a tiny pinch of yeast, it was because of an intense curiosity about whether bread techniques would work for lighter baked goods, as well as to see how the yeast would interact with sweet batter. What a surprise to find that the starter imparted a subtle new flavor to the cakes and also gave the crumb a lovely light texture, as in the Sourdough Lemon Cake. I included the recipe for Brownie Scout Chocolate Cake because it is the tastiest and simplest cake to make that I know. There are richer cakes, lighter cakes, and mousses and tortes, but this is a cake for all seasons, light and easy.

I chose to put our *tozzetti* in this chapter because they are a perfect complement to sorbet or ice cream, without danger of being heavy. To make up for all my opinionated views on desserts and sweets, I urge you to make the sinfully rich Wild Turkey Ice Cream to go with *tozzetti*. This is an unforgettable gelato that relies on the unbeatable team of bourbon and chocolate to offset the very small amount of sugar in the recipe, while imparting a richness not often found in most standard ice creams. This recipe will convince you that the simplest ice creams are the best: cream, just enough sugar, and one other ingredient are usually enough. No liqueurs or artificial flavors.

Many sweet breads and desserts are seasonal. In California we have an abundance of grapes, and so I make my own raisins, using the Red Flame grapes of autumn for Roasted Grapes in Schiacciatta. Because of their high sugar content, these grapes caramelize quickly in the oven and turn into the succulent little morsels known as raisins. And there is nothing as seductive as intense, ripe summer apricots or crisp, fragrant autumn apples caramelized into a perfect apricot tart or tarte Tatin. But these desserts derive most of their sugar from the fruit, not from cupfuls of granulated sugar.

We all love sweet tastes, be it in elaborate desserts, simple sorbet, or luscious ripe fruits. Our body needs sugar, just as it needs proteins and fats at different times. If you eat a light ricotta cake or fruit with a *tozzetto* for most of your desserts, you will be able to indulge once in a while in an irresistible high-rise of whipped cream–topped decadence. And besides, a great rationalization for eating any dessert is to tell yourself that all the chemically stored energy is going to burst forth on the treadmill—just as soon as you finish that last bite.

Classic Brioches

The brioche is to me as the madeleine is to Proust. I first encountered brioches on the *Île de France* steamship when my friend Nan and I were given a first-class stateroom because of a mix-up in the booking! We took turns lolling in the oversized gimbaled bathtub, devouring caviar at the captain's table, and enjoying our first real French brioches for breakfast each morning. Two naïve little Texans were completely transformed into worldly Francophiles (we knew "oui" and "merci") when the ship reached Calais, perhaps because we were saturated in everything French for five days, but in the end it was the brioches that won us over. Golden and rich with more butter than a croissant in every bite, the brioche is still the queen of breakfast breads.

After this momentous trip, brioches became part of my weekly baking, and I thought I had learned everything about it. It was only years later, when I met Celestino Drago, a Sicilian chef lauded in Los Angeles for his successful restaurants, that I learned the trick of using brioche in bread pudding. When made with brioche in place of bread, this very earthy dessert is to bread pudding as the *Île de France* is to a tugboat.

continued

1 tablespoon active dry yeast

½ cup warm water (85 to 95°F)

1 cup sifted all-purpose flour

BRIOCHE PASTE

2¾ cups unbleached all-purpose flour, sifted

3 tablespoons water or warm milk

3 tablespoons sugar

1 teaspoon salt

6 large eggs

20 to 24 tablespoons unsalted butter, at room temperature (with the texture of modeling clay)

1 egg yolk beaten with 1 tablespoon water

To make the sponge: Stir the yeast into the water and add the flour to make a soft dough. Place the dough in a bowl set in a larger bowl of very warm water, cover, and let it rise to the top of the bowl. Or, place the dough in a bowl, cover, and let rise for 30 minutes to become a sponge. It will then be ready to mix with the brioche paste.

To make the brioche paste: In the bowl of a mixer set on low speed, or by hand, blend 1½ cups of the flour with the water or warm milk, sugar, and salt. Beat in 1 egg at a time. Add the remaining 1¼ cups flour and blend just until the dough resembles a smooth sticky golden paste.

Carefully add the sponge and mix just until incorporated. Remove from the bowl with a spatula onto a smooth hard surface, such as marble, granite, or Formica. Now the fun begins. Wash and dry your hands well. Scoop up the brioche paste with one hand and throw it against the surface again and again, until the dough does not stick to the surface or your hands and is very elastic. It is a lovely way to work out any aggressions, but mostly the dough is so silky and buttery that it's very pleasing to handle. Dip your fingers in flour from time to time if the dough is tacky. Mix in the butter, a few tablespoons at a time, until it is incorporated, keeping the dough elastic.

Form the dough into a ball and place in a buttered bowl, cover with plastic wrap, and let rise until doubled in volume, about 1 hour. The dough will be beautifully light and golden.

Same day method: Refrigerate the dough for at least 4 hours before forming the brioche. It will rise and take on flavor. The dough will fall slightly when you shape the brioche, but will rise again in the muffin pan or brioche mold before baking.

Overnight method: Refrigerate overnight. Remove the dough and proceed with shaping instructions.

Cut X in brioche dough with scissors

Place smaller brioche ball in X, pressing it down.

Dough will bake like this

Forming the brioche: Butter a 20-cup muffin pan or 20 individual fluted brioche molds (found in kitchen shops). Using two-thirds of the dough, form it into little round balls about 2 inches in diameter or large enough to fill half of each muffin mold. Make the same number of smaller balls of dough with the remaining third of dough. With scissors, cut an X in the top of each of the larger balls (see illustration) and press the smaller ball down into the X. Cover with a dry cloth and let rise in a warm place until doubled in volume, 30 to 40 minutes.

Preheat the oven to 425°F. Brush each brioche with the beaten egg yolk mixture. (In France, this is called the *dorure*, and here, an egg wash, used as a glaze for many egg breads.) Bake for about 15 minutes or until nicely browned. Serve with fresh fruit purée.

Bigmama's Kolaches

My grandmother made all of her own breads and pastries, among them the sweet rolls called *kolaches*, stuffed with poppy seeds, fruit, or farmer's cheese. In the Czech and German community of Weimar, Texas (there was once even a tiny town called Shimek, our family name, which most likely was a couple of chicken coops and a possum trot), a lot of *kolaches* changed hands, but undeniably Bigmama's were different. Her dough fairly lifted off the table, even when weighed down with filling. The same satiny dough was made into "twisties," dipped in the heavenly combination of butter and coarse sugar, which we children devoured, fresh from the oven. Her twisties and *kolaches* were famous among her friends, many of whom often could be found chatting in Czech in her big white kitchen.

A large white enamel table stood in the center of the kitchen where Bigmama and my Aunt Isabel would stretch fine butter dough until it was paper thin, and then mix apples, cinnamon, and sugar to make the filling for airy strudel or individual pastries. Bigmama was not big at all, despite a daily diet of luscious pastries and breads from her fragrant kitchen. Her heart, however, was as big as her white kitchen table from which so many good things fell into our waiting hands.

½ cup unsalted butter, softened
4 tablespoons sugar
2 large eggs
1 cup sour cream or plain yogurt
1 teaspoon salt
1 tablespoon active dry yeast

¼ cup lukewarm water (85 to 95°F)

1 cup warm milk

5 cups unbleached all-purpose flour

About 3 tablespoons unsalted butter, melted

Poppy Seed Filling (page 132), Prune Filling (page 133), Apricot Filling (page 134), or Cottage Cheese Filling (page 134)

2 to 3 tablespoons sifted confectioners' sugar (optional)

To prepare the dough: In a large mixing bowl, beat together the butter and sugar until creamy. Add the eggs, sour cream or yogurt, and salt. Dissolve the yeast in the water and stir into the mixture. Gradually add the milk and flour and stir until the dough is smooth and satiny.

Use about 1 teaspoon of melted butter to coat a clean bowl and place the dough in the bowl. Cover tightly and refrigerate for about 2 hours or overnight. The dough will rise in the refrigerator and gain flavor.

To shape rolls: Remove dough from refrigerator and let stand, covered, in a warm place for about 45 minutes. Rub two baking sheets with melted butter.

Divide the dough in half and shape each portion into 8 little round flat cakes. Arrange the cakes 3 inches apart on the baking sheets. With your thumb, make a wide, deep indentation in the center of each for the filling. Spoon about 2 teaspoons of the filling into each indentation. Close the dough over the filling by gathering the outside of the flattened cake and pulling it together like a drawstring purse over the filling (see illustration). Brush the *kolaches* with the remaining melted butter, cover, and let rise for about 30 minutes or until doubled.

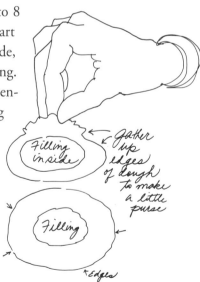

Filling inside

gather up edges of dough to make a little purse

Filling

Edges

continued

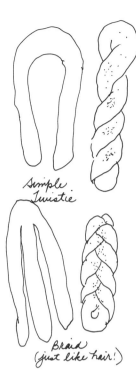

Simple
Twistie

Braid
(just like hair!)

To shape twisties: Divide dough into 6 parts and roll each with the flat of your hands into a long worm of dough about ¾ inch thick. Form each into a U shape, like a hairpin, and then twist one strand with the other (see illustration). Lay on buttered baking sheets, brushed with melted butter, and let rise until doubled.

To bake rolls and twisties: Preheat the oven to 350°F. Bake the rolls and twisties for 20 to 25 minutes, or until golden brown. Transfer to cooling racks. If desired, sift a bit of powdered sugar over them to make them festive.

NOTE: Dip twisties in melted butter, then in granulated or coarse sugar before or after baking.

Poppy Seed Filling

ABOUT 1 CUP

1 cup ground poppy seeds (see Note)
⅔ cup sugar
⅛ teaspoon salt
½ cup plus a little more milk or cream
2 tablespoons unsalted butter
½ teaspoon vanilla extract

Place the poppy seeds, sugar, and salt in a heavy saucepan and stir over low heat until the sugar is melted. Stir in the milk and butter and cook slowly for about 20 minutes until thick. Add a little more liquid if needed. Remove from the heat, stir in the vanilla, and cool. Use to fill Kolaches, as directed.

NOTE: For a slightly stronger poppy seed flavor, grind them in a coffee grinder or spice grinder. Measure before or after grinding. If you prefer, leave them whole—it makes little difference in the finished product.

Prune Filling

ABOUT 1 CUP

One 8-ounce package pitted prunes
1 teaspoon grated lemon peel
Pinch of salt
Pinch of ground cinnamon or mace

In a saucepan, combine the prunes with just enough water to cover. Add lemon peel, bring to a simmer, and cook until soft. Add the salt and cinnamon or mace and cook 1 minute longer. Drain, cool, and process in a food processor for a few seconds to blend all ingredients or mash with a fork. Use to fill Kolaches, as directed.

Apricot Filling

One 8-ounce package dried apricots, or 3 cups fresh apricot halves
⅔ cup sugar
1 teaspoon lemon juice

In a saucepan, combine the dried apricots with just enough water to cover (if using fresh or fresh frozen, combine with ½ cup of water as fresh apricots will generate juice). Bring to a simmer and cook until soft. Add the sugar and lemon juice and cook over low heat for about 20 minutes until thick and shiny. Cool and use to fill Kolaches, as directed.

Cottage Cheese Filling

1 cup large- or small-curd cottage cheese
½ cup sugar
¼ cup toasted bread crumbs (crumbs made from rosemary focaccia are good in this)
1 large egg yolk
1 tablespoon grated lemon peel
Pinch of mace
Pinch of salt

Loosen the lid on the container of cottage cheese or loosely cover a measured cup and leave it on the countertop at room temperature for about 12 hours to sour.

Mix the cottage cheese, sugar, bread crumbs, egg, lemon peel, mace, and salt until very smooth. Use to fill Kolaches, as directed.

Apricot Focaccia

ABOUT 2 FOCACCE

Every Wednesday I get a free trip to Europe when I visit the Santa Monica Farmer's Market. There I can find, in season, luscious Blenheim apricots, which are, as any grower will tell you, the crème de la crème of apricots. They are only available for three weeks in July, and it is then that I freeze flats of them, whole, and use them in this focaccia in place of dried apricots. (Wash and dry them before you freeze them in 8-ounce portions.) Their flavor is so intense it is as if they had been dried already but still retained their juice. Sometimes you can actually find the dried ones in packages marked "Blenheim," and if you do, buy plenty!

8 ounces dried apricots or frozen whole Blenheim apricots, defrosted
1½ cups water (for dried apricots only)
2 cups lukewarm water (85 to 95°F)
1 tablespoon active dry yeast
5 cups unbleached all-purpose flour
2 teaspoons salt
2 tablespoons olive oil
½ cup turbinado, raw brown sugar, or dark brown sugar
1 teaspoon ground cinnamon

To prepare the apricots: Place the dried apricots, chopped into ½-inch pieces, and water in a small saucepan and bring to a boil over medium-high heat. Reduce the heat to low and simmer, uncovered, for 10 to 15 minutes, or until tender. Drain, reserve the liquid, and set the fruit aside to cool.

If using frozen apricots: Defrost and chop them into ½-inch pieces. Do not cook.

continued

To make the bread: Measure the lukewarm water into a large bowl. Sprinkle the yeast over the water and stir until dissolved. Stir in the cooled apricot liquid, chopped apricots, flour, and salt. Stir until well blended. If necessary, stir in an additional ½ cup of flour. Cover bowl and let the dough rise in a warm place until doubled in volume, 30 to 45 minutes.

To shape the focaccia: Preheat the oven to 500°F. Oil two 13-by-18-inch baking sheets.

Carefully scrape half of the dough onto each sheet without deflating too much. Brush the dough with 1 tablespoon of olive oil.

To make the traditional focaccia with indentations, dip your fingers into cold water and insert them straight down into the dough. Make holes in the dough by pulling it to the sides about 1 inch at a time. Pull the holes at random to form little craters all over with the pan showing through where you have put your fingers. As you work, stretch the dough into a 1-inch-thick oval. Brush with the remaining 1 tablespoon of olive oil. Stir together the sugar and cinnamon and sprinkle over focaccia. Let rise in a warm place for 15 to 25 minutes.

To bake the focaccia: Place the pans in the oven and reduce temperature to 450°F. Bake for 15 to 18 minutes, or until golden brown and the smell drives you crazy. Cool on wire racks and cut into wedges or rectangles.

NOTE: You may decorate the top of the focaccia with apricots pushed into the raw dough at random before baking.

Prune and Walnut Bread

2 LOAVES

With the exception of the sourdough Filoncino Integrale on page 58, whole wheat breads have not captured my attention as much as country breads with large-holed crumb structure and nice chewy crusts. I love a BLT on whole wheat, or chappatis with my curry, but in general, I like whole wheat bread for breakfast with things in it: nuts, fruit, and other grains for texture. This one evolved one day out of chappati dough when I was fooling around with whole wheat flour, and it remains in my repertoire mostly because of its texture and for its breakfast qualities. I say breakfast only because its sweetness makes great toast, but I also eat tuna on this bread and call it my "Sicilian sandwich," as many Sicilian dishes are salty and sweet.

1½ cups warm milk
½ cup wheat bran
¼ cup unsalted butter, melted, or ¼ cup olive oil
3 tablespoons honey or molasses
1 tablespoon salt
1 teaspoon unsweetened cocoa powder
½ cup lukewarm water (85 to 95°F)
2 tablespoons active dry yeast
2 cups whole wheat flour
3 cups unbleached all-purpose flour
½ cup graham, rye, or any other dark flour
1 cup chopped stewed prunes
⅓ cup walnut pieces
⅓ cup ground walnuts

continued

To make the dough: Combine the milk, wheat bran, butter or olive oil, honey or molasses, salt, and cocoa, stir well, and set aside to cool.

Measure the water into a bowl. Sprinkle the yeast over the water and stir until dissolved. Add the milk mixture alternately with the flour, prunes, and nuts, stirring well until the dough pulls away from the sides of the bowl. If necessary, stir in an additional ½ cup of flour. Turn the dough out onto a floured board and turn it over on itself a few times to distribute the fruit and nuts evenly.

Same day method: Place the dough in an oiled bowl, cover with plastic wrap, and let the dough rise in a warm place until doubled in volume, about 1 hour. Whole wheat dough is heavier than white bread dough and needs more time to rise. Proceed with the shaping instructions.

Overnight method: Place the dough in an oiled bowl, cover, and refrigerate overnight. The dough will rise in the refrigerator and acquire flavor from the slower yeast action. Remove the dough 2 hours before shaping and let stand, covered, in a warm place. Proceed with shaping instructions.

To shape loaves: Heat the oven to 450°F. Oil two loaf pans. Carefully pour the dough into each pan and let the dough sit for about 30 minutes to rise again.

To bake loaves: Bake for about 15 minutes, turn the pans around and continue baking for 10 to 15 minutes longer, or until the bread sounds hollow when you thump it and the tops are nicely browned. If the bread falls after the first 15 minutes of baking, reduce the oven temperature to 400°F. Cool on a wire rack.

Schiacciatta* with Roasted Grapes

The schiacciatta is a Tuscan bread made most often during the grape harvest to celebrate nature's success at once again supplying the world with good wine. It is much like a focaccia, except in two layers, and sweet instead of salty, with the addition of grapes or raisins. My schiacciatta is different from most in that the dough is not as sweet and so complements the very, very sweet grapes that I use. I slow-roast the grapes, which turns them into glorified, elegant raisins that give the schiacciatta its intense flavor. I also try to make the dough as thin as possible in order to get a good crunch along the edges. In Italy, the dough is made with lard, which is high in fat but also very flavorful. However, lard also makes a heavier dough, and so I use olive oil, which contains no saturated fats or cholesterol and which gives the bread the same "short" (crisp) texture and flavor without the wear and tear on your arteries. But if you would like to taste the original flavor of schiacciatta, by all means, use lard. Once a year can't hurt you.

1½ cups lukewarm water (85 to 95°F)
1 package active dry yeast
¼ cup sugar
1 large egg, beaten (optional)
3¼ to 4 cups unbleached all-purpose flour
¼ cup olive oil, or ¼ cup lard, plus more oil for brushing
2 teaspoons salt
3 cups Suzanne's Roasted Grapes (page 141)
3 to 4 tablespoons raw turbinado or white sugar

*Pronounced *skee-ah-cha-tah*.

Schiacciatta with roasted grapes

continued

To make the dough: Measure the water into a bowl. Sprinkle the yeast over the water. Add the sugar and egg and beat well. Add the flour, ¼ cup of olive oil, and salt, and mix well, stirring until the dough is smooth and satiny and pulls away from the sides of the bowl. (If you are using lard, cut the lard into the flour, as you would for pie crust, before adding the flour to the wet mixture.) Place in an oiled bowl, brush with olive oil, cover, and refrigerate overnight. Remove dough from refrigerator and let stand, covered, in a warm place until doubled in volume, about 1 hour.

To shape dough: Rub a 13-by-18-inch baking sheet with olive oil. Place half the dough on the baking sheet and begin to stretch it into a very thin circle to the edges of the pan, as you would for pizza. Brush with olive oil and spread half of the roasted grape mixture over the dough.

On a lightly floured surface, roll out the remaining dough to a similar circle and, lifting carefully, place it over the grape layer (you may do this more easily by dusting the circle with a little flour, and rolling it up loosely, flour side in, and then unrolling it over the grapes). Press the 2 circles together to push out the air. Dip your fingers in cold water or olive oil and make indentations over the top of the dough. Make holes in the dough by pulling it to the sides of the baking sheet, about 1 inch at a time. Pulling the holes at random will form small craters all over the dough, with the pan showing through in spots. The dough should be oval and stretched to fit almost the entire baking sheet. Brush the dough with the olive oil and sprinkle the remaining grapes evenly over the dough. Sprinkle with the sugar and let rest for 15 minutes.

To bake the schiacciatta: Preheat the oven to 500°F. Bake for 5 minutes, then lower heat to 400°F and continue to bake for 20 minutes or until golden brown. (Do not allow the grapes to burn.) Transfer to a large wire baking rack to cool. Serve warm or cooled, cut into strips, with a glass of red wine.

Suzanne's Roasted Grapes

ABOUT 3 CUPS

I have never seen roasted grapes in recipes, but after I inadvertently left a pan of grapes in the oven to dry, turned the heat to 350°F instead of 150°F and, as usual, went out to the garden, I was surprised to find delectable little morsels when I returned. Roasted grapes can also be used in other dishes such as broiled quail with grapes, panettone, or plum pudding, or soaked in Cognac and spooned over ice cream, or used to make one helluva bowl of morning cereal!

1 teaspoon olive oil
3 pounds seedless Red Flame grapes (see Note)

Preheat the oven to 350°F. Oil a baking sheet with olive oil. Stem the grapes and spread over the sheet.

Roast the grapes, turning once or twice with a large spatula, for about 1 hour, or until the grapes have collapsed and begun to turn brown around the edges. Remove them from the oven before they are completely browned and dried like raisins. Set aside to cool.

NOTE: The high sugar content of Red Flame grapes makes them ideal for roasting, but experiment with other types to find your own favorite.

Sourdough Lemon Cake

This is a very simple recipe, invented one day when I remembered that I had invited a special friend to a birthday dinner but had completely forgotten the cake. My lemon trees had just given me a generous gift of fruit and I did have a little flour around. My mother's answer to such emergencies was to keep cake mixes in the cupboard, and elevate them with extra butter or spices or what have you, in this case, lemon juice and zest, but I hadn't bought a mix for years. I am now seriously reconsidering this.

Eliminate the sourdough starter if you like, but it gives a little zing to the batter and reacts well with the lemon peel. The cake is very good served with fruit purée.

STARTER

3 tablespoons buttermilk
3 tablespoons unbleached all-purpose flour
4 to 5 drops lemon juice
Tiny pinch of yeast dissolved in a tablespoon of water

CAKE

¾ cup unsalted butter
1¼ cups sugar
3 large eggs, separated
1 tablespoon lemon juice
1 teaspoon vanilla extract
1½ cups unbleached all-purpose flour
½ teaspoon baking soda
½ teaspoon salt

1 cup buttermilk or yogurt

2 teaspoons grated lemon (or orange peel, in a pinch)

To make the starter: Combine the buttermilk, flour, lemon juice, and yeast-water mixture. Stir well to aerate the mixture and form a wet dough. Cover tightly with plastic wrap and let ferment overnight at room temperature.

To make the cake: Preheat the oven to 350°F. Butter and flour a 9-inch round cake pan.

In a large bowl, cream the butter. Add the sugar, egg yolks, lemon juice, vanilla, and starter, beating until smooth.

Mix the flour, baking soda, and salt and add to the batter, alternating with the buttermilk, mixing well after each addition.

Beat the egg whites until they are glossy and hold soft peaks. Carefully fold in the beaten egg whites and the lemon or orange peel. Pour into the cake pan and bake for about 45 minutes, or until the top of the cake springs back when lightly touched.

Golden Cornmeal Torta della Nonna

ONE 9-INCH CAKE

Every "nonna" (grandmother) in Italy has a version of this cornmeal cake, and since I am a third, semi-nonna to three Italian grandchildren (thanks to my husband's daughter!), I, too, have created my own. The seductive texture and richness of cornmeal drives me mad, which is why I use it in so many dishes. It is amazing to me that the very same grainy substance that makes a soft and creamy polenta for wild mushrooms or sausages can segue right into this crumbly, rich dessert cake. The inclusion of a soured mash starter for this cake gives it a tangy flavor not often found in a cornmeal torte.

STARTER
½ cup stoneground yellow cornmeal
½ cup buttermilk or milk
Pinch of yeast

CAKE
½ cup unsalted butter
⅔ to 1 cup sugar
2 large eggs
½ teaspoon vanilla extract
½ cup stoneground yellow cornmeal
½ cup unbleached all-purpose flour
1 teaspoon baking soda
1 teaspoon baking powder
½ teaspoon salt
1 cup toasted almonds, walnuts, pecans, or pine nuts, ground fine
¼ cup buttermilk
Confectioners' sugar, for dusting

To make the starter: Combine the cornmeal, buttermilk, and yeast. Stir well to aerate the mixture and form a wet dough. Cover tightly with plastic wrap and let ferment overnight at room temperature.

To make the cake: Preheat the oven to 350°F. Butter a 9-inch round pan. In a large bowl, cream the butter. Add the sugar, eggs, and vanilla, beating until smooth. Mix the cornmeal, flour, baking soda, baking powder, and salt and add to the batter with the starter, ground nuts, and buttermilk. Mix well. Pour into the pan and bake for about 30 minutes or until firm. Cool in the pan, set on a wire rack, dust with confectioners' sugar, and serve.

Gabriella's Ricotta Cake

ONE 9-INCH CAKE

Many years ago, my husband was first married to Gabriella Piga, a Sardinian, Australian, Roman, in whose remarkable cooking all of these various cuisines are reflected. We have become fast friends over many years, and she sent me this recipe, which my stepson adores. When he is with us, I can make him feel even more at home by making his mother's ricotta torte. We cannot often find the intensely creamy ricotta here that is available in Rome, and so I let my humble cottage cheese "sour" overnight in order to give the cake richness, or I make my own fresh ricotta. It is so easy, you will make it whenever fresh ricotta is called for in a recipe, or just to eat with a little cinnamon or chocolate sprinkled on top.

continued

²⁄₃ cup sugar

5 large eggs, separated

1 pound cottage cheese or fresh ricotta (page 147)

1 tablespoon unbleached all-purpose flour

2 tablespoons sour cream, crème fraîche, or mascarpone

1 tablespoon grated lemon peel

⅛ teaspoon salt

Pinch of cinnamon

Confectioners' sugar, for dusting

Preheat the oven to 350°F. Butter and flour a 9-inch springform pan.

In a food processor, mix sugar and egg yolks until smooth. Add the cheese, flour, sour cream, crème fraîche, or mascarpone, lemon peel, salt, and cinnamon, and blend well.

In a large bowl, beat the egg whites until stiff but not dry. Fold into the batter. Pour into the springform pan and bake for about 40 minutes, or until the cake springs back easily with the touch of a finger. Let cool in the pan, remove from pan to a serving plate, dust with confectioners' sugar, and serve.

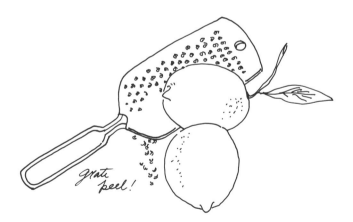

grate peel!

Fresh Ricotta

1 ½ POUNDS

This recipe was given to me by an Italian man who was tasting my breads at a demonstration one day. Naturally, we got into a deep conversation about food, and when I lamented the lack of good ricotta in the markets, he said, "Oh, you can make your own in about five minutes." This caught my attention. If you let the ricotta drip until it's very, very dry, you will have a nice fresh low-fat cheese to spread on homemade bread.

½ gallon whole milk
1 cup yogurt
½ cup fresh lemon juice
Salt

In a large stainless steel saucepan, bring the milk and yogurt to a simmer. Little bubbles will form around the edge of the pan and the surface of the milk will bulge slightly. Remove from heat and pour in the lemon juice without stirring. Let sit at room temperature for about 1 hour to allow the milk to curdle.

Line a sieve or fine colander with 4 layers of cheesecloth, leaving enough hanging over the edges to gather up and secure at the top. Place the sieve in the sink and carefully pour the milk into the cheesecloth. Gather up the cloth and secure it with string or a rubber band. (I tie mine to the sink faucet stem and let it drip directly into the sink.)

Let the cheese drip for at least 6 hours or overnight. Transfer to a bowl and add salt to taste. Store for up to a week in the refrigerator, or, after a week, wrap the cheese in cheesecloth and dry it out of the refrigerator for 1 to 2 days.

Brownie Scout Chocolate Cake

ONE 8-INCH LAYER CAKE

In its own mundane way, the gas company provided a turning point in my young career, introducing me to easy casseroles and simple desserts, small culinary achievements that eventually took me to fish soufflés and Sacher Tortes. When I was an eight-year-old Brownie Scout, the gas company in Houston offered to divulge to our raucous troop the secrets of tuna casserole (canned cream of mushroom soup and potato chip crust) and perfect chocolate cake. The precise recipes for both are long gone from my brain, but the memory of the cake's silky crumb and easy icing lingered long enough for me to develop my own recipe in tribute to that memorable lesson. And you can bet I cook with gas, 20,000 BTUs per burner! Using a starter to help leaven a cake may seem unusual, but it produces a lovely, light-textured crumb.

STARTER

½ cup lukewarm milk (85 to 95°F)
½ cup all-purpose flour or cake flour
Pinch of active dry yeast

CAKE

½ cup (1 stick) unsalted butter, softened
2 tablespoons vegetable shortening
2 cups sugar
2 large eggs
2 cups all-purpose flour or cake flour
¾ cup unsweetened Dutch-processed cocoa powder, such as Droste

2 teaspoons baking powder

2 teaspoons baking soda

¼ teaspoon salt

¾ cup milk

½ cup strong brewed coffee

1 teaspoon vanilla extract

Foolproof Chocolate Icing (page 150)

To make the starter: Measure the milk into a bowl. Add the flour and yeast and stir well to aerate the mixture and form a wet dough. Cover tightly with plastic wrap and let ferment overnight at room temperature. In the morning, it will be bubbly and fragrant.

To make the cake: Preheat the oven to 350°F. Butter and flour two 8-inch round cake pans.

In the bowl of an electric mixer set on medium speed, cream the butter, shortening, and sugar until light and fluffy. Add the eggs, one at a time, and mix until blended. Add the starter and mix just until incorporated.

Sift together the flour, cocoa, baking powder, baking soda, and salt. Add to the batter, alternating with the milk and coffee, and mix after each addition until smooth. Add the vanilla and mix well. Divide the batter between the pans. Bake for about 35 minutes or until the cake springs back when pressed gently with a finger. Turn out onto wire racks to cool. Frost when completely cool, filling and stacking the layers.

Foolproof Chocolate Icing

⅓ cup heavy cream

8 ounces bittersweet chocolate, chopped fine

⅔ cup sugar

2 tablespoons bourbon

1 teaspoon vanilla extract

¼ cup (½ stick) unsalted butter, softened

In a heavy saucepan, heat the cream over medium heat. Add the chocolate, sugar, bourbon, and vanilla, and cook, stirring, until very smooth and shiny. Let cool to barely warm. Using a handheld electric mixer set on medium high or a sturdy whisk, beat in the butter until smooth. Use immediately.

Another Foolproof Chocolate Icing

8 ounces bittersweet chocolate, chopped fine

2 cups confectioners' sugar

½ cup unsalted butter, softened

2 to 3 tablespoons bourbon or strong, brewed espresso

In the top of a double boiler set over barely simmering water, melt the chocolate, stirring, until smooth. Remove from the heat and let cool slightly. The chocolate should be cool but still soft.

Put the confectioners' sugar, butter, and chocolate in the bowl of a food processor and process until smooth. Add the bourbon or espresso to taste, pulse a few times, and use immediately.

NOTE: For creamier icing, use 1 or 2 more tablespoons of butter or cream. This icing may also be made in a mixer.

Gingerbread Cake

ONE 9-BY-13-INCH CAKE

In all my old children's books about little girls on farms or visiting grand-parents in some rustic mountain village, the heroine (always with thick, glossy, blond braids and rosy apple cheeks) was given slabs of gingerbread, hot from the oven and dripping with butter. Naturally, a glass of fresh goat's milk accompanied this delicacy. I realize now (thanks to a perceptive copy reader) that I embellished Heidi's breakfast of plain bread—I remember my mother giving *me* warm gingerbread to eat when I was reading this lovely children's book.

Pushed into obscurity by nut tortes and exotic mousse cakes, ginger-bread never graces a restaurant's dessert tray, but it remains one of the sweetest reminders of the carefree days of childhood when I (ordinary brown braids, no apple cheeks) curled up with a book, a glass of milk (cow's and out of a carton), and this wonderfully spicy brown bread.

continued

½ cup lukewarm milk or buttermilk (85 to 95°F)

½ cup unbleached all-purpose flour

1 teaspoon molasses

Pinch of active dry yeast

1 cup packed dark brown sugar

½ cup unsalted butter, softened

½ cup dark molasses

2 large eggs, separated

1½ cups unbleached all-purpose flour

2 teaspoons baking soda

2 teaspoons ground ginger

1 teaspoon ground cinnamon

½ teaspoon ground mace

¼ teaspoon grated whole nutmeg

½ cup buttermilk

Lemon Curd (page 153) or whipped cream

To make the starter: Measure the buttermilk into a bowl. Add the flour, molasses, and yeast and stir well to aerate the mixture and form a wet dough. Cover tightly with plastic wrap and let ferment overnight at room temperature. In the morning, it will be bubbly and fragrant.

To make the bread: Preheat the oven to 350°F. Butter and flour a 9-by-13-inch rectangular cake pan.

In the bowl of an electric mixer set on medium speed, cream the brown sugar, butter, and molasses until light colored. Add the egg yolks, one at a time, beating until blended. Add the starter, and mix just until incorporated.

Sift together the flour, baking soda, ginger, cinnamon, mace, and nutmeg. Add to the batter, alternating with the buttermilk, and mix well.

In a clean bowl with clean, dry beaters, beat the egg whites until stiff but not dry. Gently fold them into the batter. Pour into the pan and bake for 30 minutes, or until the bread springs back easily when pressed gently with a finger. Let cool in the pan. Serve with Lemon Curd or whipped cream.

Lemon Curd

ABOUT 1½ CUPS

This rich lemon curd has better taste and texture than thin, cornstarch-thickened lemon sauces. Those Spartan sauces are fine for a special diet or for calorie watchers, but gingerbread is such a low-fat cake that it's nice to dress it up with a richer sauce.

¾ cup sugar
2 large eggs
2 large egg yolks
½ cup fresh lemon juice
1 cup unsalted butter, softened
1 tablespoon grated lemon peel
Pinch of salt

In a heavy saucepan, combine the sugar, eggs, egg yolks, and lemon juice. Cook over low heat, whisking until glossy and thick. Remove from the heat and whisk in the butter, a little at a time, until smooth. Stir in the lemon peel and salt. Cool before serving.

NOTE: This dessert, by the way, can be as elegant as a French mousse cake if served properly. Cut the gingerbread into diamond shapes. Spoon the sauce onto a dessert plate, place the cake on top of the sauce, and toss a few fresh raspberries over the whole kit-and-caboodle. Tell your guests it's the hottest new dessert since tiramisú. The lemon curd may also be used as filling for tarts or pies.

Chocolate Tozzetti

Roman Dipping Cookies

24 TOZZETTI

These are the biscotti of Rome, but better than biscotti in my estimation, as they are much more like a cookie—not so hard and dry that they threaten to chip a tooth. I like them, too, because they are a light, elegant end to a meal. They also contain fennel, a good digestive.

As others plunge into a chocolate mousse tart or a "medley" of ice creams, I plunge my knife into a fresh Camembert or Reblochon cheese and pour another glass of good Rhone wine whenever possible. But now that I have discovered the French chocolate made in the valley of the Rhone (appropriately named Valrhona), I am a changed woman.

My personal chocolate trainer, my husband, first began to dent my attitude toward sweets by titillating me with whiffs of See's dark candies, his passion. He then began pushing little broken bits of Lindt Excellence toward me on occasion, nudging them closer and closer to my cheese board with a casual, "Just take a little. It can't hurt you. Just try it." I succumbed and let a little bit melt on my tongue, but still wanted goat cheese. Then I discovered Valrhona. My normal *tozzetti* took on a new dimension when I added this beautifully rich and subtle queen of chocolates to the recipe.

4 ounces bittersweet chocolate, such as Valrhona, or any good, bittersweet or semisweet chocolate, chopped fine
½ cup unsalted butter, softened

1 cup sugar

3 large eggs

1 teaspoon vanilla extract

3 cups unbleached all-purpose flour

2 teaspoons baking powder

Pinch of fennel

½ teaspoon salt

1 cup chopped, toasted almonds, walnuts, or pecans

Preheat the oven to 350°F. Butter a 13-by-18-inch baking sheet.

In the top of a double boiler set over barely simmering water, melt the chocolate, stirring until smooth. Remove from the heat and let cool to lukewarm.

In the bowl of an electric mixer set on medium-high speed, cream the butter and sugar until light and fluffy. Add the eggs, one at a time, beating until blended. Add the cooled chocolate and vanilla and beat until smooth.

Sift together the flour, baking powder, fennel, and salt and add to the batter with the nuts. Stir or beat on low speed until the dough is firm but malleable. Divide the dough in half and transfer each half to the baking sheet. Shape each into a roll about 16 inches long. Flatten the rolls with the palm of your hand and then use two spatulas to square off the long sides to make each roll about ¾ inch high.

Cutting tozzetti

Bake for 10 to 12 minutes or until slightly darkened. Remove from the oven and cool on wire racks for about 15 minutes.

Using a sharp, serrated knife, cut each roll into ½-inch-thick slices. Lay the slices on the baking sheet, cut side up. Bake for about 7 minutes or until browned around the edges. Cool on wire racks. Serve immediately or store in an airtight container

Turning tozzetti cut side up

continued

for up to 2 weeks. You may also wrap the cookies in foil and freeze them; they'll keep for several months.

NOTE: For plain *tozzetti*, substitute ½ cup slightly sweet white wine, such as vin Santo, Tokai, Malvasia, or Sauvignon Blanc, in place of the chocolate.

Wild Turkey Chocolate Ice Cream

6 SERVINGS

Ice cream makers are wonderful gadgets, but anyone with a freezer, a good metal container, and a wire whisk can make the best ice cream imaginable. I stir my ice creams and sorbets after 2 hours in the freezer to distribute the ice crystals evenly and improve the texture. This particular ice cream is dense and rich like a *marquise* (a frozen dessert containing butter). If you forget to stir it, don't worry.

This is an elegant ice cream that you can serve as a quick dessert to any dinner guests, including Julia Child, the Queen of England, or your mother-in-law, whoever comes first. Serve this with Chocolate Tozzetti (page 154).

2 cups heavy cream
6 ounces semisweet chocolate, chopped
½ cup plus 2 tablespoons sugar
1 large egg yolk
½ teaspoon vanilla extract
3 tablespoons Wild Turkey bourbon

In a heavy saucepan, heat the cream over medium heat until hot but not boiling. Add the chocolate and stir until melted. Lower the heat to very low, add the sugar and egg yolk, whisking quickly and fiercely so eggs will not separate, until the mixture thickens. Remove from heat and whisk in the vanilla and bourbon and pour the mixture through a sieve into a metal bowl or container.

Cover and refrigerate for at least 1 hour until chilled. Place in the freezer, stir after 1 to 2 hours, depending on your freezer, and proceed to freeze for at least 3 hours more, or until firm.

Special Breads and Bread Sticks

THESE BREADS ARE BAKED FOR special holidays or seasons—rich plum pudding, Christmas panettone, Russian Easter kulich—and are so out of the ordinary that they often are found only in expensive shops rather than home kitchens. I love to make them for gifts because there is nothing you can buy commercially that will even come close to tasting like these special breads made at home.

Plum puddings, for example, appear daunting to most, whereas they are really quite simple to make once the ingredients are assembled. Your own will be far superior to any sold in shops. The word *pudding* is the English word for dessert, and this pudding is nothing like a creamy American-style pudding. Still, many wonder why anyone would want to make this particular dessert from scratch. What on earth is a pudding steamer? Does a plum pudding really contain plums? And where do you get them in the middle of winter?

Similar questions apply to other special breads. Isn't a complicated panettone time-consuming to make? Will it taste like the Italian ones? What about candied fruits? Most are preserved and taste awful, so why use them?

I asked these same questions as a novice baker, but the first time I mixed the fruits, nuts, and spices together for a real plum pudding, I understood exactly why the process was so intriguing: the house was filled with the seductive fragrance of cinnamon, nutmeg, and cognac, and when I carried the flaming pudding to the Christmas table on its silver platter, my guests felt as though Tiny Tim were about to appear on Cratchit's shoulder! With the first bite of real plum pudding, I finally understood why an entire nation reveres a dark heap of questionable ingredients steamed into the shape of half a bowling ball and weighing about the same. And so will you. Understand, that is, not weigh the same.

For breads as exotic as kulich with pashka, it helps to know some Russians to get excited about Russian Easter. The only reason I ever made this bread was because I met some wild new Russian friends and wanted to let them know how much I enjoyed meeting them and how fascinating I found their culture. After they were long gone, I used to celebrate Russian Easter every year, just for the hell of it, so that I could make this amazing bread and cheese combination that I now serve for our Easter, too.

Almost everyone has a curry recipe in his or her repertoire, but not everyone makes bread to go with it. Ever since I met my first Indian friends at college, I have been fascinated by Indian cooking: the spices, the thousands of different curries, the lovely breads—puris, chappati, naan—the relative lack of hard-and-fast culinary rules. In short, I adore the creativity that is encouraged by Indian cuisine. And, being a Philistine at heart, I was fascinated by the custom of eating with bread rather than a fork. (As an adult, which is a questionable statement in itself, I delight in eating with my hands and licking my plate—literally—and all those things children are not supposed to do, like running with scissors.) The gestalt of it drew me deeper and deeper into Indian cooking, until I was making so many curries that my husband begged me to start reading Norman Mailer or Walt Whitman instead of the Bhagavad Gita and tomes on Indian cooking that were stacked up in the kitchen—anything that would get me back on the steak-and-potato track for a while. There is nothing like a good chappati with curry, and although these breads can be bought at Indian markets, they will never compete with your own.

When I was at Berkeley, I also met African students whose cooking was memorable for its exotic spices and unusual combinations. I was introduced to berberé, a paste of many flavors, and the marvelous cardamom bread Yewolo, which is made into a large, flat round to fit inside a basket woven expressly for it. I would like to have included my favorite exotic breads from every country, but alas, I had to choose most carefully for lack of space.

For special occasions or to pep up an antipasto table, I have included little rolls scented with white truffle oil. White *tartuffi,* as they are so charmingly called in Italy, are for me the eighth wonder of the world. As a child, I was taught the golden rule practically daily, and learned very soon that it does indeed work. Share and share alike was also thrown in for good measure, and I have always tried to adhere to both when a plate of either white truffles or black caviar is set before me and, unfortunately, others at the table. At this point I lose all morality and my mother's words are lost in the vapor. I eye the little black jewels as they are passed around from toast to toast, consciously and meticulously counting each one to make sure I have not been cheated of my share. As truffles are shaved over my steaming fettuccine, I have been known to grasp the waiter's arm that holds the truffle shaver, forcefully retaining him for just a few seconds longer than my allotted time, thereby blatantly cheating my dinner companion out of two or three of his own pungent slivers. When it comes to truffled anything, I am more than ruthless; I am dangerous. I keep truffle oil on hand as others keep salt in the shaker, to sprinkle over my focaccia for a special aperitivo accompaniment or to give subtle flavor to a roasting game hen. But I know there will come a day when my decadence will hit bottom and I will furtively pour a full jigger of it, all for myself, tossing it off like a true Texan—I'll have Urbani* 101 straight up, water back.

Who does not love bread sticks, if only for the pleasure of their snap or simply to fiddle with in restaurants? Some are good, many are tasteless, and

*A top Italian truffle-oil purveyor.

while very few are memorable, all feel good under the teeth. It is very hard not to eat a bread stick, if only because there is always hope that the next one will be different from and better than the rest.

The ones you make in your kitchen will outshine any commercial ones. You will be amazed at how varied bread sticks can be; they are, after all, just long sticks of good crust, and what you put on them is only limited by imagination. Roll them in seeds, crushed nuts, cinnamon, and sugar for breakfast, or brush them with scented olive oils or just plain melted butter for richness. In America, we have not really tuned in to bread sticks in restaurants, but when we finally learn to make good ones, I am sure they will be the next trend. I predict that there will be duels between chefs, each brandishing his own signature sword of dough, and each munching on the other's after they have called a draw. Children also love making bread sticks, and anything that engages a child in the kitchen has a very special place in my heart.

Apricot-Plum Pudding

8 SMALL (8-OUNCE) OR 4 LARGE (16-OUNCE) PUDDINGS

True plum pudding has never been as large a part of American holidays as it has been in the United Kingdom or other parts of Europe, but once you have tried this one, you will always want to include it on your holiday menu, if only for the lovely scent of marinating fruits. My husband counts the days until he has his Christmas pudding, warmed by flaming cognac and the requisite hard sauce melting over the top—a spectacular fiery finish to a grand dinner. By the way, the plums in plum pudding are actually dried prunes, but if you happen to freeze a few dozen fresh plums in the summer, you may use them in the pudding to make it more authentic.

1 cup golden raisins

1 cup currants

1 cup chopped dried apricots

1 cup chopped pitted prunes

1 cup chopped dried figs or dates, or a mixture of both

1 large tart apple, chopped fine

1 cup plum purée (see Note)

2 cups fine bread crumbs (from your own good bread, of course)

1 cup brown sugar

Zest and juice of 1 orange

Zest and juice of 1 lemon

1 teaspoon ground cardamom

1 teaspoon ground mace

1 teaspoon grated fresh nutmeg

1 teaspoon ground ginger

⅛ teaspoon ground cloves

⅛ teaspoon salt

1½ cups cognac

1½ cups sifted unbleached all-purpose flour

1½ cups chopped toasted almonds

½ pound chopped beef suet, or 1 cup unsalted butter, softened

6 large eggs, beaten

1 cup cognac, to sprinkle over baked puddings, plus ¼ cup for igniting

Hard sauce (page 165)

In a very large bowl, mix the dried fruits, apple, plum purée, bread crumbs, brown sugar, orange and lemon zest, orange and lemon juice, spices, and salt. Toss to mix and add the cognac. Stir until moistened. Cover and leave at room temperature for 24 hours, tossing once or twice.

Butter four 6-inch pudding molds or eight 5-inch heatproof 8-ounce glass dessert bowls. Have ready a large roasting pan or other pot large enough to hold the molds or bowls snugly. It should have a lid. If not, fashion one from foil.

continued

Add the flour, almonds, suet, and eggs to the fruit mixture, stirring well to distribute the eggs. Spoon the pudding mixture into the molds, packing it tightly and filling the molds nearly to the rims. Leave a 1-inch space at the top. Cover tightly with foil and put the molds in the larger pan.

Set the roasting pan on the stove and pour enough boiling water into the pan to come halfway up the sides of the molds or 1½ inches up the sides of the larger pan. Cover the pan and return the water to a boil over high heat. Reduce the heat to low and simmer for 1½ to 2 hours. Add more boiling water as necessary to maintain the correct depth, or simply add water, bring it to a boil, and then lower heat.

Remove the molds from the larger pan and let the puddings cool. Remove the foil and loosen the puddings by running a sharp knife around the inside of the molds. Invert the puddings onto a work surface and sprinkle each with some of the cup of cognac. Wrap tightly in plastic wrap or cheesecloth and then in foil. Refrigerate for at least 1 week and up to 1 year.

To serve: Preheat the oven to 350°F. Unwrap the puddings and then rewrap them in foil. Place directly in the oven and heat for about 20 minutes. Unwrap the puddings and arrange on a serving plate.

In a metal ladle, heat the remaining ¼ cup of cognac over high heat until it ignites. Pour over the puddings and carry them to the table quickly before the flame goes out. Serve with Hard Sauce.

NOTE: Seed and purée 2 pounds fresh plums for plum purée, then freeze for your puddings, or substitute applesauce.

Hard Sauce

2 cups confectioners' sugar
¼ cup unsalted butter, softened
2 tablespoons cognac or rum

In the bowl of a food processor, combine the sugar, butter, and cognac or rum and process until the consistency of soft icing. Serve with hot plum puddings.

Panettone

4 SMALL OR 2 LARGE PANETTONE

When I was living in the heart of Italy at Christmastime, I had absolutely no reason on earth to make panettone. Many bakeries offered fresh ones, and commercial brands hung from the rafters like brightly colored Chinese lanterns or were stacked in precise pyramids in the beautifully decorated windows of food shops. But back home, full of nostalgia for my Roman Christmas—musicians from the Abruzzo with their bagpipes made of sheepskins, the smoky smells of roasting chestnuts on every corner, children bundled up as round as soccer balls, warm, perfect *espresso ristretto*

continued

("corrected" with a splash of grappa) on chilly late afternoons of shopping and people watching—I cheered myself up by making my own.

Homemade panettone is unequivocally on another level from commercial bread and must be made with a lot of good butter and fresh eggs. It helps, too, if you make your own candied peel, but if you cannot, use fresh grated orange and lemon peel along with raisins plumped in rum or cognac—and toss in toasted almonds. Some bakeries sprinkle roasted pine nuts on the top of the breads before baking. I sometimes ice the panettone with the same pink sugar icing I use for Russian Easter Bread, but panettone is good as is and needs no adornments. For the correct panettone shape, I like to use empty coffee cans brushed with olive oil or melted butter, although these breads rarely stick because of the high butter content. For this recipe, you will need two 36-ounce or four 12- or 14-ounce coffee cans.

SPONGE

1 cup unbleached all-purpose flour
½ cup lukewarm milk (85 to 95°F)
2 tablespoons active dry yeast
1 teaspoon sugar

PANETTONE

1 cup golden raisins or Suzanne's Roasted Grapes (page 141)
¼ cup cognac or rum
2 large eggs, separated
1 cup unsalted butter, softened
1½ cups sugar
4 large eggs
1 tablespoon grated orange peel
1 tablespoon grated lemon peel

1 teaspoon vanilla extract

About 4½ cups unbleached all-purpose flour

1 teaspoon salt

1 cup toasted, chopped almonds

½ cup mixed Candied Orange and Lemon Zest (page 169)

¼ cup toasted pine nuts, for garnish (optional)

To make the sponge: Thirty minutes before mixing the dough, stir together the flour, milk, yeast, and sugar in a small glass bowl. Cover and set aside.

To make the panettone: In a small bowl, soak the raisins in the cognac or rum. In another bowl, beat the egg whites until they hold soft peaks. Take out 2 tablespoons to brush the tops of the panettone. In a large bowl, using an electric mixer, cream the butter and sugar until fluffy. Add the eggs and egg yolks, one at a time, and beat well after each addition. Add the grated orange and lemon peel and vanilla.

Sift the flour with the salt and add to the batter. Mix on low speed, gradually adding the sponge until incorporated. Add the raisins and their liquid, and continue to beat on low speed for a minute or so. Add half the almonds and beat until incorporated. The dough should not be too firm, but should look buttery and a little rough and ragged. Remove the bowl from the mixer and fold in the beaten egg whites.

Turn the dough out onto a floured surface and knead for 2 to 3 minutes, pushing the dough away from you with the heels of your hands folding it in half over on itself and repeating the motion. The dough will become smooth and shiny very quickly. Transfer the dough to an oiled bowl, cover, and let it rise in a warm place until doubled in volume, about 2 hours.

Turn the dough out on a work surface and flatten into a rectangle. Spread the remaining almonds and the candied zest across the dough lengthwise. Starting at the short end, roll the dough over the nuts and candied zest. As you roll the dough, knead the nuts and candied zest into it to distribute equally. This takes about 2 minutes with a steady pressing motion of the heels of the hands. Let the dough rest 15 minutes.

continued

To shape the panettone: Thoroughly butter two 36-ounce or four 12- or 14-ounce coffee cans. Divide the dough into 2 or 4 pieces, depending on the number of coffee cans. Shape each piece into a ball and place the balls in the cans (the dough should fill cans about half full). With a sharp knife or kitchen shears, cut an X in the top of each about ½ inch deep. Brush each with the egg whites. Decorate the tops with the pine nuts, pressing them into the dough. Cover and let the loaves rise until doubled in volume, or about 1 hour. The dough may be active at this point and rise quickly, so you may not need a full hour's rising, but sugar inhibits yeast so you may wait longer than 1 hour.

To bake the panettone: Preheat the oven to 400°F. Uncover the loaves, place in the oven, and reduce the oven temperature to 350°F. Bake for 40 minutes for large coffee cans, 25 to 35 minutes for the smaller cans. Cool in the pans for 15 minutes. Carefully remove the loaves from the cans and cool completely on wire racks. Serve toasted slices on Christmas day or during holidays with vin Santo. I slice mine horizontally into rounds.

NOTE: To toast the almonds, spread them on a baking sheet, spritz with a little water, sprinkle with salt, and toast in a 350°F oven for about 15 minutes, stirring once or twice. Set aside to cool.

Nuts and fruit may be added to dough during mixing if you have a mixer strong enough to incorporate them, but the first rise may take a little longer because of the weight of the dough.

Candied Orange and Lemon Zest

Candied zest, the outer peel of citrus fruits, made at home is far superior to the zest found in little plastic containers in markets at holiday time. If you can find them without preservatives or the odd flavors that sometimes surface in the commercial zest, use them, but I believe you will always taste the difference in your bread. I experimented by ordering very expensive candied zests from France. I took one sniff and tossed them all into the circular file! This is not to say good citrus peels do not exist somewhere in the world, but I haven't found them. You always can count on your own to taste the best. Tangerine zest may be used here also.

1 cup slivered or chopped assorted lemon, orange, or tangerine zest
1 cup sugar
¼ cup water

Place the zest in a heavy pot and pour enough boiling water over it to cover. Reduce the heat to medium-low and simmer for about 15 minutes or until the zest is transparent and tender. Drain well.

Add the sugar and water and boil until syrupy, about 3 to 4 minutes.

Spread the zest out on a smooth, oiled surface in one layer to cool until crystallized. Store in an airtight jar in the refrigerator or freeze. This will last indefinitely.

Russian Kulich

1 LARGE OR 4 SMALL LOAVES

When my Russian friends at Berkeley discovered that I could make kulich and pashka for Russian Easter, they *all* showed up at our yearly party, invited or not. I have made these for years, although in my family we are all Czechs with no Russian blood that I know of. I think a brief stay with a Russian nanny, Tolstoy, and especially *Dr. Zhivago* had more of an influence on my cooking than I realized. There is something about the fur hats, sleds, and mustached men dancing wildly in black boots that inspired me at an early age to research this amazing bread. I prefer it to the Italian Colomba (dove-shaped Easter bread), which is so similar to panettone. Kulich is easier to make in many ways and has the lovely flavors of saffron and cognac to go with the astonishingly rich pashka, which is traditionally served with it. Don't forget a shot of ice-cold vodka for the Czar.

SPONGE

1 tablespoon active dry yeast
¼ cup lukewarm water (85 to 95°F)
2 cups lukewarm milk (85 to 95°F)
½ cup sugar
1 teaspoon salt
1 cup all-purpose bread flour, sifted

KULICH

5 large eggs, separated
1½ cups sugar
½ teaspoon vanilla extract
6½ cups all-purpose bread flour

1 cup unsalted butter, melted

½ cup graham flour

½ cup raisins

½ cup apricots, prunes, or figs, chopped fine

1 cup ground toasted almonds or pecans

¼ cup cognac

2 tablespoons Candied Orange or Lemon Zest (page 169)

1 tablespoon lemon or orange zest

1 teaspoon ground cardamom

½ teaspoon powdered saffron

Pink Confectioners' Sugar Icing (page 172) (optional)

Pashka (page 172) (optional)

To make the sponge: In a large bowl or the bowl of an electric mixer, stir the yeast with the water until dissolved. Add the milk, sugar, and salt. Stir in the flour and mix well. Cover and let rise for 1 hour until light and foamy.

To make the kulich: Butter two 36-ounce or four 12- or 14-ounce coffee cans.

In a large bowl, whisk the egg yolks, sugar, and vanilla until smooth. Add to the sponge and stir or mix on low speed to incorporate. Add 3 cups of the bread flour, ½ cup of the butter, and the graham flour, and mix just until blended. Add the remaining 3½ cups of the bread flour and the remaining ½ cup of the butter and mix well. Add the raisins, apricots, almonds or pecans, cognac, candied peel, zest, cardamom, and saffron, and mix or stir the dough until it pulls away from the sides of the bowl and is shiny and elastic.

In a separate bowl, beat the egg whites until they hold soft peaks. Carefully fold into the dough. Scrape the dough into the coffee cans, filling each halfway. Set aside until doubled in volume, about 1 hour.

To bake the kulich: Preheat the oven to 350°F. Bake for 45 minutes to 1 hour, depending on the size of the cans. Cool in the cans for 15 minutes. Carefully remove the loaves from the cans and cool completely on wire racks. Ice with Pink Confectioners' Sugar Icing or spread with Pashka. My Russian friends slice this horizontally from the top, but I prefer to slice it more conventionally so that everyone gets some of the icing.

Pink Confectioners' Sugar Icing

ABOUT 1 CUP

2 cups confectioners' sugar
2 tablespoons unsalted butter
½ teaspoon vanilla extract
¼ cup cognac
2 drops red food coloring (optional)

In the bowl of a food processor, mix together all ingredients except the food coloring to make a creamy icing. Add the food coloring to make the traditional pink icing for kulich.

Pashka

2 POUNDS OF CHEESE

Although you can serve this without the kulich, simply spreading it on any of your own breads, it is truly magnificent with kulich. It is also especially good on rye or wheat breads or served with the Apricot Focaccia on page 135. As when almost any cheese is made, you need to drain the whey away to achieve the correct texture. I find that a plastic flowerpot or even a deep sieve with a flat bottom is perfect for draining pashka. Line the pot or sieve with two layers of damp cheesecloth and then pack the cheese mixture in it to drain overnight. Sometimes I just gather up the cheesecloth (with cheese in it, of course) and tie it securely to my faucet over the sink to drain. In the morning, when the cheese is now a neat little ball of goodness, you put it into any mold you like, refrigerate it, and then turn it out onto a plate to serve. This recipe cuts some of the fat calories, yet I find it just as tasty and rich as the Russian version.

1½ pounds cottage cheese
1 cup sugar
1 cup cream or whole milk
½ cup unsalted butter, softened
½ cup plain yogurt
½ cup toasted almonds, chopped fine
2 tablespoons cream cheese, softened, or mascarpone cheese
3 large egg yolks
¼ cup Candied Orange or Lemon Zest (page 169)
¼ cup currants or golden raisins
1 tablespoon grated lemon zest
½ teaspoon vanilla extract
Pinch of salt
Confectioners' sugar, for dusting

Leave the cottage cheese, loosely covered, at room temperature overnight or for 12 hours. In the bowl of a food processor, blend until smooth.

In a large bowl, mix all the ingredients, except the confectioners' sugar, together, stirring well. Pack the mixture into a double-cheesecloth-lined plastic flowerpot or sieve. Set over a bowl or the sink and let drain overnight at room temperature. Turn the cheese out on a plate and serve, dusted with confectioners' sugar.

Quick Chappati for Curry

16 PANCAKES; SERVES 4 TO 6

These are flat, tortilla-like wheat cakes used to scoop up curry like an edible spoon. I was taught how to make these breads and many delicious curries by an Indian friend in Berkeley during the 1960s, a time when all the corners of my house, day and night, seemed to be filled with jug bands, folksingers and musicians, travelers, and students. Bob Dylan (before fame) came by once in those early days, and I remember trimming his hair and feeding him curry. You have to eat, even when the times they are a changin'.

1½ cups whole wheat flour
½ cup unbleached bread flour
½ cup unsalted butter, melted, plus more for the skillet
1 teaspoon salt
1 cup plain yogurt

In a mixing bowl, combine the whole wheat and bread flours, ¼ cup of the butter, and salt, and rub through your fingers until grainy. This may also be done with a few pulses in the food processor. Add enough yogurt to make a fairly firm but still malleable dough, not too dry but not sticky. Stir for about 2 minutes to smooth it out. Cover and let rest for 30 minutes. It will be elastic and shiny when ready.

Take pinches of the dough and roll them into 1½-inch-diameter balls in your palms to make 32 balls. Dip each into the remaining ¼ cup of butter, flatten it slightly, and set aside. When you have used all the dough, stack in pairs, placing one ball on top of another and flattening it slightly (layering causes them to bubble) to make 16 pieces of dough, and, on a marble slab or floured board, roll each pair out into a very thin circle, just less than ⅛ of an inch thick.

Heat a skillet or griddle on medium heat and add about a teaspoon of melted butter. When it is bubbling, carefully pick up the chappati, as if you were lifting a delicate fabric, and lay it in the skillet. Cook for about 1 minute and as each circle bubbles and browns, turn it over and brown the other side for another minute or less; it should not quite reach the point of crispness, just turn a light brown. The chappati must remain supple, like flour tortillas. Stack the chappati, one on top of the other, and keep warm, covered with foil, in a very low oven until serving.

NOTE: These may be frozen with great success. This recipe is enough for 4 to 6 people, depending on how many they eat before the curry is served. When you are feeding the masses, you will need 2½ pounds of whole wheat and 1 pound of white flour to make 100 chappati.

Ye-Wolo Ambasha

African Spiced Bread

ONE 12- TO 14-INCH ROUND LOAF

I am, along with being a shoe fanatic, a basket nut. I buy baskets of all kinds, such as Japanese rice-washing baskets or Chinese fishing baskets, with no purpose other than my illusion that I might just find myself fishing in China when I get some time off. One of my best frivolous acquisitions is a beautiful round African bread basket designed to house ye-wolo (as I found out from Hamsa el Din, an amazing musician from Nubia). The basket is colored with vegetable dyes and fitted with great leather loops from which to hang it on the wall. It was the inspiration for what grew to be my African period—four months of research and cooking with marvelous berberé, a spiced paste that flavors many Ethiopian foods; nit'r k'ibe, a spiced oil; and the making of the famous ye-wolo spice bread. This bread accompanies savory doro wat, a chicken stew with red peppers, but you may eat it with practically anything and it will be a success. It is a lively detour from the plain dinner breads we know so well.

2 cups lukewarm water (85 to 95°F)
2 tablespoons active dry yeast
4 cups unbleached bread flour
½ cup whole wheat flour
¼ cup Nit'r K'ibe (page 178)
1 tablespoon ground cardamom
1 tablespoon ground coriander seeds
1 teaspoon ground black pepper

1 teaspoon Berberé (page 179)
½ teaspoon ground fenugreek
Pinch of ground cloves
Pinch of ground cinnamon
4 teaspoons olive oil

Measure the water into a large mixing bowl. Sprinkle the yeast over the water and stir until dissolved. Stir in the bread and whole wheat flours. Add the Nit'r K'ibe, cardamom, coriander, pepper, Berberé, fenugreek, cloves, and cinnamon, and stir until the dough is smooth and shiny and pulls away from the sides of the bowl. The dough will be fairly soft. Cover and refrigerate overnight to give the spices time to permeate the dough.

Let the dough come to room temperature. Turn onto an oiled baking sheet and pinch off a small piece of dough about the size of a golf ball. Set aside. Form the remaining dough into a large circle and flatten with your hand until it is about 12 inches in diameter. With a very sharp knife, cut ½-inch-deep slashes in the dough starting at the center and cutting out as if you were dividing it into wedges about 1 inch wide at the edges of the bread (see illustration). Press the ball of dough into the center of the circle. With scissors, snip across the wedges starting at the point and working to the outside to make the traditional design of the Ye-wolo (see illustration). Let rise until doubled in volume, about 45 minutes.

Preheat the oven to 400°F. Brush bread with olive oil and bake for 15 minutes. Reduce the oven temperature to 350°F. Bake for about 30 minutes longer, or until the bread is nicely browned. Cool on a wire rack.

Cutting slits in Ye Wolo Ambasha

Nit'r K'ibe

This is great in non-African dishes, too. Try a spoon of it on grilled meat, poultry, or fish. Or toss it with noodles for a very exotic pasta to serve with Southeast Asian foods. You may also use a spoon of it in any plain bread or biscuit recipe to liven it up.

2 cups unsalted butter
3 cloves garlic, chopped fine
1 small sweet onion or green onion, chopped fine
1 tablespoon peeled and grated fresh gingerroot
1 teaspoon turmeric
½ teaspoon ground cinnamon
½ teaspoon ground cardamom
½ teaspoon fresh grated nutmeg
½ teaspoon ground fenugreek
Pinch of ground cloves
Pinch of salt
Pinch of black pepper

In a heavy pot, heat the butter until it bubbles. Stir in the rest of the ingredients and let the mixture cook over very low heat until separated, about 30 minutes. Strain through a fine sieve into a glass container, making sure there are no visible butter solids. This will keep, like the Indian clarified butter, ghee, for several weeks in the refrigerator. It may be frozen.

Berberé

This is *hot!*

SPICES

1 cup sweet Hungarian or French paprika

1 tablespoon ground hot red peppers or cayenne

½ teaspoon ground cardamom

½ teaspoon ground coriander seeds

½ teaspoon ground cinnamon

½ teaspoon grated fresh nutmeg

½ teaspoon ground fenugreek

½ teaspoon powdered asafoetida (see Note)

Pinch of ground cloves

Pinch of ground black pepper

1 tablespoon olive oil

1 small onion, chopped fine

2 cloves garlic, chopped fine

1 teaspoon salt

1 teaspoon peeled and grated fresh gingerroot

Dash of red wine vinegar

1 cup water

In a heavy skillet, toast the spices over low heat for about 3 minutes, stirring constantly so they will not burn, until fragrant. Remove from the skillet and set aside.

In the same skillet, heat the olive oil over medium-high heat. Sauté the onion and garlic until golden. Add the spices, salt, ginger, vinegar, and water and cook for about 10 minutes over low heat, stirring well.

continued

Transfer to a blender or food processor and purée. Store in a glass jar with a tight lid. Pour a little olive oil over the top of the paste to preserve it for up to 3 months.

NOTE: Asafoetida is sold in Indian food stores in lump or powdered form. Use it sparingly.

Truffle Rolls

20 TO 24 ROLLS

The scent of truffles always takes me back to Cittá di Castello where, years ago when searching for the Alberto Burri museum, we wandered into an amazing Sagra di Tartuffi (truffle festival) instead. A handsome young man with the requisite brown-stained hands of a truffle hunter and a certain unmistakable aroma emanating from his stylish Italian sweater watched with interest as we sighed over the tables and tables of truffles brought to auction from the countryside. He introduced himself as owner of Il Bersaglio, a local restaurant offering a *dégustation* of ten truffle courses, of which one was a golden homemade pasta made with numerous egg yolks and unequaled in the area. We trotted along behind him to his *ristorante*, like truffle pigs in hot pursuit. Over the next two hours, we managed to lay waste to all ten courses while he sat with us, pouring both wine and his philosophy of life, which included truffle eating as part of everyday consumption. If one has the means to do it, that is. Most years, truffles are way over a thousand dollars a kilo.

"I have not needed more than four hours sleep since I became a truffle hunter," he said. "The truffle is my life, I have no time for women or family. I live only to hunt truffles and run my restaurant. I need nothing else and have the strength of two, no, three men!" Needless to say, truffles can be very seductive, but I am still wondering how many women in Cittá di Castello wish they were benefiting from this remarkable stamina....

You'll find truffle oil in the olive oil sections of larger supermarkets or in specialty food shops. Another way to have a nice stash of truffle oil is to buy a very small white truffle during the truffle season, October through December, cut it in half and put it in a bottle of good olive oil; wait about 24 hours before using it. The oil, well-stoppered, will last for months and costs less than the commercial kinds.

¾ cup lukewarm water (85 to 95°F)
1 package active dry yeast
2¼ cups unbleached all-purpose flour
1 teaspoon sugar
1 teaspoon salt
1 large egg, beaten
¼ cup unsalted butter, softened
2 teaspoons truffle oil

To make the dough: Measure the water into the bowl of an electric mixer. Sprinkle the yeast over the water and stir until dissolved. Add 1 cup of the flour, sugar, and salt and beat on low speed until smooth. Add the egg, butter, and remaining 1¼ cups of flour and beat on low speed until well blended and shiny.

Same day method: Cover the bowl and let the dough rise in a warm place until doubled in volume, 30 to 45 minutes. Stir down the dough.

continued

Overnight method: Cover the bowl and refrigerate overnight. Remove the dough from the refrigerator 30 minutes before shaping. Let stand in a warm place until doubled in volume. Stir down the dough.

To shape rolls: Grease two 9-inch round baking pans with oil. Drop the dough by generous spoonfuls into mounds about 1 inch apart into the pans, or shape into little balls, arrange in the pans, and press down slightly to flatten each one. Cover and let rise until doubled in volume, 30 to 40 minutes. Brush with 1 teaspoon of the truffle oil.

To bake rolls: Preheat the oven to 400°F. Bake for 17 to 20 minutes, or until golden brown. Remove from the oven and brush with remaining 1 teaspoon of truffle oil. Serve warm.

NOTE: If you just happen to have extra white truffles lying around, chop one and add it to the dough, or keep them all for yourself, shaved over a nice bowl of fresh fettuccine!

Nobody Knows the Truffles I've seen....

Rosemary-Pepper Bread Sticks

20 TO 24 THIN BREAD STICKS

I cannot resist the bread sticks that almost every trattoria in Rome serves along with the bread. Bread sticks are also irresistible to children, and when my brother and I were taken out to restaurants, we inevitably either "smoked" them or poked each other mercilessly until they broke. Tiring of this, we began fencing or trying to beat each other over the head with them, managing to make a sizable mess before my mother threatened to have us arrested or forgo dessert or, in my case, the shrimp cocktail. I was never a sweet eater even then, but give me a bowl of boiled Gulf shrimp, some remoulade sauce, and a few bread sticks and I would even behave myself.

In keeping with this custom, the eleven-year-old guests at my step-son's birthday party years ago on an open restaurant terrazza (thank heaven) in Rome had a bread stick–eating contest, followed by a collective laughing fit, which resulted in a shower of spewed crumbs and bemused looks from neighboring tables.

I have made straight bread sticks, rolled ones, pulled ones, bent ones, seeded ones, and sugared ones, and they all are delicious and crunchy, as seductive now as they were when I was eight years old. Of course, I would never do such silly things with them as I did then…except when I need a cigar for my Groucho Marx impersonation.

continued

1 teaspoon active dry yeast

½ cup lukewarm water (85 to 95°F)

½ cup unbleached all-purpose flour

¼ cup olive oil or melted unsalted butter

¼ cup fresh rosemary leaves, chopped fine

½ teaspoon active dry yeast dissolved in 1 tablespoon of water

1 cup unbleached all-purpose flour

¼ cup warm milk

1 teaspoon salt

2 teaspoons ground black pepper

1 teaspoon sugar (optional)

Coarse salt, for sprinkling

To make the biga: In a glass bowl, mix the yeast with the water and stir well. Add the flour to the yeast mixture, stirring well to aerate the mixture and form a wet dough. Cover tightly with plastic wrap and let ferment overnight at room temperature. In the morning, it will be bubbly and fragrant.

To make the dough: In a small saucepan, heat the olive oil over medium heat and sauté the rosemary leaves until soft, about 3 minutes. Set aside to cool.

In the bowl of a food processor combine the yeast, flour, milk, salt, pepper, and sugar, if using, and pulse until moistened, about 10 seconds. Add the rosemary and oil. Add the *biga* and process until the dough pulls away from the sides of the bowl. Do not overmix.

Oil your hands and remove the dough from the processor. Form the dough into a nice shiny ball and place in an oiled bowl. Cover and let rise until doubled in volume, about 1 hour. Push down the dough and let it rest for 15 minutes.

Flatten the dough into a rectangle about 4 inches wide and ½ inch thick. With a sharp knife, cut strips of dough 1 inch wide. Roll each strip lengthwise, as if you were rolling clay, pulling it slightly to lengthen the dough into a long, thin, even shape like a long worm. Or, if you are fairly skilled at baking, grasp each end of the long rolled piece of dough and gently flap it against the counter, lengthening the bread stick as you flap. Make the strips any width you like, fat or thin, but they must be all the same width to bake evenly.

To bake bread sticks: Preheat the oven to 400°F. Carefully lift each end of the bread sticks and place them 1 inch apart lengthwise on an ungreased baking sheet. With a spray bottle, mist the bread sticks, sprinkle with coarse salt, and let rise while oven heats. Bake for 10 to 12 minutes or until golden. Use as drumsticks, weapons, table ornaments, or cigars, or simply bite and savor.

Leftovers

Leftovers

ISN'T THERE ANOTHER WORD FOR THIS? Leftovers are, for me, the second most important part of my cooking, the first being the creation of that which will become a leftover. The wild enthusiasm that accompanies bread baking can never create too much of a good thing. One small dish of extra risotto, roast chicken drippings, or a few random slices of Housewife's Bread or brioche may well be destined for some glorious next undertaking: a quick bruschetta revived on the grill; a simple Tuscan bread soup; or a rich Chocolate Bread Pudding. Leftovers are inspiration that can propel you in new directions each day. This is what cooking is all about. And you will never be bored in the kitchen.

There are limits, of course; I am not advocating that you hoard every little bite of extraneous brioche or bread crust, but only that you start thinking ahead about what something might become later. Perhaps this is why some of the very best recipes in the world have origins in peasant or country cooking, and why I prefer a plain bowl of honest pasta to all the puff pastry–encased salmon or tournedos masked with béarnaise sauce in the world.

One can easily imagine in a household of modest means how a leftover piece of bread, a ripened tomato on the vine, and a little olive oil might catch the imagination of a hungry family and naturally evolve into a delectable dish called panzanella, or bread salad. This is the dish we serve at all Buona Forchetta events. One of the simplest of all Italian dishes, panzanella never fails to draw praise from our customers. Everyone is surprised to find that we use only bread, tomato, mozzarella, and fresh basil—in my opinion, the earth, fire, wind, and water of Italian cooking.

A bruschetta—a plain grilled slice of your own homemade day-old bread, saturated with extra-virgin dark green olive oil, a few chunks of a perfect tomato, some chopped basil, and sea salt—is, in my estimation, perfect food. Leftover bread has no limit with regard to what can be made from it: every conceivable kind of salad, fish, meat, vegetable, and pasta benefits from the addition of bread crumbs or savory bits of toasted bread. Bread soups and soufflés are some of the greatest menu stretchers to come from the kitchen, and bread in desserts has been too long overlooked.

Any one of the breads you have learned in this book make excellent little toasts, which we at Buona Forchetta call bruschettine, or little bruschette. One evening, I was at a loss for crackers, with a dinner party starting in just minutes, and so I quickly sliced up a loaf of the Kalamata Olive Filoncino and the Hazelnut-Sage Filoncino and baked the little rounds until they resembled melba toasts. Some I served with a wild arugula spread and others were crumbled into the salad. After dinner, they were passed around with the various cheeses to great appreciation, and leftovers were made into savory crumbs for sprinkling over dishes *au gratin*.

Those of us who prefer a light ending to a meal will find that caramelized fruits on toast make a kind of spartan shortcake, while those who love a little indulgence now and then may enhance the Chocolate Bread Pudding with buttery brioche in place of bread, or use toasted brioche in the recipe for Pears in Caramel with Cheese on Toast.

Transform commonplace recipes with your own superior bread crumbs and croutons. A standard Caesar salad will sing when the croutons are right, although no one seems to pay much attention to that detail—just as even well-known restaurants do not seem to think it is important to serve good bread with $100 dinners. A thin, expensive cut of veal takes on a new dimension when dipped in crumbs made from your own bread and seasoned with fresh herbs. Once you have used your own, you'll be spoiled for any others.

Bread is truly the staff of life, at least in my kitchen, and leftover bread has more uses than there are bakers on the planet. When you finally run out of ideas for what to do with lingering loaves, you can always grab the nearest child and head for a park, lake, pond, or river. Birds, ducks, and fish are the true connoisseurs of leftover bread.

Panzanella

I get maudlin describing panzanella. It is the signature dish at our bakery, Buona Forchetta, made with fresh rosemary focaccia, organic tomatoes, Virgilio Ciccone's mozzarella from Italcheese, and my 100-year-old vinegar, a gift from a Sicilian friend in San Francisco many years ago. I have kept the vinegar's mother going with red wines on those rare occasions when we have any left from a dinner party, and I now have great vats in the wine cellar filled with what, to me, is a vintage vinegar—with the color and sparkle of red garnets, tasting like toasted nuts.

Panzanella is a perfect dish, the essence of what the Italians do best, making manna from absolutely fresh ingredients with no frills. No heavy garlic. No green peppers. No ripe olives. No bacon bits. Panzanella made at the height of summer is ethereal. Learn to make this classic first, and then branch out, if you must. Remember to start with seasonal ingredients and keep them to a minimum. Your guests will remember simplicity long after they have endured complicated, trendy innovations.

One 10-ounce Focaccia (page 40) or Rosemary Filoncino (page 46), cut into 1-inch cubes

3 large ripe tomatoes, diced into ½-inch pieces, juice reserved

6 ounces fresh mozzarella packed in water, drained and diced into ½-inch pieces

1 cup fresh basil leaves, chopped fine

¾ cup olive oil
¼ cup red wine vinegar
2 tablespoons balsamic vinegar
Salt and ground pepper to taste

In a large bowl, toss together the bread cubes, tomatoes with reserved juice, mozzarella, and basil. In another small bowl, whisk together the oil, vinegars, and salt and pepper to taste. Pour over the bread mixture and toss well. If you have the time, let the salad stand for 15 minutes to develop the flavor.

Tuna Panzanella

4 TO 6 SERVINGS

One day at the bakery, when we felt we deserved a sumptuous lunch in a civilized manner, after having gotten up at 4 A.M. and worked all morning, we looked around and saw we had nothing to eat. Nothing that is except bread and a scavenged can of tuna in olive oil, which had rolled out of my grocery bags and lain forgotten under a car seat for a day or so. This panzanella was born out of starvation and necessity, so do not give up hope when your cupboard is bare. A panzanella may yet be lurking in your larder. Some people like cheese with tuna, some don't. I tend to leave it out of this one, but it is delicious either way.

continued

1 loaf Filoncino Integrale (page 58), cut into 1-inch cubes

6 ounces tuna, in water or olive oil, or 6 ounces grilled fresh tuna, diced

1 small sweet onion, chopped fine

1 tart apple, chopped fine

6 ounces fresh mozzarella packed in water, drained and diced into ½-inch pieces (optional)

⅔ cup olive oil

½ cup chopped toasted almonds, pecans, or walnuts

2 tablespoons drained capers

Juice of 2 large lemons

Salt and ground black pepper to taste

Mix first nine ingredients together, season with salt and pepper, and let sit for 15 minutes to develop the flavor.

Fresh Scallop Panzanella

4 TO 6 SERVINGS

I am not a fan of raw garlic, feeling that garlic must be used with a light hand and with thoughtfulness for the flavor of the dish. Only in aioli, a very strong garlic mayonnaise, or in the famous *rouille* of the Roussillon region in southern France will I use raw garlic, and then only the sweet garlic of summer—never the acrid sprouting garlic of winter. There is a real difference between the two, even though most people do not appear to taste it. The best way to learn the difference is to walk by a Thai restaurant in the winter and then cruise by again in the summer. The smell of garlic will be potent in January, then sweet and seductive again in August. In the winter, you may want to cut open the garlic clove and remove the little green shoot in the middle of the clove and use only the surrounding parts. This works if the garlic is not too old, but when you see little green sprouts peeking out from the bottom of a garlic bulb, do not buy it. It could ruin your delicate panzanella, or several hours of your day—sprouted garlic can stay with you a little too long.

1 pound bay scallops or sea scallops, chopped into ½-inch pieces
½ cup fresh lime juice
½ teaspoon salt
½ clove garlic (optional)
One 10-ounce Rosemary Filoncino (page 46), Filoncino Integrale (page 58), or Pane Rustico (page 70), cut into 1-inch cubes
1 small sweet onion, chopped fine
1 cup cilantro, chopped fine
⅓ cup olive oil
Cracked black pepper

In a glass or ceramic bowl, toss the scallops with the lime juice and salt. If desired, add the garlic. Cover and let stand for 30 minutes to marinate. (The lime juice will "cook" the scallops as they marinate just as it does in making ceviche.)

Drain the liquid, discard the garlic if used, and transfer the scallops to a large salad bowl. Add the bread cubes, onion, cilantro, and olive oil and toss. Season with pepper.

In the last few years, we Americans seem to be hungry for practically any new dish, and it speaks well of our taste that we embrace Italian food so wholeheartedly. Pasta dishes always seem to be at the center of a controversy about what is authentic and what goes too far. Nevertheless, it has fast become one of our main staples, perhaps nudging the hamburger aside just a bit, and now bread is nearly as popular and controversial as pasta. There are those who insist on chewy, artisan breads and those who stand by the fluffy country white breads of their childhood. Regardless of these personal preferences, I am adamant about bruschetta and what it is.

The original bruschetta was a half-inch-thick slice of substantially textured bread (which is a polite way of saying it was not sliced, packaged, or commercial cottony bread), grilled on a fire until toasted (or toasted in an oven or toaster), brushed with the best extra-virgin olive oil that could be found, and sprinkled with salt. That's all. No garlic. No onions. No innovative stuff. Often, extra-virgin olive oil was served on the side so that guests could add more to taste. Now, having said as much, I can go on to provide recipes for just about anything that will complement the same grilled bread. As always, however, it's important to know the basics before improvising.

anything on a Bruschetta

Bruschetta with Tomato and Basil

This and the following recipes are classics. None will ever let you down.

Six ½-inch-thick slices bread
3 ripe tomatoes, chopped and drained
6 tablespoons extra-virgin olive oil
¼ cup fresh basil, chopped fine
1 teaspoon balsamic vinegar
Salt and freshly ground pepper

Grill or toast the bread until browned on both sides.

In a small bowl, combine the tomatoes, olive oil, basil, and vinegar. Toss gently and season with salt and pepper. Spoon the mixture on the toast and serve immediately.

VARIATION

Garlic lovers may want to add a little chopped garlic to the tomato salad.

Bruschetta with Arugula and Prosciutto

6 SERVINGS

Six ½-inch-thick slices bread
6 tablespoons extra-virgin olive oil
6 very thin slices prosciutto
1 cup chopped arugula leaves
2 tablespoons fresh lemon juice
Salt and freshly ground pepper

Grill or toast the bread until nicely browned on both sides. Brush one side of each slice with olive oil. Lay a slice of prosciutto on each slice of bread.

In a small bowl, combine the arugula and lemon juice. Toss gently and season with salt and pepper. Spoon the mixture on the toast and serve immediately.

Bruschetta with Sweet Peppers and Tuna

6 SERVINGS

The colorful sweet peppers of summer heaped like bright toys in farmers' markets across the country are perfect for bruschetta. The deep scarlet, yellow, and dark burgundy peppers I use for this dish have a round, lovely flavor that bears no resemblance to their harsh green cousins. I confess: green peppers are as unpleasant to me as too much bay leaf or brash winter garlic. Green peppers are just that: still green. They have not been allowed to stay long enough on the plant to gather juice and build character. Stick with the red, yellow, and purple ones, which have more sugar content and consequently more flavor.

3 red or yellow sweet peppers
½ cup olive oil
4 cloves garlic, peeled and chopped
¼ cup balsamic vinegar
Salt and freshly ground pepper
One 6-ounce can tuna in olive oil or water
2 tablespoons extra-virgin olive oil
Juice of 1 lemon
4 tablespoons chopped flat-leaf (Italian) parsley
Six ½-inch-thick slices bread

Over an open gas flame or under the broiler, grill the peppers, turning them as they blacken on all sides. Transfer to a plate and cover with a damp paper towel (to avoid a mess, I just throw mine in the sink, cover them with anything around, and wait a few minutes before peeling). Slip the skins off the peppers, cut them in half, and remove the membranes and seeds. Slice the peppers into thin strips.

In a large skillet, heat the ½ cup of olive oil over medium heat and add the pepper strips. Cook, turning once or twice, until the peppers are well browned and begin to caramelize a little around the edges. (The peppers will become shiny and smell so good that it will be hard not to eat them right then.) Add the chopped garlic and continue cooking for 3 or 4 minutes, stirring. Add the vinegar and salt and pepper and cook for 2 or 3 minutes until there is only a little syrupy liquid in the pan.

In the small bowl, toss the tuna with the extra-virgin olive oil and the lemon juice. Add the peppers and sprinkle with parsley.

Grill or toast the bread until nicely browned on both sides. Spoon the mixture on the toast and serve immediately.

Bruschetta with Caponata

6 SERVINGS

I can remember that when I was a child, the thought of eating eggplant was about as tantalizing as eating liver or chitterlings. I now adore calf's liver but am still working on chitterlings. My mother, however, anticipated aversions such as these by dipping thin eggplant "fingers" in seasoned flour and then sautéeing them in olive oil. I later gilded these lilies with fresh grated Parmesan and a few drops of lemon juice. Most eggplant haters wax poetic over these crispy ones, and this recipe for caponata will elicit the same response.

1 medium eggplant, diced in ½-inch cubes
1 tablespoon salt
½ cup olive oil (you may need more)
2 medium ribs celery, chopped fine
1 sweet onion, chopped fine
1 tablespoon sugar
1 cup canned crushed tomatoes
6 tablespoons red wine vinegar
2 tablespoons balsamic vinegar
¼ cup toasted pine nuts
3 tablespoons capers, drained
Six ½-inch-thick slices bread
3 to 4 fresh basil leaves, snipped or torn

Place the eggplant in a colander set over a plate, sprinkle with salt, and let drain for about 30 minutes. With paper towels, press down on the eggplant to remove as much moisture as possible.

In a large skillet, heat the olive oil and sauté the eggplant for about 15 minutes over medium heat until very brown and shiny. Push the eggplant aside and sauté the celery and onion until transparent, about 5 minutes. Continue cooking, stirring, until the vegetables are very limp and almost caramelized. Sprinkle with sugar and add the tomatoes, vinegars, pine nuts, and capers. Cook for about 10 minutes longer. Let cool completely.

Grill or toast the bread until nicely browned on both sides. Spoon the vegetable mixture on the toast and serve immediately, garnished with basil.

Bruschetta with Olive Paste

6 SERVINGS

The olive paste that you make for Olive Filoncino may be used for this. Simply season it with the rest of the ingredients and purée to a paste. It is also wonderful over pasta.

1 cup pitted Kalamata or green martini olives
1 clove garlic, crushed
½ cup olive oil
¼ cup toasted almonds or walnuts
1 or 2 tablespoons fresh lemon juice
Pinch of hot red pepper
Six ½-inch-thick slices Kalamata Olive Filoncino (page 52) or other bread
2 tablespoons minced flat-leaf (Italian) parsley

In a small bowl, gently stir together the olives and garlic. Let sit for a few minutes and then remove and discard the garlic. Transfer to the bowl of a food processor and add the olive oil, almonds, lemon juice, and hot red pepper. Process to a paste.

continued

Grill or toast the bread until nicely browned on both sides. Spread the olive paste on the toast and serve immediately, garnished with parsley.

VARIATION

Delete the nuts and hot red pepper and substitute 2 anchovies and 1 tablespoon of capers to make tapenade.

Bruschetta with Wild Mushrooms

6 SERVINGS

Some advice about "wild mushrooms": (1) *Never* eat them without an expert around. Each mushroom season in Italy, there is always a news story about whole parties that were wiped out after having eaten the deadly nightcap or some similar culprit instead of the safe ones. (2) Mushrooms are wild when they are found under trees, in the countryside, or in the woods—in short, when found in the wild. Wild mushrooms are not found growing in flats or cultures in dark basements or on mushroom farms. While the word *wild* has a certain fascination and looks great on menus, even the lowly cultivated button mushroom can be elevated to new heights with a dash of cognac or a sliver of garlic—which is what this recipe does. Try using Anadama Bread for the bruschetta—it's like eating mushrooms on polenta!

6 tablespoons olive oil

2 cups sliced mushrooms, preferably all of one or a mixture of porcini, shiitake, morels, cremini, oyster, chanterelles, lobster, chicken of the woods, or cultivated white mushrooms

1 clove garlic, minced

¼ cup cognac or dry white wine

Juice of 1 lemon

Salt and freshly ground pepper

Six ½-inch-thick slices Pane Casereccio (page 65) or other bread

4 tablespoons minced flat-leaf (Italian) parsley

In a large skillet, heat the olive oil on high heat. Add the mushrooms and sauté until browned. Add the garlic and cook, stirring, very briefly to prevent browning. Stand back and pour the cognac into the pan, allowing it to ignite and burn out, or add the wine and reduce by half. Add the lemon juice and salt and pepper and cook over medium-high heat for 2 to 5 minutes until very little liquid is left. Remove from the heat.

Grill or toast the bread until nicely browned on both sides. Spoon the mixture on the toast and serve immediately, garnished with parsley.

VARIATION

Two tablespoons heavy cream makes a richer mixture for the bruschetta.

Bruschetta with Roasted Garlic and Parmesan

This is a dish for the summer or early fall, when the garlic is fresh and sweet. I separate the garlic cloves to roast them so that, in keeping with my belief that more surface area relative to volume makes better flavor, all sides of each clove benefit from being well cooked. If you grill the garlic, use a small square of stainless-steel mesh or a heavy-duty grill rack with small openings. An alternative to either roasting or grilling is simply to peel the garlic cloves and sauté them in a little olive oil over a very low heat for about 8 minutes, until they take on a nice golden color. Serve this bruschetta with a robust red wine, such as Amarone or Vacqueyras. This is a potent dish, so you might want to garnish each plate with a lovely little sprig of fresh flat-leaf (Italian) parsley to be chewed later.

2 bulbs fresh garlic, separated into cloves but not peeled
4 tablespoons olive oil
Salt
Six ½-inch-thick slices Pane Casereccio (page 65) or other bread
¼ pound Parmesan cheese, shaved into thin slices with a cheese server
Fresh lemon juice for each bruschetta

Preheat the oven to 400°F.

Put the garlic cloves into a baking pan large enough to hold the cloves in a single layer. Brush with 2 tablespoons of the olive oil and sprinkle with about ½ teaspoon of salt. Roast for 25 to 30 minutes until browned on the outside and soft inside.

Turn off the oven and preheat the broiler.

Slip the skins off the cloves, and mash the garlic with the remaining 2 tablespoons of the olive oil. Add more salt, if needed.

Grill or toast the bread until nicely browned on both sides. Spread the toast with the garlic and top each with Parmesan slices. Arrange on a broiler tray and broil for about 2 minutes or until the cheese is slightly melted.

NOTE: To grill the garlic, lay them on a small-meshed grill rack and grill over a very low fire.

Bruschette with Roasted garlic

Bruschetta with Rock Shrimp or Shellfish

6 SERVINGS

All shellfish are delicious on a bruschetta. Lobsters, clams, prawns, cockles, crayfish, crab, or mussels can be sautéed quickly, dressed with a little oil and lemon juice, and spooned over grilled bread. I use rock shrimp simply because I love them and because they are a little more unusual than regular shrimp. I particularly like the rosemary bread with shellfish.

½ cup plus 2 tablespoons olive oil
2 cups chopped rock shrimp
1 small clove garlic, minced
½ teaspoon fennel or anise seed
Juice of ½ lemon
Six ½-inch-thick slices Rosemary Filoncino (page 46), Pane Casereccio (page 65), or other bread
2 tablespoons minced fresh basil

In a skillet, heat ½ cup of the olive oil over high heat. Reduce the heat to medium and add the shrimp. Sauté for about 2 minutes until barely cooked. Add the garlic, fennel or anise seed, and lemon juice, and cook for 2 minutes longer or just until the shrimp turn pink and cook through. Toss with the remaining 2 tablespoons of olive oil and remove from the heat.

Grill or toast the bread until nicely browned on both sides. Spoon the shrimp mixture on the toast and serve immediately, garnished with basil.

NOTE: Rock shrimp should be rinsed quickly and drained well before using. Sometimes there is a little grit in them.

Bruschettine are just baby bruschette: thin slices of bread cut from a slender loaf, which are then toasted like crackers or melba toast. The bruschettine we sell in the bakery are made from olive and hazelnut loaves, but use any of the breads in this book. The small slices of toast are wonderful spread with olive butter or cream cheese for hors d'oeuvres, but I also eat the hazelnut bruschettine for breakfast spread with bitter marmalade. This is a low-fat, nourishing alternative to sweet rolls and butter or pancakes and syrup.

To make the bruschettine, use a good bread knife or slicer to cut an 8- to 10-ounce loaf into very thin slices, each about one-quarter of an inch thick. Preheat the oven to 350°F. Brush the slices with olive oil, if you want, and bake for about 10 minutes, or until the little bruschettine look dry and toasted. Store in an airtight container for up to two weeks or freeze for up to one month. They are also good in salads.

Spread the bruschettine with your favorite topping or one of the following:

- any of the toppings described for bruschetta on the preceding pages
- chutney
- cream cheese or any soft creamy spread
- egg spreads
- fish or shellfish spreads
- fruit purées
- guacamole
- jams, jellies, and marmalades
- mushroom spreads
- olive spreads
- pâtés of any kind
- tonnato sauce
- yogurt spreads

Bread and Cheese Soufflé

6 SERVINGS

This is one of those odd recipes that emerged somewhere in the 1960s when there always seemed to be hordes of people hanging around my kitchen and never enough food to feed them. But there were always bread, cheese, and eggs, and so the designated cook could make this soufflé, which could stretch to include new arrivals at the table. It is especially good with a nice Rhone wine and a green salad.

2 cups 1-inch bread cubes
½ cup dry white wine
2 cups milk
4 large eggs
1 clove garlic, minced and sautéed for 1 minute in a little olive oil or butter
½ teaspoon salt
Pinch of hot red pepper
1½ cups grated Cheddar, jack, Gruyère, or any melting cheese (see Variation)

Preheat the oven to 375°F. Butter a 9-inch soufflé dish.

In a large bowl, sprinkle the wine over the bread cubes and toss. In another bowl, whisk together the milk, eggs, garlic, salt, and hot red pepper. Stir in the cheese and pour over the bread, mixing well.

Pour into the soufflé dish and bake for 35 to 40 minutes, or until puffed and browned.

VARIATION

If you prefer, use ½ pound of a softer cheese, such as Taleggio or fontina.

Bread Soufflé with Salmon and Capers

6 SERVINGS

Just about anything can be added to a soufflé, as any Frenchman will tell you. I love all soufflés, but those made with bread are heartier than others and need little else served with them, except a salad or some fruit. Use any leftover fish for this dish, although I like to start with fresh fish, when possible. Many fish markets sell what is known as "chowder pieces," which are an economical and tasty way to stretch a recipe. I buy shark, tuna, whitefish, halibut, tilapia, catfish, or salmon—any will do.

Bread in souffles

¼ cup unsalted butter
4 tablespoons unbleached all-purpose flour
2 cups milk
4 large eggs, separated
1½ pounds cooked salmon
1 cup ½-inch bread cubes, toasted
4 tablespoons capers, drained
¼ teaspoon salt
Pinch of hot red pepper
Pinch of grated fresh nutmeg
Fresh lemon juice

Preheat the oven to 400°F. Butter a 9-inch soufflé dish.

continued

In a saucepan, melt the butter over medium-high heat until bubbling. Add the flour, reduce the heat to medium, and stir to form a smooth paste, or *roux*. Add the milk, stirring until thickened.

In another bowl, beat a little of the milk mixture into the egg yolks to temper them. Stir the yolks into the mixture in the saucepan, reduce the heat to medium-low, and stir briskly until the sauce is the consistency of heavy cream.

When the mixture is cool, add the salmon, bread cubes, capers, salt, hot red pepper, and nutmeg, and stir gently to mix. Season with a few drops of lemon juice.

In another bowl, beat the egg whites until soft peaks form and the whites look glossy. Fold into the salmon mixture. Spoon into the soufflé dish and bake for 30 to 40 minutes, until puffed and browned.

So many good pasta recipes include bread as an ingredient in the sauce that an entire book could be written on these dishes alone. The most famous are from Sicily, where bread crumbs were often substituted for Parmesan when times were hard. Bread crumbs add desirable texture and taste to pasta dishes. For example, bread crumbs made from olive bread give depth to pasta alla puttanesca, and rosemary-scented bread crumbs made from focaccia are delicious in pasta with broccoli rape. By experimenting, you will find many new ways to use old (slightly stale) bread.

A word on cheese: There are those who feel strongly that dishes made with garlic or fish should not include cheese, such as penne all'arrabbiata or spaghetti aglio, olio, pepperoncino. But many Sicilian dishes made with garlic do include cheese. I say, follow your taste buds and experiment with what you like. I, for one, have never seen pasta made with garlic or fish served with cheese in Rome.

All recipes that I include here serve four as a main course with perhaps a little left over for the next day. I serve my pasta as do the Italians: an adequate but not overflowing bowlful, with just enough sauce but never so much that the pasta is drowning in it. You may adjust the recipes to your taste.

Thin-strand dried pasta, such as spaghetti, linguine, or fettucine, should be boiled for 9 minutes. Larger, thicker pastas may take 10 minutes, and smaller pastas, such as fusilli or rotelle, only 7 to 8 minutes. Fresh pasta needs only 2 to 4 minutes, depending on the size of the noodle. These amounts of time cook the pasta al dente ("at the tooth")—the only way to eat it. A *nonno* I know delights his family by throwing a strand of spaghetti at the ceiling. If it sticks, it's done.

Penne with Broccoli and Anchovies

4 SERVINGS

Even the most adamant broccoli haters love this dish, although it is best not to tell them what's in it. Just serve it and wait. You may substitute cauliflower for the broccoli, for variety.

1½ pounds fresh broccoli, trimmed, cut into florets, and stems sliced

¾ cup olive oil

4 cloves garlic, minced

1 cup tomato sauce or 4 ripe tomatoes, diced

One 2-ounce tin anchovies in olive oil, drained

4 tablespoons raisins

2 tablespoons capers, drained

2 tablespoons chopped fresh mint

½ cup pine nuts

¾ cup fresh bread crumbs

16 ounces penne

Juice of 2 large lemons

Put 2 inches of salted water in a large pot and bring to a simmer. Add the broccoli, cover, and cook for about 3 to 4 minutes, just until tender. Do not overcook. Remove the broccoli with a slotted spoon and set aside. (To keep the bright green color of the broccoli, run it under cold water for 2 to 3 seconds. Drain well.)

Fill the same pot with water for the pasta and add salt to taste. Bring to a boil while you are making the sauce.

In a large skillet, heat ½ cup of the olive oil over medium heat and sauté the garlic for 1 or 2 minutes. Add the tomato sauce or tomatoes, anchovies, raisins, capers, and mint and cook for about 10 minutes, stirring until well mixed.

In a small skillet, heat the remaining ¼ cup of olive oil over medium heat and toast the pine nuts for 2 or 3 minutes, shaking the pan several times so they do not burn. Add the bread crumbs and cook for 2 or 3 minutes longer. Remove from the heat.

Cook the pasta for 9 minutes or just until al dente. Drain, leaving a few tablespoons of water in the pot. Return the pasta to the pot and toss with the broccoli, tomato sauce, and pine nut mixture. Add the lemon juice and serve immediately.

Rotelle alla Romana

I named this after a dish that is served all over Rome in the summer months, with varying degrees of ingenuity. If you want to impress your Italian friends—or anyone else for that matter—serve this. The Italians have a saying that it takes four people to make a good salad: a spendthrift with the oil; a miser with the vinegar; a wise man with the salt; and a *pazzo*, crazy man, to toss it. Remember this when you make this dish: liberal with the oil, careful with the lemon, wise about the amount of pasta, and crazy for the leftovers. For some reason there are more servings of rotelle per box than any other pasta. It's even better the next day, so this is really a leftover recipe, once removed.

8 ripe tomatoes
1 cup fresh basil leaves
½ teaspoon salt
2 cloves garlic
¾ cup olive oil
1 pound rotelle (little wheels)
½ pound Parmesan, shaved with a cheese shaver
½ cup toasted fresh bread crumbs (olive bread makes great crumbs)
Juice of 2 large lemons

Put the tomatoes, basil, and salt in the bowl of a food processor and pulse just to chop the ingredients, not purée them. Transfer to a strainer set over a bowl. Add the garlic and set aside for about 15 minutes to drain. Remove and discard the garlic. Put the tomato mixture into a large bowl and stir in the olive oil. (Drink the juice collected during draining. It will spoil you for any other tomato juice!)

Fill a large pot with salted water and bring to a boil. Cook the pasta for 6 or 7 minutes until al dente. Drain and then toss with the tomatoes, Parmesan, and bread crumbs. Add the lemon juice, toss again, and serve immediately or at room temperature.

Rotelle alla Romana

Orecchiette with Rape and Hot Peppers

4 SERVINGS

I am mad about rape, or what is called in this country, broccoli rabe. Its flavor is tinged with vanilla, like an exotic wine, and yet it is only a lowly green leafy vegetable from the mustard family. Rape is not always in markets, and if you have difficulty finding it, substitute red or green chard, kale, mustard greens, cooked broccoli, Chinese broccoli, bok choy, or cooked cauliflower in this recipe and you will still come out ahead. As well as tasting great, greens also contain enormous amounts of vitamins. The Italians appear pink-cheeked and healthy even in the dead of winter, and I am convinced it is because they eat winter greens of all kinds throughout the season.

continued

About 8 tablespoons olive oil

2 pounds broccoli rape or other greens, steamed over salted water for about 5 minutes, drained, and chopped fine

2 cloves garlic, minced

2 tiny hot red peppers, minced, or 2 pinches hot pepper flakes

1 cup chicken broth, preferably homemade, or dry white wine, or a mixture

1 pound orecchiette (little ears)

½ cup grated Pecorino or Parmesan cheese

2 plain *tozzetti* or other firm Italian dipping cookies, crushed

Juice of 1 large lemon

In a large skillet, heat all but 1 tablespoon of the olive oil over medium-high heat. Add the greens and sauté for about 5 minutes or until crisp around the edges. Make a small well (hole) in the greens so that you can see the pan and add the remaining tablespoon of olive oil. Spoon the garlic into the well and let it cook a little. Add the hot peppers and cook for 1 minute, stirring. Add the chicken broth and cook for about 5 or 6 minutes, or until the sauce is slightly reduced.

Fill a large pot with salted water and bring to a boil. Cook the pasta for 8 or 9 minutes until al dente. Drain and return to the pot. Toss with the sauce, cheese, and *tozzetti*. Season with lemon juice and serve immediately.

Pasta con le Sarde

When it is spring in the Los Angeles canyon where I live, fresh, green, airy bouquets of wild fennel adorn the hillsides, inspiring me to make this extraordinary pasta dish from Sicily. You will need to buy several bulbs of fennel to have enough feathery fronds unless you, too, have a field of wild *finocchio*. Although you should use fresh sardines, I have used canned with mild success. Even salmon, though the less intense taste is not authentic, works O.K. Try any small fish, such as whitebait or Pacific pompano. Whatever you use will taste very, very good, if only because of the other ingredients and because you made it.

1 pound fresh sardines, cleaned (see Note)
Salt and fresh ground pepper
¾ cup olive oil
1½ cups fresh bread crumbs
1 very small sweet onion, chopped fine
1 small to medium fresh fennel bulb, chopped fine
1½ cups young fennel leaves (feathers), chopped
6 anchovies, chopped
¼ cup raisins
½ cup dry white wine
½ teaspoon saffron threads or saffron powder
¼ cup chopped toasted almonds or pine nuts
1 pound spaghetti or bucatini
Juice of 1 large lemon

continued

Preheat the oven to 400°F. Butter a large, shallow baking dish.

Wash and dry the sardines and open them flat. Sprinkle with salt and pepper.

In a large skillet, heat ¼ cup of the olive oil over medium-high heat and sauté the bread crumbs for 3 or 4 minutes, or until browned. Remove from the pan and set aside.

Add ¼ cup of the olive oil to the skillet and sauté the sardines over medium-high heat for about 2 minutes on each side until nicely browned, taking care not to overcook. Carefully lift from the pan and set aside to cool.

Add the remaining ¼ cup of olive oil to the skillet. Add the onion and fennel bulb and sauté over medium-high heat for about 5 minutes until they are softened and transparent. Add the fennel feathers and cook for 1 or 2 minutes until wilted. Add the anchovies and raisins and, using the back of a fork, mash the anchovies to a paste and blend them with the fennel. Add the wine and saffron, reduce the heat to medium-low, and cook gently.

Carefully remove the skin from the sardines and slide the meat off the bones. Add half the meat to the sauce and mash into it. Cook for 7 to 8 minutes, stirring to blend. At the last minute, stir in the almonds or pine nuts and half of the bread crumbs.

Meanwhile, fill a large pot with salted water and bring to a boil. Cook the pasta for 9 minutes until al dente. Drain and toss with the sauce.

Spoon half the pasta mixture into the baking dish. Lay the remaining sardine meat on the pasta and top with the remaining pasta. Spread the remaining bread crumbs over the pasta and bake for about 10 minutes until nicely browned and heated through. Sprinkle with lemon juice and serve immediately.

NOTE: Ask the fishmonger to bone and clean the sardines for you. If you clean them yourself, remove the heads and tails and slit the underbellies with scissors. Run your fingers down the slit to remove the innards.

Supplí

These little balls of leftover rice—creamy with a surprise of mozzarella in the middle and rolled in bread crumbs—are one of the best first courses you will ever taste. Any leftover risotto made with Arborio or any round-grained rice is best for supplí. Long-grained rice just does not work as well. I always make more risotto than I need so that we can have these for lunch or dinner the next day. As an alternative to the morning pizza bianca in Italy, the supplí are a quick energy boost without spoiling the prospects of a magnificent lunch. The next worst thing to losing your suitcase while traveling is to lose your appetite—especially in Italy!

3 large eggs
2 cups cooked round-grain rice (any leftover risotto is best)
¼ cup grated Parmesan
2 cups fine bread crumbs (see Note)
Six 1-inch pieces fresh mozzarella, fontina, or Taleggio
½ cup extra-virgin olive oil
6 lemon wedges

In a mixing bowl, stir 1 egg into the rice. In another bowl, beat the remaining egg with the Parmesan. Spread the bread crumbs on a flat plate.

With your hands, shape the rice into 6 balls, pressing a piece of cheese into the center of each one. Dip a supplí in the egg mixture and then coat it well with the bread crumbs. Set aside, while dipping and coating the rest of the balls.

continued

In a large skillet, heat the olive oil over medium heat. Sauté each supplí until nicely browned on all sides, about 3 to 4 minutes. Serve with lemon wedges.

NOTE: When making these bread crumbs, I sometimes add 2 tablespoons of chopped parsley and 1 small garlic clove, minced, to the bowl of the food processor.

When times are hard, people born to the kitchen come up with inexpensive, delectable ways to make good food. It is the simplicity of these recipes that sets them apart from the complicated, overworked dishes that often steal the limelight. In Italy, a soup made from whatever was on hand, plus a few pieces of bread to fill it out, became one of the best regional dishes of Tuscany. Versions of a similar soup can be found in other regions, but I particularly like this one. It is a hearty dish, best on a winter's day served by a warm hearth—but bread soups are light enough for the other seasons, too. Tuscan Bread Soup is a basic recipe on which to build your own repertoire.

Tuscan Bread Soup

6 SERVINGS

½ cup olive oil

2 large leeks, white part only, sliced thin, or 2 sweet onions, sliced thin

4 cloves garlic, chopped

2 large russet potatoes, peeled, halved, and sliced thin

1 large head cauliflower, halved and sliced thin

2 quarts chicken stock, preferably homemade (page 225)

Two 8-ounce cans crushed tomatoes, or 6 large fresh tomatoes, diced

Four 1-inch-thick slices bread, toasted and cut into 1-inch cubes

Juice of 1 large lemon

Salt and freshly ground pepper

½ cup grated Parmesan cheese

½ cup chopped flat-leaf (Italian) parsley or fresh basil

continued

In a large soup pot, heat the olive oil over medium-high heat. Add the leeks and sauté for 5 to 7 minutes until golden. Add the garlic and cook, stirring, for 2 or 3 minutes. Add the potatoes and cauliflower and cook, stirring, for about 5 minutes, or until the edges of the potato slices begin to brown. Add the stock, tomatoes, half of the bread cubes, and lemon juice, and season with salt and pepper. Stir gently, reduce the heat to medium, and simmer for 20 to 25 minutes until the potatoes and cauliflower are very tender. Add the rest of the bread cubes, stir to mix, and spoon into bowls. Top with Parmesan and parsley or basil and serve immediately. If you like, you may add the parsley or basil to each bowl after you have browned the soup, sprinkled with Parmesan, under the broiler.

Carrot, Celery Root, Onion, and Parmesan Soup

6 SERVINGS

I rarely find celery root in cookbooks. It is the odd man out, staying in the wings while such vegetables as radicchio di Treviso or Turkish squash take the limelight. I love it steamed and mashed into potatoes or mixed with carrots into a purée. I also love it sautéed in olive oil like artichoke hearts until very crisp, but where it really shines is in a bread soup, creating body and richness in the broth and imparting its subtle flavor. Any vegetables in combination are the beginnings of a bread soup, but these three in particular are never a crowd.

¾ cup olive oil

6 carrots, sliced thin

1 celery root, peeled and diced

1 large sweet onion, sliced

2 cloves garlic, minced

½ cup marsala wine

½ cup white wine

1½ quarts chicken or vegetable stock, preferably homemade (page 225)

Pinch of grated fresh nutmeg

Pinch of hot pepper flakes

2 cups 1-inch bread cubes

Juice of 2 lemons

½ cup shaved Parmesan cheese

In a large soup pot, heat ½ cup olive oil over medium-high heat. Add the carrots, celery root, and onion, and sauté for 5 or 6 minutes until nicely browned. Add the garlic and cook for 2 minutes longer until golden. Stand back and pour the marsala and white wine into the pot; the marsala may ignite. Add the stock, nutmeg, and red pepper. Stir to mix, reduce the heat to medium, and simmer for about 30 to 40 minutes until the vegetables are tender.

In a large skillet, heat the remaining ¼ cup of olive oil and sauté the bread cubes for about 5 minutes until browned. Add half the bread cubes to the soup, stir, and cook for about 10 minutes. Add the rest of the bread cubes, stir in the lemon juice, sprinkle with Parmesan, and serve immediately.

Pappa al Pomodoro

There are as many versions of this thick soup made in Italy as there are grandmothers, and it is a soup meant to soothe and lift the spirits as a nonna often can. It is sometimes made for ailing children or the infirm elderly, but I love it on a cold day or when I am feeling a little blue. The marriage of tomatoes and bread is eternal, in sickness or in health!

¾ cup olive oil
2 cups 1-inch bread cubes
6 cloves garlic, minced
1 tablespoon minced sweet onion
4 large ripe tomatoes
3 cups chicken stock, preferably homemade (page 225)
Salt and freshly ground pepper, or pinch of hot pepper flakes
½ cup shaved Parmesan cheese
2 sprigs fresh basil, chopped fine

In a large skillet, heat ½ cup of the olive oil over medium-high heat. Add the bread cubes and sauté for 8 to 10 minutes, until browned and crunchy. Add the remaining olive oil, the garlic, and the onion, and cook for about 5 minutes longer, until the onion is golden.

Put the tomatoes in the bowl of a food processor and process until pulpy.

Put the bread mixture, the tomatoes, and stock in a large soup pot and cook for about 20 minutes until thick. Season with salt and pepper, ladle into soup bowls, and garnish with Parmesan and basil.

White Bean and Balsamic Vinegar Soup

6 SERVINGS

My love of beans ensures that we have them in the house at all times. I usually cook them until tender, add sautéed onion and fresh toasted sage, and then serve them with tuna or roasted red or yellow peppers and a large splash of olive oil. One day I needed to stretch my beans to include several sudden dinner guests, and so I added the ingredients below to make a rich main course (fortunately we always have bread around and rampant arugula for salad in the garden).

1½ cups dried white beans (cannellini, or small Great Northern preferably)
2 sweet onions, chopped fine
1 cup beer, white wine, or Champagne (see Note 1)
2 cups chicken or vegetable stock, preferably homemade (page 225)
1 teaspoon salt
6 tablespoons olive oil
⅔ cup fresh bread crumbs
10 fresh sage leaves
3 cloves garlic, minced
6 tablespoons of extra-virgin olive oil
6 tablespoons balsamic vinegar (see Note 2)
2 tablespoons mascarpone or sour cream (optional)

Put the beans in a large pot and cover with cold water. Bring to a boil over high heat, remove from the heat, and let the beans cool in the water. Drain, and add fresh water to cover. Add half of the chopped onion. Bring to a boil over high heat, skimming any foam that rises to the surface. As soon as the water boils, reduce the heat, add the beer, wine, or Champagne, and simmer for about 1½ hours until the beans are tender. Add the chicken stock as

continued

needed to keep the beans completely covered. When the beans are tender, add the salt, and stir well.

Transfer ½ the bean mixture to the bowl of a food processor and process until nearly smooth. There should be some texture to the soup. (This may have to be done in batches.) Return the puréed beans to the pot.

In a medium skillet, heat 2 tablespoons of olive oil over high heat and cook the bread crumbs, stirring, for 5 to 7 minutes until crunchy. Remove from the pan and set aside.

In the same skillet, heat the remaining 4 tablespoons olive oil and sauté the remaining onion for about 5 minutes until just golden. Add the sage leaves and cook for about 5 minutes until just crisp. Add the garlic and cook for about 2 minutes longer until golden. Add the bread crumbs and stir the mixture. Add to the soup, stir, bring to a simmer over medium heat, and cook for about 10 minutes until heated through and blended.

Spoon a tablespoon of olive oil and balsamic vinegar into each soup bowl before ladling the soup into the bowls. Garnish each with a teaspoon of mascarpone, if desired, and serve.

NOTE 1: Use any kind of leftover beer or Champagne for this recipe; it makes no difference if it is flat.

NOTE 2: For the best flavor, use the finest balsamic vinegar you can afford. This vinegar varies wildly in flavor and texture, with the finest being intensely flavored and syrupy.

Suzanne's Rich Chicken Stock

I make my chicken stock with breast bones, no necks, no backs, no feet. Breast bones are usually thrown away at butcher shops, so ask for them free before paying. Breast bones make a very fast, low-fat broth with clear, pure flavor. I told my cooking class where to get them and now there are never any left for me! But, they are making their own stock.

1 large sweet onion, chopped
3 stalks celery with leaves, chopped
4 large carrots, sliced
10 pounds chicken breast bones
Salt

In a very large soup pot, place the vegetables on the bottom, then the chicken bones, and then fill with cold water to just cover the bones. Bring rapidly to a boil over high heat, lower the heat to medium, and skim off the brown foam that rises until it is gone. Simmer on low heat for 1½ to 2 hours. Add salt to taste and strain. Cool before refrigerating. Freeze whatever you don't plan to use in the next week. I use several smaller containers, to freeze different amounts for different purposes.

Bread for Dessert

Leftover bread can always be used in desserts such as sweet bread puddings or trifles. I happen to love bread with fruit and so have invented recipes for leftover bread that becomes a kind of low-fat shortcake made with fresh fruit or cooked fruit and its syrup. Unlike pastry, bread soaks up the juices and flavors of the fruit giving the dessert a moist, almost cakelike consistency. Add a dollop of whipped cream, a caramel or chocolate sauce, or your favorite cheese to complement the fruit and bread, which I think is a heavenly alternative to heavy, sometimes overly sweet desserts.

Classic Bread and Butter Pudding

6 SERVINGS

My bread and butter pudding is lavish with butter and uses an especially rich, cream-based crème Anglaise instead of custard. I figure if you're going to make an earthy dessert such as bread pudding, you might as well make one that knocks your socks off. If you use leftover Classic Brioche (page 127), Panettone (page 165), or Russian Kulich (page 170) in place of bread, you will elevate the pudding even more.

7 tablespoons unsalted butter
Four 1-inch-thick slices plain white bread, cut into 1-inch cubes (see Note)
1½ cups milk
1½ cups heavy cream
⅔ cup sugar
3 large eggs

3 large egg yolks
1 teaspoon vanilla extract
Pinch of salt
Pinch grated fresh nutmeg

Preheat the oven to 350°F. Generously butter a 9-inch-square baking dish. Sprinkle liberally with sugar.

In a large skillet, melt 6 tablespoons of the butter over medium-high heat. Add the bread cubes and sauté for about 5 minutes, until browned on all sides. Transfer to the prepared baking dish.

In a saucepan, combine the milk and cream over medium heat. When warm, lower heat and whisk in the sugar, eggs, egg yolks, vanilla, and salt. Cook for 2 or 3 minutes, or until thickened, stirring constantly. Pour through a strainer into the baking dish and let the mixture sit for about 15 minutes so that the bread can absorb the liquid. Sprinkle with nutmeg and dot with the remaining tablespoon of butter.

Put the baking dish in a larger pan and pour in enough hot water to come halfway up the sides of the baking dish. Bake for about 30 minutes, or until nicely browned. Lift the baking dish from the water bath and let it sit for about 15 minutes before serving.

NOTE: You may, if you choose, simply toast and butter the bread liberally and lay the slices in the baking dish.

VARIATIONS

1. Add ⅔ cup Roasted Grapes (page 141), pitted cherries, sliced bananas, or sautéed apples to the bread mixture. You could also fold in ½ cup toasted nuts, such as walnuts, pecans, or almonds.

2. For a more refined dish, process the bread into bread crumbs, then separate the eggs, beat the whites to soft, glossy peaks, and fold them into the cream–egg yolk mixture just before baking.

Chocolate Bread Pudding

Here we have true hedonism and decadence at its finest. This was one of the many desserts I put together just after I had discovered Valrhona chocolate and was on the verge of addiction. The coffee and Cognac really push it to the limit, but it is equally sinful without them. Little chocolate shavings are pretty over the top—just don't ever use those little things my mother called "mouse tracks…."

6 tablespoons unsalted butter
4 to 6 Classic Brioches (page 127), cut into ½-inch slices
1 cup milk
2 cups heavy cream
4 to 6 ounces bittersweet chocolate, chopped
2 tablespoons strong brewed espresso or coffee
½ cup sugar
3 large eggs
3 large egg yolks
2 tablespoons cognac or rum
½ teaspoon vanilla extract

Preheat the oven to 350°F. Generously butter a 9-inch square or oval baking dish.

Butter the brioche slices and lay them in the baking dish.

In a saucepan, combine the milk and cream over medium heat and when warm, add the chocolate and coffee. Reduce heat to low and cook until the chocolate melts, stirring constantly.

Whisk in the sugar, eggs, egg yolks, cognac, and vanilla. Cook over low heat for 2 or 3 minutes, or until slightly thickened. Pour through a strainer into the baking dish and let the mixture sit for about 15 minutes so that the bread can absorb the liquid.

Put the baking dish in a larger pan and pour in enough hot water to come halfway up the sides of the baking dish. Bake for about 30 minutes, or until nicely browned. Lift the baking dish from the water bath and let it sit for about 15 minutes before serving.

Sautéed Apples and Cream on Toast

6 SERVINGS

These are the same apples I use for my tarte Tatin, but I have found that a piece of good bread, toasted and buttered, is sometimes a welcome change from rich pastry. The addition of a little cream dresses up this dessert, or you can serve it with a good piece of sharp Cheddar.

¼ cup unsalted butter
¼ cup sugar
4 tart apples, peeled, cored, and sliced very thin
Pinch of cinnamon
Dash of lemon juice
4 tablespoons heavy cream
Six 1-inch-thick slices bread, toasted and buttered
Sharp Cheddar cheese (optional)

continued

In a skillet, melt the butter over medium-high heat. Add the sugar and cook, stirring, for about 2 minutes until the sugar is dissolved. Add the apples, cinnamon, and lemon juice, and cook for about 2 minutes, stirring gently to coat apple slices with butter. Cover the skillet, reduce the heat to medium, and cook for 3 or 4 minutes.

Uncover the skillet and cook the mixture, which will be very juicy, for about 5 minutes until the apples caramelize and look glossy. Stir in the cream. Spoon over the toast and serve with or without the cheese.

Pears in Caramel with Cheese on Toast

6 SERVINGS

There is a saying in Italy that you don't have to teach a farmer to eat pear with his Parmesan. Or, in other words, any farmer worth his salt knows that Parmesan and pears are made for each other. This recipe came of that natural pairing.

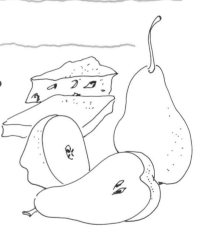

Pears on toast with cheese

6 ripe firm Bosc or Comice pears, peeled, cored, and halved

6 tablespoons unsalted butter

6 tablespoons sugar

1 cup heavy cream

½ teaspoon vanilla extract

Six 1-inch-thick slices bread, toasted and buttered

6 ounces aged Parmesan or Gouda

Preheat the oven to 425°F. Butter a shallow baking dish large enough to hold the pear halves in a single layer.

Arrange the pears, cut side down, in the dish so that they fit snugly in one layer. Dot with butter and sprinkle with sugar. Bake on the lowest oven rack for 20 to 30 minutes, or until the pears are light brown and the sauce caramelized (see Note).

Remove the pears from the oven but do not turn the oven off. Add the cream and vanilla. Tilt the pan to swirl the cream and sauce together. Return to the oven for about 5 minutes to heat the cream and allow the flavors to blend. Lay the bread on top of the pears and continue baking for about 3 minutes longer. Serve with chunks of cheese on the side.

NOTE: If the sauce does not caramelize, increase the oven temperature to 475°F and watch carefully to prevent burning. The sauce can also be caramelized, if needed, on top of the stove in a large saucepan.

I believe that texture along with flavor are the two most important elements of a good dish. Since my first bite of Caesar salad at Trader Vic's in San Francisco years ago, I have adored the crunch of what is, essentially, fried bread. As a child, I learned to love salad by listening to my mother bite down on celery and lettuce—it sounded so good I wanted to make my own noises. Croutons and bread crumbs make good noises and provide great texture.

All of the breads in this book make delicious and unusual croutons and bread crumbs. Here I explain the basic techniques for making both. Once you master them, elaborate with your own favorite seasonings to create new tastes for salads, dishes *au gratin*, casseroles, soups, or bruschettine (little toasts) for spreads and for dipping.

I like to first toast the crumbs I use in pastas or sprinkle over salads. If the bread crumbs are sprinkled on dishes that will be baked, there is no need to toast them first. If you use spices or dried herbs to coat the crumbs or croutons, always sauté them in a little olive oil first or toast them in a dry pan for a short time to release their flavors and make a dish more palatable and digestible. Fresh herbs need only to be chopped fine, tossed with the croutons or crumbs, and then cooked for a minute or two in a little olive oil.

Croutons and Bread Crumbs

One 8- to 10-ounce loaf of bread
6 tablespoons olive oil, or to your taste (see Note)
Salt and freshly ground pepper (optional)

To make croutons: Slice the bread into ½-inch-thick slices and remove the crusts or not (I do not). Slice into cubes. Toss with the olive oil and any seasonings, including salt and pepper, you choose (see Variations). Transfer to a large skillet and cook over medium heat, stirring, for 6 to 8 minutes or until browned and crunchy. Remove from the pan and cool.

Another alternative is to heat the olive oil in the skillet, add the dry bread cubes, and cook over medium heat for 6 to 8 minutes or until browned and crunchy. Remove from the pan and cool.

Finally, you can spread the cubes mixed with oil on a baking sheet and bake in a preheated 350°F oven for about 15 minutes to crisp, then turn off the oven, open the oven door, and leave cubes to dry for 5 to 10 minutes.

To make bread crumbs: Slice the bread into 1-inch-thick slices and then cut into large pieces. Remove the crusts or not (I do not). Put the bread into the bowl of a food processor and process until the crumbs are the size you need for a recipe: fine, medium, or coarse. Toss with the olive oil and any seasonings, including salt and pepper, you choose (see Variations). Transfer to a large skillet and cook over medium heat, stirring, for 5 to 7 minutes or until browned and crunchy. Remove from the pan and cool.

Another choice is to heat the olive oil in the skillet, add the dry crumbs, and cook over medium heat for 5 to 7 minutes or until browned and crunchy. Remove from the pan and cool.

Finally, you can spread the crumbs mixed with oil on a baking sheet and bake in a preheated 350°F oven for about 10 minutes to crisp.

continued

NOTE: Depending on the recipe, use butter in place of olive oil. Buttered crumbs are better for most desserts and for recipes that specify them.

VARIATIONS: RECOMMENDED SEASONINGS FOR CROUTONS AND BREAD CRUMBS

Spices and dried herbs

Heat spices or dried herbs in a small amount of olive oil or in a dry pan set over medium-high heat, usually for less than a minute, until fragrant. Shake the pan to prevent scorching. Transfer to a plate to cool and halt the cooking. Toss with the croutons or bread crumbs. Proceed with the toasting processes just described. Use the following to enhance bread used in or to accompany the suggested dishes or preparations.

allspice—use in sweet dishes

cardamom—use to flavor bread stuffings, fruit salads, and soups

cinnamon—use in sweet dishes

cloves—use in sweet dishes

coriander seeds—use in Indian dishes, bread stuffings, and soups

cumin—use in Mexican and Indian dishes and soups

curry powder—use for some salads, Indian dishes, egg dishes, and soups

nutmeg—use in sweet dishes or with some greens, such as spinach, rape, chard, and beet tops

saffron—use for soups, fish chowders, and egg dishes (dissolve it first in water and spray it over the bread)

sage—use in bread stuffings, pasta, and casseroles

sweet paprika—use to give color and flavor

thyme—use in bread stuffings, salads, soups, poultry, meat, and fish dishes

Fresh herbs and other fresh greens

For all of the following, chop the fresh herbs or greens very fine and toss with the croutons or bread crumbs. Proceed with the toasting process described earlier. Any of the following can be used to enhance bread used in or to accompany salads, soups, poultry, meat, or fish dishes.

- arugula
- basil
- celery leaves
- chives
- cilantro (also known as fresh coriander)
- garlic chives
- marjoram
- oregano
- parsley
- rosemary
- sage
- thyme (lemon thyme is my favorite)

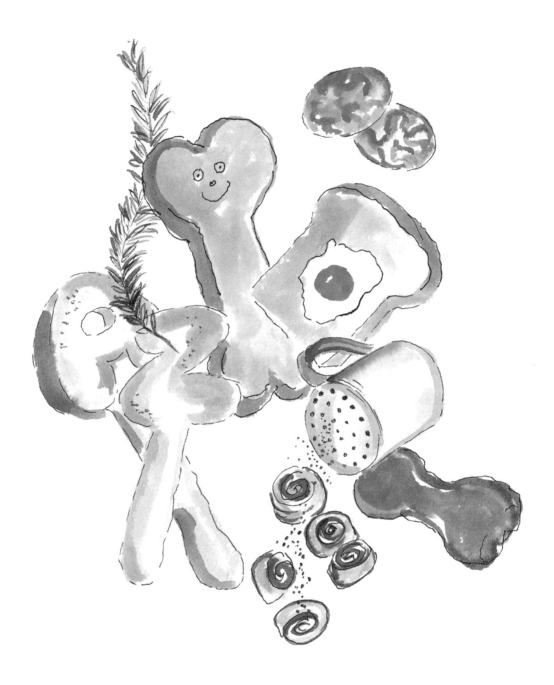

Bread for Children

GET THOSE KIDS IN THE KITCHEN! Children have such fun making mud pies and pretend doughs that real pizza crust or simple breads do not seem that different. A child who is helping you in the kitchen is learning not only how to cook but how to cooperate with others, work at a job, have responsibility, and not be bored. Even when babies are one or two years old, they love to rattle measuring spoons and bang on pots and pans, and I am sure that these images and sensations find a place in their tiny brains, stored away for the day when they will whip up their own country loaves or make a terrific bread pudding. Even if you are skeptical about my reasoning, you will have a liberated child who is self-sufficient in the kitchen and not a slave to fast foods, if you start teaching him or her at an early age to shell peas and devil eggs. Besides, it's great fun.

These breads for children are also for adults who still like sitting around a campfire or having a little bit of childhood creep into their all too serious grown-up days. Egyptian eggs are still my favorite, over and above anything poached, boiled, or otherwise, but the Log Cabin Scrambles hold second place. I remember the marvelous scrambled eggs served in the University of Texas cafeteria; in those days the eggs were from the country-side and *fresh*, and we starving students could eat 5 or 6 scoops at a sitting. I know these recipes will stimulate your own ideas about cooking with kids. You may soon have a child who gives up TV for timbales. Remember that it is often only you who can point your child toward the oven.

Pie Crust Pinwheels

MANY LITTLE PINWHEELS, DEPENDING ON HOW THEY ARE CUT (AT LEAST 24)

At last, the famous inspirational pinwheels of my childhood! These are not bread, but they are an easy way to get your kids interested in baking, and a recipe that accomplishes that is one to keep. Any kid in his right mind will love to play with this pie crust, which is exactly the texture of Play-Doh or modeling clay. This dough, rolled thin, makes a beautiful pie or tarte Tatin, in case the supervising cook wants to bake along, but take out what you need before the kids go at it. Even under a watchful eye, kids tend to want to roll dough out over and over again (which is the fun of it, after all) and after that, it will make great shoe leather but not be fit for a dinner party dessert.

2¼ cups all-purpose flour

1 teaspoon salt

Pinch of sugar (optional)

6 ounces very cold butter, cut into generous ¾-inch cubes

¼ cup very cold vegetable shortening

About ¼ cup ice water

4 tablespoons melted butter

¾ cup brown or white sugar

1 teaspoon cinnamon

A small pastry brush or clean paintbrush

Sift dry ingredients into the bowl of a food processor. Add butter and short-ening and pulse only 5 to 6 seconds or until mixture is coarse, not fine. Add water as you pulse again but only until mixture is moistened, *not* mixed. On a piece of plastic wrap, turn out the mixture (which will be very crumbly) and with one or two pushes of your palm, bring the dough together into a rough circle. Place another piece of plastic wrap on top and press the circle flat. Gather up the edges of the plastic wrap, wrap the dough well, and place in a plastic bag in the refrigerator for at least 30 minutes, keeping the dough flat.

For kid use: Remove from plastic bag, flour a surface short enough to work on, remove plastic wrap, and let kids wail. Roll dough out into a big piece, then cut off the sides to make a rectangle. Brush with melted butter, sprinkle with sugar and cinnamon, and roll up like a jelly roll. Cut across the roll and lay each piece flat on a baking sheet. The pieces will look like little pinwheels. Brush with butter again if you want. Bake at 400°F for 15 minutes.

For adult use: Remove from the plastic bag and using the plastic wrap both under and over the dough to hold it in place, roll out the dough into a thin circle. Proceed with recipe for pies.

Your Very Own Bread

2 LITTLE LOAVES

Children can whip up most of my simple bread recipes with a little super-vision, but I think they like having their own recipe to follow while the head baker follows his or hers. Make a copy for them (if they can read, that is) to start off their own cookbooks. My first recipe for "bread," even before the pinwheels, was this: butter 2 saltines and put them in play oven. Believe it or not, my little red and white oven heated to 300°F and there were no disclaimers on the side! Those saltines were first class, but the bread I made after that pushed them into second place.

1 large bowl
1 whisk
1 large spoon

1 cup water, the temperature of your bath
1 tablespoon dry yeast
1 teaspoon sugar (optional)
2 cups flour, any kind that is white
1 teaspoon salt

Get out the bowl, whisk, and spoon, and place them on your work surface. Put the water in the bowl and whisk in the yeast until it is foamy. If you want to see live yeast dance around, put in the sugar and wait a few minutes. The yeast will bubble and foam. Stir in the flour carefully and slowly so as not to slosh it out of the bowl. Stir and stir and then sprinkle in the salt and stir until it is very hard to turn the spoon. The dough will pull away from the sides of the bowl. Put some oil on your hands and lift the dough out of the bowl onto a floured surface. Push on the dough to make it flat and then make a book by folding one side over on the other and then make an even smaller book by folding that part again. Wash and dry your bowl and rub the inside with a little oil. Put the dough back in the bowl to rise. Cover it with plastic wrap and go play for 1 hour. Come back to see that your dough is twice its original size! Uncover it and poke it around just to see it deflate. Cover and go play again for 1 hour. Come back and make your bread into sandwich loaves or bones or cinnamon focaccia or hearts or letters or whatever you like. Have your mother turn on the oven to 400°F. Put the shapes you make on a greased cookie sheet and go play for half an hour. Come back and put your bread in the oven to bake for 30 minutes. Eat slices plain or with butter or butter and sugar, the way my grandmother gave fresh bread to me.

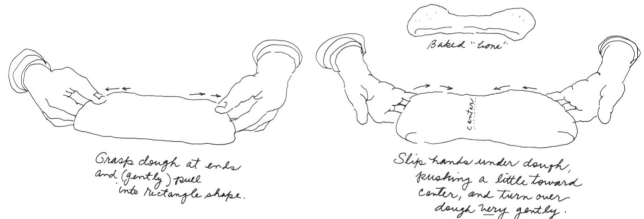

Grasp dough at ends and (gently) pull into rectangle shape.

Baked "bone"

Slip hands under dough, pushing a little toward center, and turn over dough very gently.

To make bones: Divide the dough into 4 pieces. Pull on the ends of each one to make a long shape. Place on a floured baking sheet. Let rise 30 minutes and then turn each bread over, pulling again into a "bone"—the bread will get skinny in the middle and big at the ends like a dinosaur bone. Bake immediately.

Bone bread

Egyptian Eggs

I have made these for my husband, stepchildren, and grandchildren for years. I have never known their origin, but I think the name must have come from the Egyptian friezes that depict wise men walking sideways with only one eye showing, or even from the staff with one "eye," the ankh, held by Egyptian rulers. This may be a stretch of the imagination but it makes perfect sense to me. You may give full sight to this dish by cutting slices from larger bread loaves, making the hole wider, and using two eggs. These eggs will cause no ankhxiety.

1 slice of day-old bread for each person
1 tablespoon unsalted butter for each slice of bread plus 1 teaspoon for hole
1 large egg for each slice of bread
Salt and pepper

With a cookie cutter or glass, cut the center out of each slice of bread, leaving the outer area intact. Butter both sides of the bread.

Heat a large skillet over medium heat. When hot, place the bread in the skillet. Put the teaspoon of butter inside the cut-out hole, and when it is bubbling, break the egg into the hole. Season with salt and pepper. Let the bread cook on one side for about 2 minutes or just until the egg is set. With a spatula, carefully turn over the bread and cook on the other side. Serve this sprinkled with confectioners' sugar if you like, or better yet, with fresh fruit.

Egyptian Eggs

Log Cabin Scrambles

This recipe was inspired by my brother, who built amazing cabins and compounds with his Lincoln Logs. Somewhere in my memory there is a picture of him at breakfast, making all sorts of structures from his toast—but then again, this may be a trick of memory. I can clearly see little carefully cut strips of buttery toast, alternately laid upon each other and forming a perfect little house for my scrambled eggs. The game was to chop down the house, eating as you go, to get to the savory golden treasure inside.

4 tablespoons unsalted butter
4 large eggs
¼ cup heavy cream
Salt and freshly ground pepper
8 slices bread, toasted and buttered

Very carefully, heat a medium-size skillet, and put in the butter. Beat eggs, cream, salt, and pepper with a fork until well mixed, and pour into the skillet. With a spatula, pull the eggs from one side to the other, allowing the uncooked egg to run onto the exposed skillet. Do this quickly until the eggs are still runny on top but cooked underneath. Remove from the heat and continue to pull the eggs to one side to cook the rest of the liquid egg. This way the eggs will never overcook and be hard, and the skillet is still hot enough to finish cooking the eggs gently.

Quickly spoon eggs onto each of four plates in a little pile. Make buttered toast and cut into four "logs" each. Lay two of these logs on opposite sides of the eggs and then place the next two on top of them, continuing to place two more each time on top of the previous two, making a square "cabin" around the eggs. You can make all kinds of structures with toast logs.

Alphabet Bread Sticks—Basic Recipe

ABOUT 26 BREAD STICKS, FROM A TO Z

These easy bread sticks can be shaped into letters, or even your name, with a little practice. They can be unadorned or sprinkled with all sorts of good things. Bend the dough into the shapes of cats or stars or pigs or flowers or whatever you like. You may also use them to make edible bracelets and necklaces, but they will be a little fragile so be prepared to eat them quickly. If you lower the oven temperature to 300°F and let the bread sticks bake for 45 minutes, they will last longer as jewelry but will not be edible (they are too hard on the teeth!).

2 cups lukewarm water (85 to 95°F)
2 teaspoons yeast
2 teaspoons sugar (optional)
3¾ to 4 cups unbleached bread or all-purpose flour
¼ cup extra-virgin olive oil, or ¼ cup unsalted butter, melted
1 heaping teaspoon salt

In a large bowl, mix water and yeast (add sugar here for sweet bread sticks). Mix in the flour, oil or butter, and salt and mix well until smooth and shiny. Dough should not be too sticky but easily pull away from fingers. Use a little more flour if needed. Cover and let rise until double in a warm place, about 1 hour. You can speed this up by putting the dough on top of a water heater or in a low, low oven (100°F).

Preheat oven to 450°F. Push the dough down and turn it out onto a floured surface. Flatten it with your hands into a rectangle about 1 inch thick. With a sharp knife or scissors, cut strips 1 inch wide down the long side of the dough (see illustration). Roll it like clay into a long snake. Place the bread-stick snake on an oiled cookie sheet and use an end of the snake to shape any letter you like, pinching off small pieces of dough to make the crossbars on an *A,* for example, or the tail on a *Q.* Or bend the dough into flowers with stems, stars, and so on. Spritz with water before baking. When cool, place in a tall container and let your friends choose a bread stick that is a letter in their names.

cut here

To make strips to roll for breadsticks

VARIATIONS

For cinnamon bread sticks

Before baking, brush with 2 tablespoons olive oil or melted butter and sprinkle with a mixture of ½ cup turbinado or white sugar mixed with 1 teaspoon cinnamon.

Various sprinkles for bread sticks

Toasted seeds of all kinds, crushed nuts, chocolate sprinkles (mouse tracks), candy sprinkles, or Parmesan, grated fine (other cheeses are too soft).

Pain Perdu

Lost Bread

6 SERVINGS

When I asked John Deville, the chef at Antoine's in New Orleans, about the origin of Pain Perdu's name, he said (in a soft Cajun drawl), "Well, it's just one of those things you know about in New Orleans. You just put that bread in the batter and then you brown it up on the grill and it's pain perdu. I don't know why they call it that, but you just want to eat it like dessert and with your eggs and grits and that's the pain perdu." Which was enough for me. Maybe the name refers to old bread that felt sort of "lost" or rejected in the kitchen. Even my New Orleans friends could not discover the origin. Now there's a job for you.

2 cups milk, or milk and heavy cream
½ cup sugar
Pinch of cinnamon or fresh grated nutmeg
3 large eggs, beaten with a little salt and a pinch of baking powder
6 slices day-old bread, cut 1-inch thick
6 tablespoons unsalted butter
Confectioners' sugar

Heat the oven to 425°F. In a glass bowl, beat the milk or milk and cream, sugar, cinnamon or nutmeg, and eggs together well. Place the slices of bread in the mixture for 10 minutes to soak up the liquid, coating them well. In a large ovenproof skillet, heat the butter and sauté the bread slices quickly on each side for 2 to 3 minutes until golden brown. Put the skillet in the oven for 5 to 6 minutes to finish cooking the bread. Dust with powdered sugar and serve, or serve with Fresh Fruit Purée (page 88). Don't forget the eggs and grits!

Campfire Roly-Polys

My Girl Scout troop was divided into two groups: the cremated-marsh-mallow madwomen and the toasted-coco-nuts. You leaned toward one or the other, and I was definitely a marshmallow fan. But those who could make a good roly-poly, the coco-nuts, were always in demand. This is a really decadent dessert but fun to make around the campfire (after the fresh fruit!).

6 thin slices of fresh soft bread, crusts removed
One 6-ounce can sweetened condensed milk
One 6-ounce package grated, sweetened coconut, or 1 cup grated fresh coconut mixed with 2 tablespoons sugar
A campfire

When the hamburgers are finished and the coals are still glowing, cut a nice long branch for a skewer for each person. Sharpen one end. Roll each slice of bread around the sharp end of the stick using the point to help secure the bread, then squeeze the bread firmly to seal, or secure it with a toothpick. Alternately, roll up each slice of bread into a tight cylinder and poke the stick through it from top to bottom, threading the bread on the stick firmly.

Put the milk and coconut in two separate flat, shallow dishes. Roll the bread first through the milk, sopping up as much as you can, and then coat well with the coconut.

Or, put the milk in a deep container and dip the bread end of the stick into it. Coat well with the coconut.

Hold the stick over the coals, turning it slowly to toast the coconut and bake the bread and milk onto the stick. Let cool and eat.

Adam and Eve on a Raft

I once had to draw Adam and Eve on a Raft (which means eggs over easy on toast) for an article on short-order cooking. The image of these two taking the sun on their sturdy bread boat makes me smile every time I make this dish. I do not turn my eggs over, but instead add a little water to the skillet and "blindfold" them. Any way you make this dish, it is fun to serve and a great way to get kids to eat eggs.

1 slice toast
2 teaspoons butter
2 large eggs
2 teaspoons water
1 slice fried bacon
A toothpick

Butter toast.

In a skillet, heat the rest of the butter over medium heat. Break the eggs into the skillet and cook for 2 minutes. Add 2 teaspoons of water to the skillet and cover the eggs with a lid for 2 more minutes, or until the yellow of the egg is steamed to a pale pink-gray color but still soft. With a spatula, remove the eggs, place on the toast, and make a "sail" by sticking the bacon lengthwise on the toothpick. Push the toothpick into the edge of the toast to complete the raft.

Acknowledgments

In memory:

Sandra Graham, who kept telling me that it's all good.

Myra Livingston, who started the whole thing.

Thanks to:

Betsy Amster, my patient agent, who tickled my fancy with a book proposal and then relentlessly made me do it.

Will Schwalbe, much more than an editor, who always speaks as he eats.

Halley MacNaughton whose illustration list saved the day.

Mary Goodbody, a steady, meticulous cookbook wizard who helped me find my way to clarity with her rampant red pencil.

Adrian James, copy editor extraordinaire, whose challenging notes and questions made me look further.

My stepdaughter, Nicole, for her many tips on cooking, and my stepson, Simon, for tasting.

Their mother, Gabriella Piga, for ricotta cake and a special friendship.

Alida Shimek who inspired the *tozzetti*, and my brother, Joe Shimek, who presses on, regardless.

Paula and William Merwin, my advice squad.

Jane Louise Curry for her weekly *coraggio*!

Annabel Baker who always knows a good thing when she sees it.

Cameron Graham, Robert Kulewicz, Samantha Graham, and Gary Vura for being such loyal fans.

Annie Ray Poth for her smiles and wisdom.

Judy Rosen and her doves, for TLC, TV, and PR, and Milt who made us laugh.

Judy and Marvin Zeidler for just about everything.

Caroline Bates for her lively humor and vast knowledge.

Lee Lorenz at *The New Yorker*, who bought my first spot art.

Irwin Glusker who told me to draw with color and pushed my brush in new directions.

Joe and Betty Rosa at Beverly Glen Marketplace who bought my first focaccia.

Susan McAlindon, our magnificent manager, who held the fort.

Our loyal customers who came to the bakery and put us on the map.

The American Institute of Wine and Food; Tom and Ann Martin, Noel Riley Fitch, Bert Sonnenfeld, and so many more.

Every market and restaurant that contributes to our success.

Joan Luther and Jill Sandin for their PR prowess.

Carolyn Johnson, who waited until we were ready for Mrs. Gooch's eight markets!

Sarah Black for helping me make the holes bigger.

Celestino Drago for the secret to bread pudding.

Claudia McQuillan, who knows everyone.

Gregory Job, for keeping my home Dacor ovens humming while they turned out one thousand loaves a week.

Grazia Caroselli for a great *Slice of Life*.

My adventuresome recipe testers: Mary Mann, Patti Bauman, Phyliss Leavitt, Jacquie Gengé, Dobbie Heimer, Dossie Gilbert, and Alida Shimek.

My cooking students who came to dinner and stayed seven years: Tracy Fairhurst, Charmaine Balian, Linda Terris, Kathy McBroom, Susan Vogelfang, Ann Naymie, Beth Lichter, Sue Wilson, Donna Griffes, Cynthia Eicher, Laurie Murphy, Jane Curry, Mary Ellen Klee, Louise Schwartz, Camille Wall, Teresa Laursen, Francie Moore, Richard Renaldo, Richard Goodman, and Diana Goodman, who inspired the whole operation.

My demo women and men who always showed up smiling.

Barbara Barschak who knows when to wear white shoes.

Les Dames d'Escoffier, a very special group of people in food and wine: indefatigable Karen Berk of The Seasonal Table, and Ruthie Graham of Bonny Doon Winery, whose enthusiasm knows no bounds; Nancy Arum, Jean Barrett, Mitzie Cutler, Susan Duquette, Annie Boutin, Renny Darling-Klein, Cecilia de Castro, Margaret Ferrazzi, Kora Gail, Lina Gerometta, Christine Graham, Betty Harwood, Halle Gould, Zov Karamardian, Carole Klincke, Lauren Krim, Mary Clare Mulhall, Neela Paniz, Peggy Rahn, Joy Shefter, Tara Thomas, Loretta Griffiths-Hwong, Jane Matyas, Judy Ornstein, Phyliss Vacarelli of Let's Get Cooking, Jan Weimer, Andrea Werbel, Mary Sue Milliken and Susan Feniger, two hot tamales.

Charles Perry, my generous food guru.

KCRW for making my day.

Lena Mae Newsome, my other cooking teacher.

Special thanks to Leonel Ramos, our head baker, who was there from the beginning with dedication and a smile; his great team of amazing bakers; Carlos Ruiz, always ready: Helen and the fast baggers and dependable drivers who make Buona Forchetta run like a fine-tuned engine; Daniel and Oto who make the bakery shine.

And to everyone on Chrysanthemum Lane. You are my daily bread.

If I forgot anyone, it's because I'm over thirty.

Index

Page numbers in **boldface** indicate recipe.

Adam and Eve on a Raft, **248**
Additives, 5
African cooking, 161
African Spiced Bread, 39, **176–77**
Almonds, 25
  toasting, 168
Alphabet Bread Sticks, **244–45**
Anadama Bread, **80–81**, 200
Anchovies, 112
  Penne with Broccoli and, **210–11**
Another Foolproof Chocolate Icing, **150–51**
Apples, 26, 227
  caramelized, 126
  Sautéed, and Cream on Toast, **229–30**
Apricot(s), 26, 30
  caramelized, 126
  Filling, **134**
  Focaccia, 25, 26, **135–36**, 172
  -Plum Pudding, **162–64**
Art of Eating, The (newsletter), 22

Artichokes, 115–16
Arugula, 120, 223
  and Prosciutto, Bruschetta with, **196**
  Paste, Very Thin Pizza with, **120–21**

Baguette(s), 8, 19, 38
  French, **73–75**
  olive, 52
  Rosemary Filoncino, **46–48**
Baked beans, 78, 97
  Suzanne's Version of Boston, **99**
Baking, 12
  holiday, 2
  reasons for, 6–7
  tactile pleasures of, 17
  tenets for, 7–13
  tips on, 31–32
Balsamic Vinegar
  term, 31
  White Bean and, Soup, **223–24**
Bananas, 26, 227
Basic Pizza Crust, **105–7**
Basil, 112
  Bruschetta with Tomato and, **195**

Beans
  in soup, 223
  see also Baked beans
Beaten Biscuits, My Grandmother's, 18, 29–30, 79, **89–91**
Beer yeasts, 33
Behr, Edward, 22
Berberé, 176, **179–80**
Biga, 14, 21, 33, 34
  Buttermilk Bread, 84, 85
  Ciabatta, 50
  English Muffins, 100–1
  Filoncino Integrale, 59, 60
  My Grandmother's Beaten Biscuits, 90
  My Mother's Sourdough Biscuits, 86, 87
  Pane Casereccio, 66
  Pane Rustico, 71
  Pizza Bianca alla Romana, 108, 109
  Rosemary-Pepper Bread Sticks, 183
  Sourdough Caraway Rye, 62
Bigmama's Kolaches, 25, **130–32**
Biscotti, 37

Biscuits, 1, 2, 27, 79
    My Grandmother's
        Beaten, 18, 29–30,
        79, **89–91**
    My Mother's Sourdough,
        86–87
Blini, Buckwheat, **96–97**
Boston Baked Beans,
        Suzanne's Version of,
        99
Boston Brown Bread, 2,
        13, 78, **97–98**
Boule, 8, 10
Bread(s), 2, 3–5, 9
    basic, 4, 5, 20, 35
    and Butter Pudding,
        Classic, **226–27**
    and Cheese Soufflé, 19,
        206
    for children, 237–48
    commercial, 25, 38
    crisp, 40
    daily, 4, 20, 37–75
    for dessert, 226–31
    Hazelnut-Sage, 52
    in pasta and rice, 209–18
    quick, 105
    salt-free, 24
    temperatures, 18
Bread crumbs, 188, 189,
        209, 217, 218, 227,
        233–35
    exotic, 232–34
Bread pudding(s), 226
    brioche in, 127
    Chocolate, 187, 188,
        228–29
Bread salads, 188, 190–93
Bread soufflé(s), 94, 188,
        206–8
Bread and Cheese, 19, **206**
    with Salmon and Capers,
        207–8
Bread soup(s), 187, 188,
        219–25

Tuscan, **219–20**
Bread sticks, 17, 40, 159–
        85
    Alphabet, **244–45**
    Rosemary-Pepper, 19,
        183–85
Breakfast breads, 25, 127
    focaccia, 43
Brewer's yeast, 33
Brioche, 7, 28, 187, 188
    Classic, 17, **127–29**, 226
    dough, 34
Broccoli and Anchovies,
        Penne with, **210–11**
Broccoli rape, 209, 213
Brownie Scout Chocolate
        Cake, 125, **148–49**
Bruschetta, 25, 187, 188
    with Arugula and
        Prosciutto, **196**
    with Caponata, **198–99**
    Hazelnut-Sage and goat
        cheese, 56
    with Olive Paste,
        199–200
    with Roasted Garlic and
        Parmesan, **202–3**
    with Rock Shrimp or
        Shellfish, **204**
    with Sweet Peppers and
        Tuna, **196–97**
    with Tomato and Basil,
        195
    with Wild Mushrooms,
        200–1
Bruschette, 70, 194–204
Bruschettine, 52, 188,
        205, 232
Buckwheat Blini, **96–97**
Bulgur wheat, 25–26
Bunyettes, 44
Buona Forchetta Hand
        Made Breads, 3, 4, 5,
        17, 24, 27, 28, 38,
        52, 188, 190

Butter, 2, 28, 125, 226
    for bread crumbs, 234
    in panettone, 166
    term, 30
Buttermilk Bread, **84–85**

Caen, Herb, 20
Cake(s), 125, 126
    Brownie Scout
        Chocolate, 125, **148–49**
    cornmeal, 144
    Gabriella's Ricotta, 25,
        125, **145–46**
    Gingerbread, **151–53**
    Sourdough Lemon, 125,
        142–43
Campfire Roly-Polys,
        247
Candied Orange and
        Lemon Zest, **169**
Candied peel, 166
Capers, Bread Soufflé with
        Salmon and, **207–8**
Caponata, Bruschetta with,
        198–99
Caramel, Pears in, with
        Cheese on Toast, 26, 188,
        230–31
Carbohydrates, 21
Carrot, Celery Root,
        Onion, and Parmesan
        Soup, **220–21**
Cashews, 25
Cassata, 124
Caviar, 96, 161
Celery Root, Onion,
        Carrot, and Parmesan
        Soup, **220–21**
Chappati, 160, 161
    dough, 137
    Quick, for Curry, 19,
        174–75
Cheese, 4, 27
    Bread and, Soufflé, 19,
        206

and pasta dishes, 209
Pears in Caramel with,
 on Toast, 26, 188,
 230–31
on pizza, 117
Cheesecakes, cottage
 cheese in, 25
Chicken Stock, Suzanne's
 Rich, **225**
Children, 17, 38, 79
 bread for, 237–48
 bread sticks, 162
Chili pepper, 5
 corn bread, 2
Chili powder, 30, 92
Chocolate Bread Pudding,
 187, 188, **228–29**
Chocolate Cake, Brownie
 Scout, 125, **148–49**
Chocolate Ice Cream,
 Wild Turkey, **156–57**
Chocolate Icing
 Another Foolproof,
 150–51
 Foolproof, **150**
Chocolate Tozzetti,
 154–56
"Chowder pieces," 207
Christmas, 2
 panettone, 165
Ciabatta, 11, 20, 28,
 49–51
Ciccone, Virgilio, 110, 190
Cilantro, 121
Cinnamon
 bread sticks, 245
 focaccia, 25
 pinwheels, 1
Classic Bread and Butter
 Pudding, **226–27**
Classic Brioche, 17,
 127–29, 226
Coffee (term), 31
Cold dough method, 5–6
Collioure, 44

Colombo, 170
Confectioners' Sugar Icing,
 Pink, 171, **172**
Cooke, John, 14
Cooking, tips on, 31–32
Cooking diary, 13–14
Cooking implements,
 13–16
Corn Bread, Skillet, 5, 30,
 79, **91–92**
Cornmeal, 80
 Spoon Bread, **93–94**
 Torta della Nonna,
 Golden, **144–45**
Cottage cheese, 25, 145
 Filling, **134**
Covered bread pan
 method, 68
Cracked wheat, 25–26
Cracker dough, 7
Cream
 Sautéed Apples and, on
 Toast, **229–30**
 term, 31
Cream bread, 2
 My Mother's (Pain de
 Mie), 68, 79, **82–83**
Créme fraîche, 31
Croutons, 56, 189,
 233–35
 exotic, 232–34
Crumb, 3, 8, 9, 10, 11, 29,
 52
 Brownie Scout
 Chocolate Cake, 148
 Pane Rustico, 70
 Rosemary Filoncino, 46
 rye bread, 61
 texture, 28
 Whole Wheat Bread, 68
Crust, 3, 8, 9, 10, 29, 33
 Basic Pizza, **105–7**
 Fougasse de Collioure, 44
 Pane Rustico, 70
 rye bread, 61

Cumin, 26
Currants, 26
Curry, 26, 160–61
 Quick Chappati for, 19,
 174–75

Dairy products, 5, 20,
 24–25
Dash (term), 31
Dates, 26
Desserts, 124, 126
 bread, 188, 226–31
 children's recipes, 247
Deville, John, 246
Diced (term), 30
Diet, 21
Dill Pickles, Shimek,
 64–65
Dough
 additions to, 3–4
 basic, 4, 40–43
 intuition regarding, 29
 mixing, 27–28
 shaping, 18–19
 temperatures, 18
 wetter than conventional,
 7, 8, 10–11, 28, 33,
 49
 yeast in, 23–24
Drago, Celestino, 127
Dried fruits, 26, 68
Dried herbs, 234
Dried spices, 30
Dried vegetables, 27
Durum flour, 21

Easter kulich, 159
Eating as art, 2
Eggplant, 27, 198
Eggs, 25, 28, 166, 243, 248
 Egyptian, 238, **242**
 term, 30
Egyptian eggs, 238, **242**
el Din, Hamsa, 176
Elasticity, 28, 29, 30

Emotions
  and bread baking, 89
  and cooking, 19
English Muffins, 78, **100–1**

Failures, 30
Fats, 5, 20–21, 24–25
Fennel, wild, 215
Fermentations, 33, 35, 59
Figs, 26
Filling
  Apricot, **134**
  Cottage Cheese, 25, **134**
  for Kolaches, 132–34
  Poppy Seed, **132–33**
  Prune, **133**
Filoncini, 4, 8
Filoncino
  Hazelnut-Sage, 27, 30,
    55–57, 188
  Integrale, **58–61**, 68, 137
  Kalamata Olive, **52–54**,
    188
  Olive, 38, 199
  Rosemary, 20, 29, 38,
    46–48
Fish
  in pasta dishes, 215
  in soufflé, 207
Flapjacks, Sourdough,
  94–95
Flatbreads, 5, 8, 52
  basic dough for, 40–43
Flavor(s), 40, 232
  Ciabatta, 49
  combining, 5
  starters and, 35
Flaxseeds, 26
Flour(s), 20, 21–22, 24,
    27, 30, 32, 33, 35, 44
  in baguettes, 73
  in pizza, 104, 105
  rye, 61
  term, 30
Focacce, 4, 13

Focaccette, 40
Focaccia, 3, 5, 8, 11–12,
    17, 20, 24, 29, 33,
    35, 39, 52, 139
  antipasto, 106
  Apricot, 26, **135–36**, 172
  apricots in, 30
  basic dough for flatbreads
    or loaves, 40–43
  bread crumbs for, 209
  Kalamata, 26
  mixing dough for, 28
  old dough method for,
    34
  rosemary, 190
Foolproof Chocolate Icing,
  150
Fougasse, 5, 8, 18, 40
  de Collioure, 39, **44–45**
Four Seasons pizza, 116–17
French Baguette, **73–75**
French toast, 56, 70
Fresh Fruit Purée, **88**, 246
Fresh Ricotta, **147**
Fresh Scallop Panzanella,
  192–93
Fruit(s), 137, 168, 226
  caramelized, 188
  dried and fresh, 26, 68
  Fresh, Purée, **88**, 246
  purée, 142
Fruitcakes, 2

Gabriella's Ricotta Cake,
    25, 125, **145–46**
Garlic, 27, 192–93, 195,
    209
  Bruschetta with Roasted,
    and Parmesan, **202–3**
  grilling, 203
Genzano, breads of, 66
Gingerbread Cake, **151–53**
Golden Cornmeal Torta
    della Nonna, **144–45**
Grains, 25–26, 68, 137

Grapes, roasted
  see Roasted Grapes
Greens, 213
  for croutons and bread
    crumbs, 235

Hamburger buns, 40
Hands, 16–20
Hard Sauce, 164, **165**
Hazelnut(s), 21, 30
  -Sage Bread, 52
  -Sage Filoncino, 27, 39,
    55–57, 188
Health food stores, 22, 24
Heaping (term), 31
Herbs, 68, 232
  dried, 234
  fresh, 235
Hot Peppers, Orecchiette
  with Rape and,
  213–14
Housewife's Bread, 5, 11,
  20, **65–67**, 187
Houston, 86
Hush puppies, 91

Ice Cream, Wild Turkey
  Chocolate, 125–26,
  156–57
Icing
  Another Foolproof
    Chocolate, **150–51**
  Pink Confectioners'
    Sugar, 166, 171, **172**
  Foolproof Chocolate,
    150
Indian cuisine, 160–61
Ingredients, 3, 4
Intuition, 26, 27, 29–30
Italcheese (co.), 110, 190
Italian breads, 13, 38
  textures of, 11
Italy
  flours of, 21
  water, 22–23

Johnnycake pans, 14, 91
Journal of Gastronomy, The,
104

Kalamata
    focaccia, 26
    Olive Filoncino, **52–54**,
        188
Kneading, 4, 27, 33
    limiting, 7, 11–13, 19, 28
Kolaches
    Bigmama's, 25, **130–32**
    dough, 1
    fillings for, 132–34
    My Czech Grandmother's,
        125
Kulich, 160
    Russian, 5, **170–71**, 226

Lactobacillus sanfrancisco,
    32, 58
Ladder breads, 39, 40, 44
Lago di Como, 49
Lard, 139
Leftovers, 187–235
    in desserts, 226
Lemon
    Cake, Sourdough, 125,
        142–43
    Candied Orange and,
        Zest, **169**
    Curd, **153**
Like Water for Chocolate,
    19
Little toasts, 188
Loaves
    basic dough for, **40–43**
Log Cabin Scrambles, 238,
    243
Lost Bread, **246**

McGee, Harold, 18, 22,
    23, 33, 35, 124
Mascarpone, 124
    term, 31

Mashed (term), 30
Milk (term), 31
Millet, 26
Minced (term), 30
Mixing, 27–28, 29
Molasses, 124
Mozzarella, 103, 104, 105,
    110, 112, 190, 217
    term, 31
Muffins, 25
    English, 78, **100–1**
Mushrooms, Bruschetta
    with Wild, **200–1**
My Czech Grandmother's
    Kolaches, 125
My Grandmother's Beaten
    Biscuits, 18, 29–30,
    79, **89–91**
My Mother's Cream Bread
    (Pain de Mie), 68,
    79, **82–83**, 96
My Mother's Sourdough
    Biscuits, **86–87**

Naan, 160
Naples, pizza of, 105
Nit'r K'ibe, 176, **178**
Nuts, 25–26, 68, 137, 168

Oil, Rosemary, **48**
Old dough method, 33,
    34, 35
Olive(s), 21, 26–27
    bread(s), 205, 209
    Filoncino, 38, 199
    Filoncino, Kalamata,
        52–54, 188
Olive oil, 105, 108, 139
    extra-virgin, 12, 194
    term, 31
Olive paste, 121
    Bruschetta with,
        199–200
On Food and Cooking
    (McGee), 18, 22, 33

Onion, 27, 114
    Carrot, Celery Root, and
        Parmesan Soup,
        220–21
Orange and Lemon Zest,
    Candied, **169**
Orecchiette with Rape and
    Hot Peppers, **213–14**
Organic flour, 22
Ortiz, Joe, 33
Overnight method
    daily breads, 47, 49,
        53, 57, 63, 67, 69,
        71, 74
    focaccia, 41
    pizza, 106
    special breads, 182
    sweet loaves, 129, 138
    traditional breads, 81,
        101

Pagnotta, 66, 72
Pain de Mie, 28, 68,
    82–83
Pain Perdu, 2, **246**
Pancakes, 25, 27
Pane Casereccio
    (Housewife's Bread),
    5, 11, 20, 37, **65–67**
    biga for, 34
Pane Osso, 39, 66
Pane Rustico, **70–72**, 96
Pane Trattoria, 39
    biga for, 34
Panettone, 5, 13, 159, 160,
    165–68, 226
    sponge for, 34
Panzanella (bread salad),
    188, **190–91**
    Fresh Scallop, **192–93**
    Tuna, **191–92**
Pappa di Pomodoro, **222**
Parmesan, 230
    Bruschetta with Roasted
        Grapes and, **202–3**

Carrot, Celery Root, Onion and, Soup, **220–21**
term, 31
Pashka, 160, 170, 171, **172–73**
Pasta
  al dente, 209
  alla puttanesca, 209
  bread in, 209–18
  con Sarde, 20, **215–16**
Pasta sauces, 25
Peaches, 26
Pears, 26
  in Caramel with Cheese on Toast, 26, 188, **230–31**
Pecans, 25
Penne
  all'arrabbiata, 209
  with Broccoli and Anchovies, **210–11**
Pepper (term), 31
Peppers, 27
  Bruschetta with Sweet, and Tuna, **196–97**
  grilled, 118, 119
  Orecchiette with Rape and Hot, **213–24**
Perry, Charles, 104
Pickles, Shimek Dill, **64–65**
Pie Crust Pinwheels, **238–39**
Piemonte, 5
Piga, Gabriella, 145
Pine nuts, 25
Pink Confectioners' Sugar Icing, 171, **172**
Pistacchi, 25
Pizza, 8, 23, 103–21
  ai Funghi, 110
  alla Griglia, **118–19**
  bianca, 11, 37, 217

Bianca alla Romana, **108–10**
con Carciofi, **115–16**
con Cipolle, 109
con Olio di Tartuffo, 109
con Patate e Rosemarino, **113–14**
con Rughetta (arugula) or Salvia (sage), 109
Crust, Basic, **105–7**
dough, 5, 17, 22, 30
Margherita, **110–11**
Napoletana, **112–13**
Quattro Stagione, **116–17**
Pizza stone, 107
Pizze, 13
  square, 18–19
Plasticity, 28
Plum puddings, 159–60, 162, 165
  Apricot-Plum, **162–64**
Plums, 26
Pomodori al Riso, 20
Poppy Seed Filling, 1, **132–34**
Poppy seeds, 26
Potatoes
  on pizza, 114, 116
Pottery mixing bowl, 14
Preservatives, 4
Prosciutto, Bruschetta with Arugula and, **196**
Proteins, 21
  in flour, 22, 27
Prune
  and Walnut Bread, **137–38**
  Filling, **133**
Pudding
  Apricot-Plum, **162–64**
  Chocolate Bread, 188, **228–29**
  Classic Bread and Butter, **226–27**
Pudding molds, 14

Purée, Fresh Fruit, **88**, 246
Puris, 160

Quick Chappati for Curry, 19, **174–75**

Rape and Hot Peppers, Orecchiette with, **213–14**
Raisins, 68, 126, 139
  dried, 26
Ramos, Leonel, 3
Red Flame grapes, 5, 126, 141
Red wine, 21
Reggiano Rocca, 31
Rice
  bread in, 209–18
Ricotta, 145
  Cake, Gabriella's, 25, 125, **145–46**
  Fresh, **147**
Roasted Grapes, 30, 227
  Schiacciata with, 5, 26, 125, 126, **139–40**
  Suzanne's, **141**
Rock Shrimp or Shellfish, Bruschetta with, **204**
Rolls, 2, 8, 25
  Truffle, 5, 19, **180–82**
Roman Dipping Cookies, **154–56**
Rome, 37
  pizza of, 103, 105
Rosemary, 12, 46
  bread, 204
  Filoncini, 29
  Filoncino, 20, 38, **46–48**
  Oil, **48**
  -Pepper Bread Sticks, 19, **183–85**
  on pizza, 114
Rotelle alla Romana, **212–13**

Rough and ragged (term), 31
Russian Easter, 160
Russian Kulich, 5, **170–71**, 226
Rye, 26
Rye breads, 2
   Sourdough Caraway Rye, **61–63**

Sabadas, 124
Sage, 27, 30
   Hazelnut-, Bread, 52
   Hazelnut-, Filoncino, 27, 39, **55–57**, 188
Salads, bread, 188, 190–93
Salmon, 215
   and Capers, Bread Soufflé with, **207–8**
Salt, 20, 21, 24, 27, 33
   term, 31
Same day method
   daily breads, 47, 53, 57, 63, 66–67, 71, 74
   focaccia, 41
   pizza, 106
   special breads, 181
   sweet loaves, 129, 138
   traditional breads, 81, 101
San Francisco, 32, 58
Sand toks, 2
Sandwich bread/rolls, 40, 68, 70
Sardines, 215
   cleaning, 216
Sautéed Apples and Cream on Toast, **229–30**
Schiacciatta with Roasted Grapes, 5, 26, 30, 126, **139–40**
Seasonings
   for croutons and bread crumbs, 234–35
Seeds, 25–26, 68

Sesame seeds, 26
Shellfish, Bruschetta with Rock Shrimp or, **204**
Shimek Dill Pickles, **64–65**
Sicily, 209
Simplicity, 12, 13, 190
Simply Perfect Tomato Sauce, **121**
Skillet Corn Bread, 5, 30, 79, **91–92**
Slipper Bread, **49–51**
Soufflé(s), 94, 188, 206–8
   Bread, with Salmon and Capers, **207–8**
   Bread and Cheese, 19, **206**
Soups, bread, 187, 188, 219–25
   Tuscan, **219–20**
Sourdough, 32, 58–59
   Flapjacks, **94–95**
   Lemon Cake, 125, **142–43**
   starter, 33, 35, 59, 86, 87
Sourdough biscuits, 2
   My Mother's, **86–87**
Sourdough breads, 32
   Caraway Rye, 5, **61–63**
   Filoncino Integrale, **58–61**
Spaghetti alio, olio, pepperoncino, 209
Special breads, 159–85
Spices
   for croutons and bread crumbs, 232, 234
   dried, 27
Sponge, 33, 34, 35, 39
   Classic Brioche, 128
   panettone, 166, 167
   special breads, 170, 171
Spoon bread, 1
   Cornmeal, **93–94**
Sprinkles
   for bread sticks, 245

Starters, 32–33
   in cakes, 125, 142, 143, 144, 145, 148, 149, 152
   gauging temperatures of, 18
   sourdough, 33, 35, 59, 86, 87
   Sourdough Flapjacks, 94, 95
   things to remember about, 35
   why use, 35
   yeast for, 23
   see also Biga
Stirring, 28
Straight dough method, 33, 35, 68
Stuffing, 91
   corn bread, 91, 92
   Hazelnut-Sage Filoncino for, 56
Surface area in relation to volume, maximizing, 7–10, 202
Sugar, 5, 20, 24–25, 123–25, 126
   added to yeast, 24, 29
Supplí, **217–18**
Suzanne's Rich Chicken Stock, **225**
Suzanne's Roasted Grapes, **141**
Suzanne's Version of Boston Baked Beans, **99**
Sweet loaves, 123–57
Sweet Peppers, Bruschetta with, and Tuna, **196–97**

Tabbouleh, 26
Tangerine zest, 169
Tarte Tatin, 229, 238
Taste, 7–8

Taster(s), 14
Tea sandwiches, 82
Temperatures, 18
Terms, clarification of (list),
    30–31
Texture, 17, 25, 28, 30, 33,
    39, 232
  Ciabatta, 49
  pasta dishes, 209
  pizza dough, 105
  rye bread, 61
  sweet breads, 139
Thanksgiving, 2
Tiramisú, 124
Toast, 137
  Pears in Caramel with
    Cheese on, 26, 188,
    230–31
  Sautéed Apples and
    Cream on, **229–30**
Toasted ingredients, 26
Tomato and Basil,
    Bruschetta with, **195**
Tomato sauce, 105
  Simply Perfect, **121**
Tomatoes, 27, 190, 222
Tools, 13–16
  necessities (list), 15
  other useful items (list),
    15–16
Toppings
  for bruschettine, 205
Tozzetti, 20–21, 125, 214
  Chocolate, **154–56**

Tozzetto, 126
Traditional breads, 77–101
Tramezzini, 82
Trifles, 226
Truffle(s), 180–81
  oil, 5, 161, 181
  Rolls, 5, 19, **180–82**
Tuna
  Bruschetta with Sweet
    Peppers and, **196–97**
  Panzanella, **191–92**
Tuscan Bread Soup, 187,
    219–20
Tuscany, 24, 219
"Twisties," 130, 132

Umbria, 5

Valrhona chocolate, 154,
    228
Vegetable shortening, 30
Vegetables, 26–27
  in bread soup, 220
  on pizza, 117, 118
Very Thin Pizza with
    Arugula Paste, **120–21**
Village Baker, The (Ortiz),
    33
Vinegar, 190
  see also Balsamic Vinegar

Walnut(s), 25
  Prune and, Bread, **137–38**

Water, 20, 21, 22–23, 24,
    27, 30, 32, 33, 35
Wheat bread flour, 22
Wheats, 22
White Bean and Balsamic
    Vinegar Soup, **223–24**
White breads, 2, 82
White truffle oil, 5, 161
Whole Wheat Bread,
    68–69, 137
  sourdough, 59, 68
Wild Mushrooms,
    Bruschetta with, **200–1**
Wild Turkey Chocolate Ice
    Cream, 125–26,
    156–57

Yeast, 11–12, 20, 21,
    23–24, 27, 29, 32,
    33, 35, 105
  in cakes, 125
  quick-rising, 107
  in starters, 32–33
  sugar and, 25
  wild, 23
Ye-Wolo Ambasha, 161,
    176–77
Your Very Own Bread,
    240–41

Zest, candied, 169

641.815   Dunaway, Suzanne,
DUN   1940-

          No need to knead.

$24.95

DATE			